Witnesses to change

Families, learning difficulties and history

Edited by

Sheena Rolph,
Dorothy Atkinson,
Melanie Nind,
John Welshman,
Lindsay Brigham,
Rohhss Chapman,
Nigel Ingham,
Sue Ledger and
Jan Walmsley

British Library Cataloguing in Publication Data

A CIP record for this book is available from
the Public Library

© BILD Publications 2005

BILD Publications is the imprint of:
British Institute of Learning Disabilities
Campion House
Green Street
Kidderminster
Worcestershire DY10 1JL

Telephone: 01562 723010
Fax: 01562 723029
E-mail: enquiries@bild.org.uk

Website: www.bild.org.uk

ISBN 1 904082 75 0

BILD publications are distributed by:
BookSource
50 Cambuslang Road
Cambuslang
Glasgow G32 8NB

Telephone: 0845 370 0067
Fax: 0845 370 0064

For a publications catalogue with details of
all BILD books and journals telephone
01562 723010, e-mail enquiries@bild.org.uk
or visit the BILD website www.bild.org.uk

The British Institute of Learning
Disabilities is committed to improving
the quality of life for people with a
learning disability by involving them
and their families in all aspects of our
work, working with government and
public bodies to achieve full citizenship,
undertaking beneficial research and
development projects and helping
service providers to develop and share
good practice.

Contents

Part 1
The pioneers of change 1920–59
Edited by Lindsay Brigham, Sheena Rolph and Jan Walmsley

Part 2
Change ... and continuity 1959–71
Edited by Dorothy Atkinson, Nigel Ingham and John Welshman

Part 3
Participation ... the promise of change at last?
1971–2001
Edited by Rohhss Chapman, Sue Ledger and Melanie Nind

Note on terminology

The history of learning disability from a family perspective inevitably takes us into the realm of shifting ideas and discourses about people with learning difficulties, and the potential implications of different labels. Many of the authors of the personal accounts are acutely aware of the changes to labels and language they have witnessed in their lifetimes. We see the ways in which the terms used to describe the people they live with and care for are not of their choosing, but often part of a separate discourse. We notice the ways in which they interact with these changing labels and changing attitudes, influencing and being influenced by them. Accounts in the book use a variety of terms. We have not adjusted these, as they reflect prevailing ideas, though some may appear offensive to people today. In setting the historical context in the general introduction, we also use the terms in vogue at the time when we are addressing historical subject matter. This is for authenticity, and we recognise that the terms may be offensive to some people. For our part, we prefer in all other discussions to adopt the terms 'learning disability' and 'learning difficulty' with the difference being only in context, not meaning.

Poems by Tom Hulley

stevenage pool

this is her pool
this is where she splashes
in the cool
dives through the chill
to the side

she crossed this water
for a purple ribbon
when she was eight
the weight of twenty years
has not turned the tide
on her smooth glide
through the deep

this is her pool
this is where she floats
restoring her hopes
mending her hurts
the sharks applaud
the dolphins whistle with delight

(respects to maxi jazz and faithless)

sometimes she sleeps

sometimes she sleeps
her alibis are drawn
from late nights vivid dreams
and the wrap-around warmth
of covers

meg the cat is out
investigating frost
on familiar plants
or shyly stalking
imaginary giants

but curiosity rushes home
and bounds upstairs
when sam awakes,
leaping on the pillow
purring madly

the nose now peeping out
checks for the smell
of new made coffee
sees a dish of oats
the cat expects to share

the joys of shopping

she buys slides
picture frames and soap
bunches of red flowers
socks for friendly feet
fine cut dark tobacco

unpacking these treasures
her delight outweighs the cost
each small token a triumph
each gift a celebration
so much from little paper bags

General introduction

John Welshman, Melanie Nind and Sheena Rolph

Aims of the book

This book is about the stories of families, and the range of perspectives that family members can bring to bear on the experiences of people with learning difficulties in the twentieth century. The aim is to enable families to tell a history of learning disability and family life – to show how learning disabilities impacted on family life and relationships, how challenges were approached, and how families acted as advocates. The book illustrates diversity and variety in family life, aiming to be inclusive and to challenge stereotypes. It highlights past mistakes as well as successes in managing learning disability by various services. Above all, it celebrates the lives of the families who have contributed their stories.

Great strides have been made in the past decade in uncovering the history of learning disability using in part oral sources (Atkinson et al, 1997; Brigham et al, 2000; Walmsley and Atkinson, 2000). The focus has been on recovering the voice of the service user in order to correct a tendency towards the 'official' sources (Atkinson and Cooper, 2000). However, in this movement families have, until now, not been seen as key contributors. This book seeks to alter that. We want to move away from a social policy-driven agenda, to look at 'care in the community' and its consequences for families, to consider the experiences of families in historical context, to look at change over time, and to explore whether, in all the huge changes of the second half of the twentieth century in relation to the way services for people with learning difficulties are set up, anything has really changed, as far as families are concerned. In drawing up the history of learning disability there are many stakeholders, many voices to be heard. The voices of families are part of that evolving account of the past.

Why families, and why now?

We are currently in a period when the 'voice' of people with learning difficulties is gaining a place in research and even government policy such as *Valuing People* (DoH, 2001; Walmsley and Johnson, 2003). So it may seem like returning to an earlier tradition to view the experiences of families as the main vehicle for uncovering the impact of having a child with learning difficulties. Our argument for the book is that, in recent years, the experiences of families have been put on a back burner as far as research in learning disability is concerned. While research in the 1970s and 1980s probably drew on family voices at the expense of those of people with learning difficulties, leading to the construction of their sons and daughters as 'burdens', the pendulum in the 1990s swung the other way. Families were often characterised as overprotective and as standing in the way of independent living and full and fulfilling lives for their sons and daughters. We argue that what families actually did, thought and experienced has been lost.

Recent literature has highlighted 'the continuing centrality' of the family in the lives of people with learning difficulties and its important traditional role (Traustadottir and Johnson, 2000). However, a great deal of the 1970s literature concerning families emphasised a particular viewpoint – that of the burden and the 'daily grind' of caring for sons or daughters with a learning disability (Hannam, 1975; Edgerton, 1976). When the parents themselves were interviewed in the 1970s, many spoke of the 'burden', though denying 'tragedy' and emphasising the positive aspects of having a child with learning difficulties (Bayley, 1973; McCormack, 1978; Seed, 1980). Others dwelt on the 'joys' of caring and denied the stigma of the 'burden' label (Hebden, 1985; Boston, 1981). Nevertheless the discussion of care as a burden continued in the 1980s (Glendinning, 1983; Ayer and Alaszewski, 1984; Abbot and Sapsford, 1987). This was taken up particularly by feminist writers who pointed out that care in the community had shifted the 'burden' of caring on to the women in the family (Finch and Groves, 1980; Graham, 1983). The counter-challenge from some writers in the disability field was the right of disabled parents to enjoy caring for their children (Morris, 1993; 1994).

The dangers inherent in rejecting the idea of the 'burden' have been discussed in some recent research (Mitchell, 1998) and is an issue raised by this book. The tragic case of the mother on the Isle of Wight who smothered her two adult sons, and the picture that emerged at her trial of a family at the end of its tether, and of serious gaps in services and support, highlights the continuing hardships of many family lives (*Guardian*, June 2000). More recently, the gaps in services in Wandsworth have been highlighted by a group of local families desperate to ensure equality for their children (*Observer*, 23 February 2003). These examples alone are evidence that, although scholars are continuing to research family needs and social patterns, including the situation of older parents, it is vitally important to enable parents themselves to discuss their lives and needs from the standpoint of the twenty-first century, as well as reflecting on the past. Misunderstandings and stigma are still pervasive throughout some services, with families sometimes being driven to desperate measures to retain control over their lives and those of their children. Another recent illustration of this was an incident in a hospital where family members, including parents and other relatives, assaulted doctors who, they felt, had given up hope of saving their disabled child. The relatives were sent to prison as a result (*Guardian*, July 2000).

There are many stories waiting to be told, therefore, which have had a limited forum and which present a fuller and more rounded picture of family life than the stereotyped 'burden' story. The recently published *Caring for Kathleen* (Fray, 2000), for example, a life story written by a sister, offers a different viewpoint, one in which the family rejoiced in their daughter and her unique qualities. It tells a story of everyday life and daily activities, as well as acknowledging serious difficulties and Kathleen's suffering as a result of her impairment and later illnesses. Fray was able to convey very well the historical context and the legal and attitudinal changes the family experienced during the 70 years of Kathleen's life, and this book is distinctive for the author's clear historical perspective. *Home at Last* (Fitton, O'Brien and Willson, 1995) is another example – a celebratory account by two mothers of daughters with profound and multiple disabilities, which does not gloss over the difficulties.

Witnesses to Change has a broader base than these individual biographies. It makes a different contribution by including stories told over various time periods by different family members, by families from different ethnic groups, and by non-traditional families including foster-parents, and friends and advocates who are like family. These groups have been largely neglected in the literature, though some authors have begun to address ethnicity (Shah, 1992; Nadirshaw, 1999; Di Terlizzi, 1999).

How families are defined, and the role of the family, have clearly changed much in the course of the twentieth century. We are often told that the 'family is in crisis', or we are encouraged to return to a mythical age of 'family values'. In some cases, there are important statistical and demographic differences between families past and present. Marriage, for example, is much less common than it once was, divorce much more frequent, and families themselves smaller. There is evidence of family networks of care in the past. Greater social and geographical mobility means that families are now much more disparate than they once were. And greater affluence has also affected the way in which families live their lives. But it is also arguable that despite these differences, relationships between family members show much greater continuities over time. One of the key themes of the book, then, is that of continuity versus change – which term provides the more apt description of the experiences of families in the course of the twentieth century?

Public and professional attention has tended to focus on the movement of people from hospital to the community, obscuring the reality that over half the adults with learning disabilities in Britain live, and throughout the last three decades have always lived, with their families. This makes the witness stories of these often silent supporters and care providers so crucial for gaining as full an understanding as possible of the history of learning disability.

There is evidence that many parents are now asking for support in telling their family history (Rolph, 2002). Accounts by parents covering the whole post-war period are rare, and there is considerable urgency in ensuring that this important era of learning disability history does not disappear. The period has seen considerable social change and in particular enormous changes in relation to attitudes to learning disability and to the family, to the family's role in community care, in control and surveillance and care. It seems timely to explore how these changes have impinged on families and how parents have reacted to changes in legislation and local policy changes.

Our methods and approach

The methodology for this book is a combination of the life-history approach pioneered by the Social History of Learning Disability Research Group at the Open University, alongside more traditional historical research techniques based on archives and documentary sources. There has been much work on the methodology of life history accounts and oral history with people with learning disabilities (Walmsley, 1995; Fido and Potts, 1997; Walmsley and Atkinson, 2000). Researchers have also considered the potential use of autobiographical accounts (Atkinson, 1998; Atkinson et al, 2000). The ethics of oral interviews with people with learning disabilities are also receiving attention (Rolph, 1998). And photographs have been used in an interesting way to challenge official accounts or enrich life stories (Jackson, 1996; 1997). However, little has been written on the methodology of oral interviews with families with members with learning difficulties.

In different local areas, the editors used organisational and personal contacts to find families keen to 'tell their story'. These included local Social Services Departments, adult colleges, voluntary organisations and other contacts. The main sites for the collection of the stories were the London Borough of Kensington, Milton Keynes and Bedfordshire, Norwich and East Anglia, Lancaster and Carlisle, Leeds, Cornwall and Croydon. In some cases, these contacts had been used for earlier projects, in others they were completely new. Although the history we explore, therefore, is the history of England, there is much in people's experiences that is indicative of a wider truth. This is borne out by the stories written by contacts in Australia and the Netherlands, which support the English stories gathered mainly through interview.

A number of people wrote their own life stories. In other cases, interviews were arranged with the families once the aims of the book and procedures had been clarified. A few people wished to use pseudonyms, but most wanted to be acknowledged as authors under their own names. Confidentiality issues meant that in several instances legal departments were involved in giving permission for material to be included. Information sheets and consent forms were given out to families and signed by them. Transcripts of interviews were returned to families for checking and minor corrections made. Then interviews were reshaped into narratives of manageable size along themes that had been identified as important by the editorial group. During this process, attention was given to retaining the interviewee's own words. Inevitably, a wide range of views is expressed and, though some of the witnesses use terms and labels that are not commonly used today, we have felt it important that the richness and diversity of these stories, with their indication of change over time, is retained and celebrated.

Attempts were made to correct imbalances, for example for different chronological periods, geographical locations, or on account of class, gender or ethnic biases. Even so, many gaps remain and it is important to point out that this was largely a sample of contacts of convenience. We regret that we have relatively few black and minority ethnic families, and few fathers. But our experience has been that it is white mothers who have been more willing to volunteer and to offer their stories to white researchers. Despite this, fathers are represented in each section – and the poems of Tom Hulley, a father, enrich the book. Several minority ethnic families have contributed life stories to two of the sections. Perhaps not surprisingly, relatively little is said in the stories about sexuality, and family relationships. But diversity of class is a feature of the life stories in each section. We argue that the strength of the narratives lies in the stories that the families have to tell rather than in any claim to representativeness.

The book is historical in that it focuses on the experiences of families between roughly the 1930s and the present day. We have divided the stories into three sections: the period up to 1959; the period between 1959 and 1971; and the period from 1971 to 2001. Stories were allocated to the three chronological periods according to the date of birth of the person with learning difficulties. In part, the division into sections reflects the availability of families to interview. But it also uses two dates to demarcate historical periods. The 1959 Mental Health Act was the legislative equivalent to the Royal Commission on the Law Relating to Mental Illness and Mental Deficiency – it tried to put into law the important legal principles that the Royal Commission had advanced. Similarly, 1971 saw reorganisation at the local level; an acceptance that children with learning disabilities should have access to a full education; and the publication of the White Paper *Better Services for the Mentally Handicapped* (DHSS, 1971). We use these chronological periods as a framework within which we present the stories, but even so, we do not necessarily see them as important turning points, acknowledging that there may have been as much continuity as change. We now preview some of the themes and the historical context for the book.

From 'mental deficiency' to *Valuing People*

The history of learning disability (and mental health) has been dominated by the institution. There are many reasons for this. Institutions have physical presences which community alternatives often lack. Similarly they often have written records, while those of families are much more widely dispersed. Institutional lifestyles have attracted attention because they have been so different to 'normal' life, and stories of resistance to these practices have been similarly heroised. Normalisation theories have been based on the abnormality of institutional life, where there is an implied contrast with normal life (Walmsley and Rolph, 2001). The result has been that life 'outside the walls of the asylum' has been neglected by historians, especially for the period before the 1950s. Recent work on the history of care in the community has revealed that families have always had an important role in care in the community, and that the boundaries between institutions and the community, and between the statutory and voluntary sectors, have never been fixed (Bartlett and Wright, 1999; Wright, 1998; Thomson, 1998b; Rolph, 2002).

In the first of our eras, local authorities had a duty to ascertain, certify and institutionalise 'mental defectives'. This followed the 1913 Mental Deficiency Act, which has been seen as the main legislative triumph of the eugenics movement. It both promoted institutional care, but also set up a system of care in the community. Three types of formal care, supervision, and control were created – institutional care, guardianship, and supervision. Institutional care was seen as a means of providing instruction and training, so that people might be prepared for outside life. To this end, a system of licensing was created. Guardianship meant that individuals could be placed in the control of suitable people in the community, and local authorities could provide financial assistance to them. Statutory supervision consisted of the visiting of defectives in their homes by salaried local authority officials, such as enquiry officers, health visitors and district nurses, and also by the members of local voluntary organisations. These visitors prepared quarterly reports for local Mental Deficiency Committees. In addition, the 1927 Mental Deficiency Act made it a duty of local authorities to provide training for 'defectives', through occupation centres (Walmsley and Rolph, 2001).

The start of the National Health Service, in July 1948, appeared to mark a distinctive break with the past. Section 28 stated that local authorities could 'make arrangements for the purpose of the prevention of illness, the care of persons suffering from illness or mental defectiveness, or the aftercare of such persons' (National Health Service Act 1946, Section 28). This meant that responsibility for mental health and mental deficiency was divided between the new Regional Hospital Boards that controlled hospital services, and the local authorities who continued to have responsibility for public health.

The 1950s saw important developments in relation to mental health and, by extension, to the wider community of people provided for by hospitals and local authorities. Hospitals continued to provide inpatient and outpatient treatment, but local authorities became responsible for preventive services and community care. The Royal Commission argued that local authority community services should be available to all who needed them and that formal 'ascertainment' could be dispensed with: 'the whole approach should be a positive one offering help and obtaining the co-operation of the patient and his family' (Royal Commission, 1957, p.101, para. 294). An important principle was that, where possible, patients should make use of general services. There was a shift in emphasis from hospitals to community care: it was not 'in the best interests of patients' that they should live for long periods in large or remote institutions, cut off from the 'normal' world and from mixing with other people (Royal Commission, 1957, p.207, para. 601).

Community care has a much longer history both as family care and as official policy than has previously been acknowledged. Whilst it is easy to see it as a feature of the 1950s, it is clear it was already a policy option in the 1920s, set in the legislation of 1913 and the following decade. Nonetheless, the Royal Commission was highly significant. Its legislative counterpart, the 1959 Mental Health Act, laid the basis for community care services such as training and occupation centres, social centres and clubs, home visiting services, and residential homes and hostels. However, the commitment of the Royal Commission was not matched by the Act, which failed to make provision of local authority services compulsory, or to make financial provision for additional capital expenditure (Busfield, 1986).

The early 1960s seemed to be marked by a new emphasis on planning. Enoch Powell's famous 'water towers' speech of 1961 had made it clear that the Government favoured a reduction in the number of hospital beds. This was clarified in the 1962 Hospital Plan and the equivalent for local authorities, the 1963 *Health and Welfare* White Paper (Ministry of Health, 1962; 1963). These indicate the extent of services in the early 1960s and the large increases in the number of centres and places planned for in the subsequent ten years. *Health and Welfare* also noted large regional variations in the number of referrals and people receiving services, indicating there was much need that had not come to light.

The other major organisational change of this period was set in train by the Seebohm Report of 1968, which recommended that new Social Services Departments should be created, and some services transferred to them from the local authority Public Health Departments. Specific recommendations included that Local Education Authorities (LEAs) should become responsible for the education and training of all 'mentally subnormal' children; mental health services should become the responsibility of the new Social Services Departments; areas of social and medical services should be co-terminous; and the phrase 'Junior Training Centre' should be dropped, in favour of 'Special School' (DHSS, 1968, pp. 116–17). These recommendations were taken up in the 1970 Local Authority Social Services Act.

The 1971 White Paper *Better Services for the Mentally Handicapped* further exemplified the continued desire to move away from the model of hospital living. It set the course which it believed policy on services for mentally handicapped people should follow into the early 1990s, and started the process of setting target dates for the implementation of a move from hospital to community care. More generally, the period 1971–2000 saw a shift in welfare ideology in which the role of health services and the public sector was to diminish in favour of enhanced roles for families, the voluntary sector, and the private sector. The Jay Report, *Report of the Committee of Inquiry into Mental Handicap Nursing and Care*, argued that all people with 'mental handicap' should live in the community with support from the non-medical caring profession. It recommended the ending of the dual system of hospital and local care and a shift to local care, with a corresponding transfer of resources from the National Health Service to local authorities (DHSS, 1979). The commitment to community care and places to facilitate it was announced in *Care in the Community* (DHSS, 1981). Long-term admission of children to hospitals was to be avoided, and services were to be provided for children to live in families or supportive local settings.

Endorsement of the community care policy came with the Griffiths Report – *Caring for People – Community Care in the Next Decade and Beyond* – and subsequent White Paper, which outlined the government's objectives (DHSS, 1989). These included the provision of practical support for carers and respite services. The 1990 NHS and Community Care Act and the White Paper *Valuing People* (DoH, 2001) progressed further the notion of participation in the community.

In this summary of policy development and organisational change over a period spanning almost a hundred years, some main trends seem self-evident. From the legislative and policy picture, a gradual transition is presented from predominantly institutionally based, medically provided and group-focused care through to the most recent *Valuing People* strategy where the emphasis is on person-centred planning, with people with learning difficulties gaining control of service design and delivery. While we acknowledge that this 'official history' of learning disability is important, we are also keen to juxtapose it with the experiences of the families. The extent to which the evolution of policy impinged on the lives of the families will be seen in the stories themselves. These help us to resist the assumption of a notion of progress, where *Valuing People* represents the triumph of liberal values. Rather we are more hesitant about the idea of 'progress', acknowledging that while some 'improvements' have been made, in other respects the picture is more mixed.

From testing 'educational subnormality' to inclusion and diversity
The official history of education tells a similar story of shifting attitudes, discourses and priorities. Following the 1944 Education Act, children were tested for 'mental deficiency' from the age of two. 'Defectives' were classified and schools had a duty to notify local authorities when they were leaving school. To try to make notification less stigmatising, new regulations replaced the label of 'mental defective' with that of 'educationally subnormal' and 'maladjusted'. Those who were assessed as possessing an IQ of 50 or above could be admitted to state education as 'educationally subnormal' and attend special schools. Children below this assessment were designated 'ineducable' and unless spaces were found for them at occupation centres, the parents had either to find private education for them, or keep them at home (Thomson, 1998a). Children living at home were the responsibility of the local authority public health departments and were offered places in occupation centres (where available) and later, in junior training centres, especially if they had 'Special Care Units'. Such local provision, originally urged on local authorities in the 1920s (Report of the Mental Deficiency Committee, 1929) was seen as a key factor in community care and, by giving a measure of daily respite to families, was intended to help to keep at home children who would otherwise need hospital placement. Children living in hospital were the responsibility of the hospital authority and sometimes attended on-site provision when it was available.

The absolute right to a full education for all children without exception was only established in England and Wales by the 1970 Education (Handicapped Children) Act. This finally brought all children, no matter what their disability or degree of learning difficulty, within the framework of education. With a new optimism, partly influenced by behavioural psychology, no children were officially considered any longer as 'ineducable'.

A medical framework in the form of the 11 categories of handicap of the 1944 Act continued to dominate special education, however, until the Warnock Report (DES, 1978) sought to replace this with a more educational framework. Many of Warnock's recommendations and ideas made their way into the 1981 Education Act, including the concept of a continuum of need rather than categories of handicap, and an educational definition of special needs and learning difficulties. The Warnock Report also raised the profile of early intervention, recommending that the education of under-fives with special educational needs should be a priority area. The concept of investment in the early years as a preventive measure proved to be a lasting one, reiterated for example in the Green Paper *Excellence for All Children* (DfEE, 1997).

Following the 1981 Education Act, children and young people defined by the law as having (or possibly having) 'special educational needs' were given a number of entitlements. Most significantly, they were entitled to have their needs identified, to be formally assessed for a statement of special educational need, to have access to provision set out in any statement of 'special educational needs' and to have the statement regularly reviewed. This legal entitlement was extended to under-fives. The Act also introduced a legal duty on LEAs to place children identified as having special educational needs in mainstream schools, though this duty was qualified by three conditions or 'caveats', any one of which LEAs could cite as a reason for placing a child in a Special School. The 1993 and 1996 Education Acts endorsed these caveats.

It was not until the 2001 Special Educational Needs and Disability Act that two of the caveats were removed, thus creating a strengthened, though still qualified, right to a mainstream placement, which can only be denied on the grounds of incompatibility with the efficient education of other children. The disability provisions of the Act make it unlawful for schools and LEAs to discriminate against disabled pupils, in particular in relation to admission arrangements and the educational provision offered at school. With the disability anti-discrimination legislation now extended to schools, colleges, universities and providers of adult education, the 2001 Act gave parents new rights of appeal to the renamed Special Educational Needs and Disability Tribunal, if they felt that a disabled child had suffered discrimination.

The history of education is one of increasing access to education, ultimately within mainstream schools. The discourse has changed somewhat from needs to rights, influenced by the international drive for inclusive education as articulated in the Salamanca agreement. This commitment emerged from the World Conference on Education for All, signed up to by 92 participating governments and 25 participating international organisations. It committed participants to recognise 'the necessity and urgency of providing education for children, youth and adults with special educational needs within the regular education system'. Any assumed notions we may have of straightforward progress, however, may disguise the realities of families' varied experiences of schools as providers of education, support and inclusion on the one hand, or centres of stigma and exclusion on the other.

Families and influence

Another theme in the book is that of the implementation of policy, and the extent to which families have been able to influence this. In education and in life issues generally, families have campaigned at various levels. Most accounts of social policy, however, have tended to focus on the 'high politics' of policy evolution, with much less known about implementation at local level, including the role played by service users, families and local communities. Historians have occasionally raised questions about health and welfare outside institutions, but the 'mixed economy of care' has received less attention generally, with the result that the role of the family has again been underestimated (Lewis, 1995). Nonetheless, it is clear that in the interwar period, the family had a central role in mental deficiency policy (Thomson, 1996; Walmsley and Rolph, 2001).

Ironically, more is known about the role of the family in relation to the early period of mental deficiency than more recently. The Mental Deficiency Acts of 1913 and 1927 determined the lives of mental defectives and their families, and an array of officers were charged with their care and control either in institutions or in the community (Potts and Fido, 1991; Barron, 1996; Thomson, 1998a). As a result, there are many reports written by these officers and now archived in local record offices. Those families with a member who had been certified were subject to regular scrutiny from officials for their ability to both care for and control them. In particular, families were asked by visitors about their ability to prevent defectives from associating with the opposite sex. Families were scrutinised when decisions were about to be made about discharges from institutions, home leave from institutions, and in regard to suitability for licensing (Thomson, 1998a; Walmsley and Rolph, 2001).

The emphasis was on the 'defective' remaining 'safely' in the family, while at the same time providing different types of 'assistance' to the family. Many individuals did remain with their families, who retained some influence over them. For example, statistics provided by the Board of Control showed that in 1939, there were 46,054 defectives in institutions, and 43,850 under statutory supervision in the community (Thomson, 1996). However, it was often very difficult for families to resist the pressure to institutionalise, and local archives tell the stories of mothers writing to Mental Deficiency Committees asking for their children to be allowed home again (Atkinson et al, 1997; Brigham et al, 2000).

Assumptions about family life shaped mental deficiency provision. In one way, the control of defectives took away from the independence of the family; but at the same time, official policy was also shaped by a desire to assert the centrality of the family. Thus, the family had a complex role in the construction of policy. Some families used the 1913 Mental Deficiency Act to control the behaviour of defective dependants; higher numbers of notifications of female defectives may have reflected concerns about the sexuality of adolescent daughters. But families may also have used the legislation to manage their children so that their care in the family could continue. In this respect, care and control could be two sides of the same coin. There were some cases of mental defectives being institutionalised against the wishes of the family, cases of families effectively resisting institutional care, but also cases of families asking for institutional care and being turned down. 'Idiots' or 'imbeciles' (in the official terminology of the time, the most profoundly disabled) who posed no threat to public order were particularly likely to be left at home and to receive minimal care (Walmsley and Rolph, 2001).

It is debatable how far families had the opportunity to shape provision in institutions. Oral history accounts indicate that families had little room for manoeuvre, since officials tended to act in an autocratic way (Potts and Fido, 1991). The agreement of families was needed for admission of defectives into institutions unless certain conditions prevailed, but once placed, it seems families had little say over their future. Letters attempting any influence had to be sent through a bureaucratic maze (Thomson, 1996).

Families' role in shaping provision came partly with the negotiation that was necessary for the supervision of defectives in the community: parental guardianship could be negotiated between families and the state; and families and the state negotiated community care provided by occupation centres (Thomson, 1996). There are examples where the authorities acceded to the wishes of parents that their children did not have to attend occupation centres. Similarly, the regime, with its mixture of discipline and recreation, may have become more attuned to the wishes of parents. Thus families may have requested aid, resisted provision or tried to modify policy to serve their needs more closely. Nevertheless the weight of power was on the side of the authorities.

What does seem to be clear is that the social status of the family was important in determining what care their mentally defective family members received. In Bedfordshire, it appears that families deemed to be 'respectable' were supported, whereas those where poverty and poor home management was in evidence were more likely to attract greater attention and the prospect of institutionalisation (Walmsley and Rolph, 2001). Similarly, the absence of the mother could be important, and such families were more likely to be persuaded of the benefits of institutional care. Better-off families may have been more likely to come into contact with voluntary organisations, such as the National Association for Promoting the Welfare of the Feeble Minded (1896), later the Central Association for Mental Welfare, which were also active in supervision and in supporting families. The mainly female members of the organisation visited Poor Law institutions, arranged home tuition, advertised for guardians, and maintained links with people out on licence. But again, little is known about how these visits were viewed by the families themselves. Fragmentary evidence suggests that families did resent, if not resist, the visits of officials (Walmsley and Rolph, 2001).

After the Second World War, families continued to be involved as members of early pressure groups and as advocates for improved services. They began, in the late 1940s and 1950s, individually to challenge professional and public attitudes and the actions (or inaction) of local authorities, and to take steps towards change. This resulted in the formation of local voluntary organisations such as the National Association of Parents of Backward Children (NAPBC) in 1946, later better known as Mencap, one of the largest grass-roots voluntary movements to be formed in postwar Britain (Shennan, 1980). As regards the more public achievements of the parents themselves, many of the stories tell of the new services which the local societies either provided themselves or persuaded local authorities to establish, such as respite care, residential homes, swimming pools and employment opportunities. But above all in this early period, families pushed for more and better education in the form of occupation centres and industrial centres, often paid for and run by themselves.

If we take an individual area of provision, such as occupation centres and training centres, then it is clear that the role of families as witnesses to change opens up important questions to which we currently don't know the answers. Provision regarded as 'progressive' by central government departments may not have been experienced positively by families or their children. It might, for instance, have been preferable for individuals and their families to be left undetected and unprovided for (Walmsley, Atkinson, and Rolph, 1999). We are beginning to learn what parents thought of the type of training that was provided for their children, and how much they were involved and consulted, but there are still large gaps in our knowledge (Rolph, 2002) .

The Disability Rights Movement began in the 1970s, and the struggle for self-determination and an end to 'dependency born of powerlessness, poverty, degradation and institutionalisation' (Charlton, 1998, p.3) gathered momentum throughout the final period covered in the book. Rights-based perspectives came to the fore, enabling disabled people, and to some extent their families, to retain dignity in demanding rights rather than begging for acts of kindness (Bandman, 1973). Disabled people led a campaign for disability rights legislation and raised awareness through the social model of disability – showing that it is society, and not a person's impairment, that is disabling (Finkelstein, 1980; Oliver, 1983). With this there has been a change in the way in which power and decision-making are perceived. The vocabulary of services, and of people's expectations, became more rights-based as independent advocacy in its various forms developed.

Families gained more visible influence where they were organised as part of the advocacy movement. However, whilst Wolfensberger developed the idea of citizen advocacy – the partnership of a 'valued' person speaking on behalf of a vulnerable person – the self-advocacy movement focused on people speaking for themselves. London People First was established after a visit to a self-advocacy conference in America in 1984, and by the late 1980s many more regional self-advocacy groups had been set up, and informal networks were beginning to develop. The recognition that the social model applies to people with learning difficulties, who also are oppressed by environments and attitudes, has been an area of campaign for some self-advocates (Campbell and Oliver, 1996; Goodley, 2001). Self-advocacy organisations have demanded and expected rights for people with learning disabilities, and for them to be at the centre of the decision-making process, as illustrated by slogans such as 'we are the experts' and 'nothing about us without us' (Charlton, 1998).

The development and writing of the *Valuing People* strategy was the first attempt by Government to include the voices of carers and individuals with learning difficulties. A task group was set up of people with learning difficulties who travelled the country visiting self-advocacy groups and collecting evidence of quality and often, disparity, in local services. Following on from the launch of the strategy, a National Forum of people with learning difficulties was set up with four representatives elected to the Taskforce, the body set up to oversee the implementation of the strategy. This put the voice of people with learning difficulties at the centre of government process. The force behind *Valuing People* was therefore the active engagement with carers and people receiving services in the development of national policy, and the simultaneous encouragement of an interdepartmental approach to moving services for people with learning disabilities on to a more mainstream basis. Likewise, local Partnership Boards and the Taskgroups that fed into them involved representatives of people with learning difficulties and carers. The strategy represented a change in attitude to 'person-centredness' and a more participative approach to policy-making.

Families have also begun to have influence in recent years because there has been an increasing acknowledgement of the experiences and specific needs of families from black and minority ethnic and cultural groups. Following a number of key studies which researched the experiences of such groups (Shah, 1992), concerns began to be voiced regarding the double discrimination often encountered. Families' experiences of being socially excluded by language barriers, racism, negative stereotypes and attitudes (Baxter et al, 1990; Mir et al, 2001) have emerged as important issues for policy-makers, most noticeably in *Valuing People*.

Additionally, following the major shifts in the 1990s to the organisation of services with providers and purchasers, and the increased stress on consumerism generally, some, but not all, parents have gained an influence in the market place for education and services.

Language and labels

The changes in language in the period that the book covers, from 'mental deficiency' to 'learning disability' or 'learning difficulties', also hints at the important changes in ideas that lay behind these terms. The book looks at these shifting ideas and discourses and at the potential implications of different labels and dominant social attitudes.

The stories in the first section of the book, with the eugenic language of mental deficiency, show that 'fear of the unknown' and 'fear of unspeakable things' was certainly behind some of the reactions by families to the birth of their child. In the 1940s and early 1950s, mental welfare officers were also instructed to be on the lookout for 'dangers' to the local community. And although eugenist ideas began to be discredited during and after the Second World War, in part because of the use of eugenics in Nazi Germany, the stigma remained and 'mental deficiency' still carried overtones of heredity and disgrace (Jones, 1986; Thomson, 1998a).

Although eugenic language became less evident during the Second World War, 'mental defectives' continued to be viewed as a social danger, and blamed for a wide range of social problems. The 'social problem group' of the interwar period, for example, was transformed into the 'problem family' of the 1950s, the concentration of social problems in particular families now being explained with reference to the low intelligence of the parents, even if not to genetic inheritance (Macnicol, 1987; Welshman, 1996; Macnicol, 1999). Eugenic anxieties were therefore still evident in the postwar debate about declining national intelligence. Many of the individuals and groups active in eugenics in the 1930s transferred to new services and, given these continuities in personnel, it seems likely that ideas also persisted.

The vocabulary concerning learning difficulties changed dramatically during the three periods included in the book. The 1959 Mental Health Act replaced the terminology of 'mental defective', 'feeble-minded', 'idiot' and 'imbecile' with the label of 'mental subnormality'. This was intended to be liberalising. Similarly the language of 'community care' replaced that of 'supervision', although this was something of an illusion, as this 'community care' was 'really residential care under a new name' (Thomson, 1998a, p.294). The meaning of care in the community remained ambiguous and much of its popularity was on account of its ambiguity (Titmuss, 1962). Care in the community was not defined consistently, but meant different things at different times, and was applied to different groups: people who had mental health problems; older people; and those with learning disabilities.

In turn, the language of 'mental subnormality' was replaced by 'learning difficulties'. The disability rights movement, the normalisation movement and, more recently, People First, all influenced the language of the time. In the case of children, it was the Warnock Committee (1978) that sought to remove the stigma of children being labelled in terms of a single attribute or deficit, such as 'educationally subnormal', and instead proposed a continuum of special educational needs (DES, 1978). This reflected a conscious desire to remove distinct categories and to see what diverse children had in common with each other. The People First movement took its name from the desire to be seen as people and not just defined by their disability.

Normalisation ideologies, espoused by Nirje (1969; 1970) and Bank-Mikkelson (1980) in Scandinavia and by Wolfensberger (1972) in the USA, brought with them the discourse of ordinary living. Originally, normalisation was regarded as creating 'an existence for the mentally retarded as close to normal living conditions as possible … making normal, mentally retarded people's housing, education, working and leisure conditions' (Bank-Mikkelson, 1980, p.56). This approach called for normalisation of 'the rhythm of the day', a recognition of the right of people with learning difficulties to normal patterns of life. In practice this meant challenging institutional segregation, either as a matter of right or, in Wolfensberger's (1983) 'social role valorisation', because to do so meant enhancing people's behaviour, appearances, experiences, status and reputation so that they would not be socially devalued.

Normalisation did not go unchallenged. On the one hand, dissent was heard from the parents in 'Rescare' who wanted to protect their children's placements in the institutions. On the other hand, and from a different standpoint, some feminist sociologists spoke out against what they perceived as the unquestioned dogma of normalisation which could, if unchecked, lead to a desire to 'normalise' people's individual differences and a requirement that they should conform in order to gain acceptance (Chappell, 1992; Brown and Smith, 1992).

In this book we are concerned, first, with the ways in which changing language and labels impacted on the families of people with learning difficulties, and second, with the influence of ideas. How far were families aware of the changing ideas that lay behind the new labels, and what influence did these ideas have on their experiences? Is there, for example, evidence of a lag in the way the new language filtered down to the local level, so that terms such as 'mental defective' persisted in popular memory long after it had been eradicated from policy documents? Did the families regard changing discourses as supportive, or did they seek to challenge them? And did they regard the ideas as important, or were they simply more bound up with the day-to-day struggle for survival?

People and places

The final theme in the book that we shall consider in this introduction is that of the relationship between people and places. The families' stories tell of transitions – of movements into institutions, and then back to the community again – and of the migrations that people with learning disabilities have taken in the past. To some extent they echo the stories of people like Alice Chapman (Rolph, 1999), who was born in 1897 in the Norwich Poor Law Institution, sent to live in the Girls' Orphanage in Norwich, then moved to Stoke Park Colony in Bristol, some 220 miles away, before being brought back to Norwich in 1930, to a new hostel for women with learning disabilities. It seems likely that such migrations and boundary crossings were a feature of our period as a whole.

It is striking how far earlier work on the history of learning disability has been strongly identified with particular localities. Kathleen Jones found as early as the 1950s that services were quite highly organised in Manchester, Salford, Liverpool and Oldham, but less so elsewhere in Lancashire (Jones, 1954). This kind of regional variation in services has persisted. While some local authorities forged ahead with their mental deficiency services, others lagged behind. We can trace variations in particular institutions in different locations, and in care in the community in the London County Council (Thomson, 1996; 1998) and rural areas, including East Anglia, Bedfordshire and Somerset (Walmsley, 1997; Atkinson, 1997; Rolph, Walmsley, and Atkinson, 2002; 2003).

One thing that recent oral testimonies illustrate is the importance of place compared with the significance of dates, which are much less prominent. It is important to ask ourselves, as we read the stories: did it matter whether people found themselves living in a rural area, or in a town or major city? Is there evidence of families moving to areas where they perceived services for people with learning disabilities were better? And, given that this is a book very much about the experiences of families in England, is there an identifiably 'English' dimension to the experience of the families?

Summary

The book is about the experiences of families with members who have learning difficulties, and their narratives. We give space to voices that have been absent or marginalised. We deal with a period of important change in the history of learning disability both in terms of organisational structures, and shifting ideas and discourses. We look at both change and continuity across the decades. We believe that narratives – telling stories – hold key insights into people's experiences, and offer a powerful way of relating them. Our stories throw light on changing social patterns generally and changes in family life in particular.

The structure of the book in three sections reflects the three historical periods we have identified. As will be seen from the stories, for the families of children born during these periods, the picture is more complex than might be first thought. For this reason, at the end of each section we draw out the themes that emerge and relate them to the official history of the period. Overall, we argue that the stories add layers of detail missing from the usual history that is told. They also sometimes contradict it and give alternative perspectives on what life was like for the families, and the nature of the services that were actually provided. The chapters that follow enrich our understanding of this recent period of history. Moreover, they remind us of the attitudes and practices of some professionals that go unchanged from earlier decades. But it is to the experiences of the families as witnesses to change that we now turn.

References

Abbott, Pamela and Sapsford, Roger (1987) *Community Care for Mentally Handicapped Children.* Buckingham: Open University Press

Atkinson, Dorothy (1997) Learning from Local History: Evidence from Somerset. In Dorothy Atkinson et al, *Forgotten Lives: Exploring the History of Learning Disability.* Kidderminster: BILD, pp. 107–26

Atkinson, Dorothy (1998) Autobiography and Learning Disability. *Oral History, 26* 73–9

Atkinson, Dorothy et al (1997) *Forgotten Lives: Exploring the History of Learning Disability,* Kidderminster: BILD

Atkinson, Dorothy et al (2000) *Good Times, Bad Times:Women with Learning Difficulties Telling Their Stories.* Kidderminster: BILD

Atkinson, Dorothy and Cooper, Mabel (2000) Parallel Stories. In Lindsay Brigham et al (eds.), *Crossing Boundaries: Change and Continuity in the History of Learning Disability.* Kidderminster: BILD, pp. 15–26

Ayer, Sam and Alaszewski, Andy (1984) *Community Care for the Mentally Handicapped: Services for Mothers and their Mentally Handicapped Children.* London: Croom Helm

Bandman, B. (1973) Do Children Have Any Natural Rights? *Proceedings of the 29th Annual General Meeting of the Philosophy of Education Society,* pp. 234–42

Bank-Mikkelson, N. (1980) Denmark. In R. J Flynn and K. E Nitsch (eds.), *Normalisation, Social Integration and Community Services.* Baltimore, MD: University Park Press, pp. 51–70

Barron, David (1996) *A Price to be Born.* Huddersfield: H. Charlesworth & Co

Bartlett, Peter and Wright, David (1999) Community Care and its Antecedents. In Peter Bartlett and David Wright (eds.), *Outside the Walls of the Asylum: The History of Care in the Community 1750-2000.* London: Athlone, pp. 1–18

Baxter, C. et al (1990) *Double Discrimination: Issues and Services for People with Learning Disabilities from Black and Ethnic Minority Communities.* London: King's Fund

Bayley, Michael (1973) *Mental Handicap and Community Care: A Study of Mentally Handicapped People in Sheffield.* London: Routledge & Kegan Paul

Boston, S. (1981) *Will, My Son.* London: Pluto Press

Brigham, Lindsay et al (2000) (eds.) *Crossing Boundaries: Change and Continuity in the History of Learning Disability.* Kidderminster: BILD

Brown, Hilary and Smith, Helen (eds.) (1992) *Normalisation: A Reader for the Nineties.* London: Routledge

Busfield, Joan (1986) *Managing Madness: Changing Ideas and Practice.* London: Hutchinson

Campbell, Jane and Oliver, Mike (1996) *Disability Politics: Understanding Our Past, Changing our Future.* London: Routledge

Chappell, A. L. (1992) Towards a Sociological Critique of the Normalisation Principle. *Disability, Handicap and Society, 7*(1), 35–51

Charlton, J. (1998) *Nothing About Us Without Us. Disability, Oppression and Empowerment.* Berkeley, CA: University of California Press

DES (1978) Committee of Enquiry into the Education of Handicapped Children and Young People, *Special Educational Needs: A Report* (Cmnd 7212). London: HMSO

DfEE (1997) *Excellence for All Children.* London: HMSO

Di Terlizzi, M. et al (1999) Gender, Ethnicity and Challenging Behaviour: A Literature Review and Exploratory Study. *Tizard Learning Disability Review,* 4(4), 33–44

DoH (2001) *Valuing People: A New Strategy for Learning Disability for the 21st Century.* London: Stationery Office

DHSS (1968) *Report of the Committee on Local Authority and Allied Personal Social Services.* London: HMSO

DHSS (1971) *Better Services for the Mentally Handicapped* (Cmnd. 4683). London: HMSO

DHSS (1979) *Report of Committee of Inquiry into Mental Handicap Nursing and Care.* London: HMSO

DHSS (1981) *Care in the Community: A Consultative Document on Moving Resources for Care in England.* London: HMSO

DHSS (1989) *Caring for People – Community Care in the Next Decade and Beyond.* London: HMSO

Edgerton, Robert B. (1976) *Deviance: A Cross Cultural Perspective.* Mento Park, CA: Cummings Publishing Co

Fido, Rebecca and Potts, Maggie (1997) Using Oral Histories. In Dorothy Atkinson et al, *Forgotten Lives: Exploring the History of Learning Disability.* Kidderminster: BILD, pp. 35–46

Finch, Janet and Groves, Dulcie (1980) Community Care and the Family – A Case for Equal Opportunities? *Journal of Social Policy,* 9(4), 487–511

Finkelstein, V. (1980) *Attitudes and Disabled People: Issues for Discussion.* New York: World Rehabilitation Fund

Fitton, Pat, O'Brien, Carol, and Willson, Jean (1995) *Home at Last: How Two Young Women with Profound Intellectual and Multiple Disabilities Achieved their own Home.* London: Jessica Kingsley

Fray, Margaret (2000) *Caring for Kathleen.* Kidderminster: BILD

Glendinning, Caroline (1983) *Unshared Care: Parents and their Disabled Children.* London: Routledge & Kegan Paul

Goodley, D. (2001) 'Learning Difficulties', The Social Model of Disability and Impairment: Challenging Epistemologies', *Disability and Society,* 16 (2), 207–31

Graham, Hilary (1983) 'Caring: A Labour of Love' in J. Finch and D. Groves (eds) *A Labour of Love: Women, Work and Caring.* London: Routledge & Kegan Paul

Hannam, Charles (1975) *Parents and Mentally Handicapped Children.* Harmondsworth: Penguin

Hebden, Joan, (1985) *'She'll Never Do Anything, Dear'.* London: Souvenir Press

Jackson, Mark (1996) Institutional Provision for the Feeble-Minded in Edwardian England: Sandlebridge and the Scientific Morality of Permanent Care. In Anne Digby and David Wright (eds.), *From Idiocy to Mental Deficiency: Historical Perspectives on People with Learning Difficulties.* London: Routledge, pp. 161–83

Jackson, Mark (1997) Using Photographs. In Dorothy Atkinson et al, *Forgotten Lives: Exploring the History of Learning Disability.* Kidderminster: BILD, pp. 65–74

Jones, Greta (1986) *Social Hygiene in Twentieth Century Britain.* London: Croom Helm

Jones, Kathleen (1954) Problems of Mental After-Care in Lancashire. *Sociological Review,* 2, 34–56

Lewis, Jane (1995) Family Provision of Health and Welfare in the Mixed Economy of Care in the Late Nineteenth and Twentieth Centuries. *Social History of Medicine*, 8(1), 1–16

Macnicol, John (1987) In Pursuit of the Underclass. *Journal of Social Policy*, 16(3), 293–318

Macnicol, John (1999) From 'Problem Family' to 'Underclass', 1945–95. In R. Lowe and H. Fawcett (eds.), *Welfare Policy in Britain: The Road From 1945.* London: Institute of Contemporary British History, pp. 69–93

McCormack, Mary (1978) *A Mentally Handicapped Child in the Family.* London: Constable

Ministry of Health (1962) *A Hospital Plan for England and Wales* (Cmnd. 1604). London: HMSO

Ministry of Health (1963) *Health and Welfare: The Development of Community Care: Plans for the Health and Welfare Services of the Local Authorities in England and Wales* (Cmnd. 1962). London: HMSO

Mir, G. et al (2001) *Learning Difficulties and Ethnicity: Report to the Department of Health.* London: Department of Health

Mitchell, Paula (1998) *Advocacy and families.* Milton Keynes: Open University. Unpublished thesis.

Morris, Jenny (1993) Gender and disability. In J. Swain et al (eds) *Disabling Barriers – Enabling Environments.* London: Sage

Morris, Jenny (1994) Community Care or independent living? *Critical Social Policy,* 40(14), 24–45

Nadirshaw, Zenobia (1999) Editorial in Special Issue: Race, Ethnicity and Learning Disability, Tizard Learning Disability Review 4(4), 2–5

Nirje, B. (1969) The Normalisation Principle and its Human Management Implications. In R. B. Kugel and W. Wolfensburger (eds.), *Changing Patterns in Residential Services for the Mentally Retarded.* Washington, DC: Presidential Committee on Mental Retardation, pp. 231–52

Nirje, B. (1970) The Normalisation Principle – Implications and Comments. *Journal of Mental Subnormality,* 16, 62–70

Oliver, M. (1983) *Social Work and Disabled People.* Basingstoke: Macmillan

Potts, M., and Fido, R. (1991) *A Fit Person to be Removed.* Plymouth: Northcote House.

Report of the Mental Deficiency Committee (the Wood Report) (1929) London: HMSO, Part 3

Rolph, Sheena (1998) Ethical Dilemmas: Oral History Work with People with Learning Difficulties. *Oral History,* 26(2), 65–72

Rolph, Sheena (1999) Enforced Migrations By People with Learning Difficulties: A Case Study. *Oral History,* 47–56

Rolph, Sheena (2002) *Reclaiming the Past: the Role of Local Mencap Societies in the Development of Community Care in East Anglia, 1946–1980.* Milton Keynes, The Open University

Rolph, Sheena, Walmsley, Jan and Atkinson, Dorothy (2002) 'A Man's Job'?: Gender Issues and the Role of Mental Welfare Officers, 1948–1970. *Oral History,* 30(1), 28–41

Rolph, Sheena, Walmsley, Jan and Atkinson, Dorothy (2003) 'A Pair of Stout Shoes and an Umbrella': The Role of the Mental Welfare Officer in Delivering Community Care in East Anglia, 1946–1970. *British Journal of Social Work,* 33, 3, 339–359

Royal Commission on the Law Relating to Mental Illness and Mental Deficiency 1954–1957 (1957) (Cmnd. 169). London: HMSO

Seed, Philip (1980) *Mental Handicap: Who Helps in Rural and Remote Communities.* Tunbridge Wells: Costello Educational

Shah, Robina (1992) *The Silent Minority: Children with Disabilities in Asian Families.* London: National Children's Bureau

Shennan, Victoria (1980) *Our Concern. The Story of the National Society for Mentally Handicapped Children and Adults, 1946–1980*. London: Mencap

Thomson, Mathew (1996) Family, Community, and State: The Micro-Politics of Mental Deficiency. In Anne Digby and David Wright (eds.), *From Idiocy to Mental Deficiency: Historical Perspectives on People with Learning Difficulties*. London: Routledge, 207–30

Thomson, Mathew (1998a) *The Problem of Mental Deficiency: Eugenics, Democracy, and Social Policy in Britain c.1870–1959*. Oxford: Clarendon Press

Thomson, Mathew (1998b) Community Care and the Control of Mental Defectives in Inter-War Britain. In Peregrine Hordern and Richard Smith (eds.), *The Locus of Care: Communities, Institutions and the Provision of Welfare since Antiquity*. London: Routledge

Titmuss, R. M. (1962) Community Care – Fact or Fiction? In H. Freeman and J. Farndale (eds.), *Trends in the Mental Health Services: A Symposium of Original and Reprinted Papers*. Oxford: Pergamon, pp. 221–5

Traustadottir, Rannveig and Johnson, Kelley (eds) (2000) *Women with Intellectual Disabilities: Finding a Place in the World*. London: Jessica Kingsley

Walmsley, Jan (1995) Life History Interviews with People with Learning Disabilities. *Oral History*, 23(1), 71–7

Walmsley, Jan (1997) Telling the History of Learning Disability from Local Sources. In Dorothy Atkinson et al, *Forgotten Lives: Exploring the History of Learning Disability*. Kidderminster: BILD, pp. 83–94

Walmsley, Jan and Atkinson, Dorothy (2000) Oral History and the History of Learning Disability. In J. Bornat, R. Perks, P. Thompson and J. Walmsley (eds.), *Oral History, Health and Welfare*. London: Routledge, pp. 180–202

Walmsley, Jan, Atkinson, Dorothy and Rolph, Sheena (1999) Community Care and Mental Deficiency 1913 to 1945. In Peter Bartlett and David Wright (eds.), *Outside the Walls of the Asylum: The History of Care in the Community 1750–2000*. London: Athlone, pp. 181–203

Walmsley, Jan and Johnson, Kelley (2003) *Inclusive Research in Learning Disability: Past, Present and Future*. London: Jessica Kingsley

Walmsley, Jan and Rolph, Sheena (2001) The Development of Community Care for People with Learning Difficulties 1913 to 1946. *Critical Social Policy*, 21(1), 59–80

Welshman, John (1996) In Search of the 'Problem Family': Public Health and Social Work in England and Wales, 1940–70. *Social History of Medicine*, 9(3): 447–65

Wolfensberger, W. (1972) *The Principle of Normalisation in Human Services*. Toronto: National Institute on Mental Retardation

Wolfensberger, W. (1983) Social Role Valorization: A Proposed New Term for the Principle of Normalization. *Mental Retardation*, 21(6): 234–9

Wright, David (1998) Familial Care of 'Idiot' Children in Victorian England. In Peregrine Hordern and Richard Smith (eds.), *The Locus of Care: Families, Communities, Institutions and the Provision of Welfare since Antiquity*. London and New York: Routledge

Part 1

The pioneers of change 1920–59

Edited by Lindsay Brigham, Sheena Rolph and Jan Walmsley

Introduction

A sense of isolation, as well as bewilderment, fear and confusion, marks these early life stories. Lack of information, advice and support of any kind characterises many of the interactions between families and professionals. At first reading, this appears to be a paradox, as the period is that governed by the most explicit, stringent and controlling policies regarding 'mental deficiency'. The Mental Deficiency Acts of 1913 and 1927 remained in place until 1959, with the purpose of determining the lives of 'mental defectives' and their families in considerable detail and maintaining segregation and control. An array of officers – duly authorised officers, mental welfare officers, occupation centre supervisors, enquiry officers, as well as superintendents and psychiatrists – were charged with the care and control of families and their children or young people labelled as 'mentally deficient', either in institutions, or in the community. The family itself was 'to be co-opted to supply "effective control"' of 'mental defectives' in the community (Walmsley and Rolph, 2001). Evelyn Fox, Secretary of the Central Association for Mental Welfare, placed the family at the centre of community care, with the State intervening to give both 'friendly advice and help' and 'guardianship with compulsory powers' (Fox, 1930).

In Part 1, therefore, we might expect to see care and control carried out by many different professionals, with families advised carefully not only as to diagnosis, but also as to their fate and that of their children, monitored accordingly, and playing a pre-ordained role themselves in the official policy of community care. In fact, the stories are often surprising and diverse, offering a different aspect of the history of the period from that which might be expected from an investigation of legislative and social policy developments, and highlighting instead the families' pioneering efforts in bringing about change and improving the lives of their children with learning difficulties.

Part 1 Timeline

Year	Legislation and national events	Major policy developments
1920s	1927 Mental Deficiency Act	1920s–1940s Local Authority (hospital) building programme
1930s	Campaign for voluntary sterilisation Eugenicist movement at its height	New colonies opened: Little Plumstead (1930), South Ockenden, Bromham, etc. (1931) In 1930 the average number of patients in the 98 'County, County Borough and City Asylums' was 1,221 (Jones 1972, 357)
1940s	1944 Education Act 1944 Disabled Person's Employment Act Labour landslide 1946 National Insurance Act 1946 National Health Service Act 1948 National Health Service Act came into operation The excluding Welfare State: 'ineducable' children	Beveridge establishes framework for the Welfare State Development of Occupation Centres Mental Health Subcommittees replaced Mental Deficiency Committees Duly Authorised Officers (later MWOs) appointed by Local Authorities – but few resources made available Eugenics discredited after World War 2, but eugenicist concerns still in evidence in local and national policies
1950s	Royal Commission on the Law Relating to Mental Illness and Mental Deficiency (1954 to 1957), under Lord Percy, appointed 1959 Mental Health Act (England and Wales) repealed the Mental Deficiency Acts; espoused 'community care' but still little funding	1951: NCCL's 50,000 *Outside the Law* drew attention to civil liberties breaches and hospital scandals 1953: Nearly half the National Health Service's hospital beds were for 'mental illness or mental defect'. Concerns about the level of spending were likely to be a factor in shifting government thinking towards Community Care policies

Publications	Professional parent and user groups and voluntary groups	Changing labels	World events
1929: Wood Report	Voluntary organisation, Central Association of Mental Welfare (CAMW), active	'Mental defective' in use	The Depression
1934: Brock Report 1934: Alva and Gunnar Myrdal's *Crisis of the Population* 1937: Cyril Burt's *The Backward Child* 1937: Tregold's *Textbook of Mental Deficiency* (new edition)			Spanish Civil War Approximately 60,000 people subjected to eugenic sterilisation in Sweden between 1935 and 1976 World War 2
Beveridge Report	National Association of Parents of Backward Children (NAPBC) founded Local Mencap societies founded CAMW voluntary organisation still active Growth of parents' societies	'Ineducable' label used	Peace Women 'back into the home' Rationing continues
1956 Tizard and O'Connor's *The Social Problem of Mental Deficiency*	NAPBC gave evidence to Royal Commission 1958 NAPBCs 'Brookland's Experiment' 'Little Stephen' logo adopted by NAPBC – representing pathos instead of fear	'Backward' label used 'Subnormal' label used in 1959 Act	Korean War On the cusp of the 'swinging sixties'

Chapter 1
You have been a mother to him: we could only have been an uncle

Gladys Abbs

I interviewed Gladys Abbs in 1999 when I first started to explore the history of local Mencap societies in East Anglia. She was the founder of the Norwich Society in 1954. Her son Rodney was born in 1947. What follows is part of her story, compiled from the interview, and told in her own words.

Sheena Rolph

Rodney

Rodney was called a Mongol.[1] It wasn't until he was 12 years old that they transferred over and it was called Down's syndrome. He was born in 1947. He is the oldest Down's syndrome in the area! He has always lived at home with us. We didn't know until he was about 11 months old, although we thought there was something wrong. Friends used to say, "He never cries." Of course, we found out he didn't cry because he couldn't. I couldn't either. We both have Sjögren's syndrome, named after a Swedish doctor, Hendrik Sjögren, who described it in 1932. Mine didn't come on till I was at school, but Rodney was born with it. Rodney has never shed tears, and I can't – very embarrassing. So we had all that to contend with.

   What happened during that first part of his life was that there was a specialist who came to Norwich and he said, "I run a home and my advice is to let Rodney come with us and I would advise you to write this off as 'just one of those things'. Don't come and visit him and don't enquire anything about him, just acknowledge that that was that." I couldn't believe it. My husband and I talked it over, and Rodney belonged to us and we were going to see it through – which we have done. It has been hard of course. Nobody came. We didn't have anybody. We just did it all ourselves. Nobody bothered us, though we did have a very good doctor.

   The headmistress at the infant school said, "Would you like to try Rodney at the school?" I said, "Yes, of course", and he was there for a little while, but then some of the parents said they didn't think he should be there.

1 See Note on terminology, p.vii

37

It was very difficult, to say the least. In those days when they said 'mentally handicapped' lots of people didn't know what it meant. They needn't have worried because they wouldn't have any trouble from them, or the ones today. I must admit we felt very lonely. When Rodney was eight or nine the superintendent of the local hospital tried hard to get me to say he could go into the hospital and I said "No." Some years later the superintendent said "Well, I would like to apologise to you. We could never have got Rodney to the state that he is. You have been a mother to him: we could only have been an uncle."

Rodney in 1993

The Society

The Norfolk and Norwich Society for Mentally Handicapped Children was formed on 3 July 1954. I started it going. There was no one to talk to at all. Even the doctors just didn't know. So we called this meeting. Judy Fryd[2] was really the start-up of it all. I saw her letter in the *Nursery World* and wrote to her and decided to start a society in Norwich. I talked to her a lot on the telephone. We had only six members, and we had £2.10s in the funds and lots of faith. We had parties, outings and we set up a committee. Gradually people joined from all over Norfolk, though transport wasn't easy. In those days we used to go round and visit parents in their own homes, too, throughout the county, to see if we could help, or just to talk and support them in that way. My whole life at that time was the local society. We had three major projects. One was a training centre workshop for mentally handicapped boys over 16 years, and after much hard work we did manage to get St Swithin's Hall and this was opened in January 1958. We received a grant from both the Norwich City and Norfolk County Council to help run the place. We started with 10 boys and built up to 24. They did all sorts of things. I used to go and see some of the factory people in order to get jobs. Tom Smith's Crackers were very good – the boys used to fold paper hats for Christmas. At that time we had supervisors. In September 1960 the Council accepted full responsibility and transferred the boys to a new centre in Norwich known as St Mark's Hall.

Now project number two: the Society opened a Girls' Centre. Now that the boys had gone, we had the girls into St Swithin's and ran it until December 1962 when the authorities again took over and transferred the girls to the

2 Judy Fryd was the founder of the National Association of Parents of Backward Children (now Mencap) in 1946

St Mark's Centre with the boys. At first we didn't have the help we should have. I was very disappointed in the Lady Mayoress, because after they took the boys over, she was furious. She said, "I don't know what you are thinking of in setting up a workshop for the girls. Those girls can be of help to their mothers – there are all sorts of things they can do at home." So I am afraid we didn't get the help.

Then, the third project. We started looking out for suitable premises to start up a residential home and after some time we were able to buy Burlingham House. The boys and girls had to be over 16 years of age, and then there were 17 residents to start with. We also had a short-stay bed for holidays and emergencies. The stable block was converted in 1979, giving us another 19 beds. When we bought Burlingham House, we didn't have any money and the Committee thought I was mad!

So that was how it all started, with six people, and it built up to about 130. Now it has gone down. We have had some wonderful times, wonderful outings. We have been on the funfair at Yarmouth, to circuses, but not now. The young parents don't want to join. There has been so much done for them, they don't feel the need for it.

Chapter 2
Our life with Margaret

Don Hardy

I first met Vi and Don Hardy when I was doing research for a project on the history of local Mencap societies in East Anglia. They were most generous with their time, and shared with me not only their memories of their daughter, Margaret, but also their wonderful collection of very early archives and photographs concerning the Cambridge Mencap Society. Although I interviewed them for my project – an interview that provided most interesting and valuable historical material – Don decided on a different approach for this book, choosing to take the opportunity to write the chapter himself, while including some of the material from the interview.

Sheena Rolph

My wife, Vi, and I moved from London to Cambridge with our two-year-old daughter in December 1948. We wanted other children and, after we settled down, Margaret was born prematurely at home on Christmas Eve 1949. She was very ill from the start and we often had to share the night to be with her. She was taken to hospital where we were told by doctors that they "thought she was a Mongol" (although it was known that Dr Down, in 1866, called them 'Mongols', the much better description of 'Down's syndrome' was not adopted until about the early 1970s). We had not heard about Mongols before, although Vi had a recollection of hearing about them in an anatomy lesson at school. The paediatrician said that she would be a loveable child who would "never let you down" but might only live to about the age of ten and would never be able to do very much (Margaret lived to be 46). This, of course, was a shock to us but we faced the future determined to do what we could for her.

Margaret's early years

At that time there was a small department in the Medical Officer of Health's Department of the Cambridgeshire County Council which dealt with the mentally ill and mentally handicapped. The service was poor and Margaret was again described as a "very low-grade mongol". A Mental Welfare Officer visited to help Margaret, who at the time was crawling about on the floor. She gave Margaret a toy to help her use her fingers. Vi said, "What a marvellous idea."

It was little pegs to go into holes. The visitor said, "I will call to see Margaret in a fortnight." Vi next saw her in 11 months' time. She was really useless.

There was, however, an Occupation Centre which we visited in the early 1950s. It was in a church hall rented to the County Council. It was not ideal as the staff had to pack everything away on Friday and take it out again on Monday. The theme at that time was to occupy rather than to train. The supervisor, Miss Isobel Simon, was very good and in addition to giving them jobs, she taught them personal hygiene. We got to know her quite well – she lived to be over 90. Margaret did not go there but when she grew older she went to a special school and later to a new Training Centre which opened in 1958 in Coldham's Lane, Cambridge. A second centre was opened in Ditton Walk in 1976.

We had a very helpful District Nurse. She said to Vi, "You work with her because she might go much further than people expect." Vi's sister, who was a teacher, also said, "Don't take any notice of what they say, you teach her to read." How right they were, because as time went on Margaret was able to read and write simple sentences. She could be relied upon to do a job with great care and accuracy. For example, when we ran off the Cambridge local society's newsletter at home, Margaret would put the sheets together and any black or smudged ones would be thrown out. She could also assemble a large jigsaw puzzle without the picture and sometimes upside down. On one occasion when her grandmother was staying with us there was a commotion from the kitchen because Grandma was putting things in the wrong places after washing up.

Margaret doing a jigsaw puzzle, early 1990s

Margaret was always so happy. We cannot recall ever seeing her miserable except perhaps on a very rare occasion if somebody teased her too much, or if somebody was a bit cross with her, or if one of the others in the Training Centre gave her a push, but otherwise she was always happy. She was a friend to all and could see no evil. She could have been left quite safely alone in the house but we did not leave her because she would have invited anybody in who happened to knock on the door.

Vi remembers pushing her in a pram, when she waved to a lady who went by. Vi said, "Don't worry, darling, the lady doesn't know you." When the lady returned she waved and Margaret said, "There you are, she does know me!" Margaret loved travelling by car. She would sit in the back and wave to other drivers, including lorry drivers. When they waved back she said, "They are my friends." It was as simple as that.

We often drove to London for the day to see the two grandmothers. She used to sleep on the back seat and when the car stopped on arriving home she would say, "Where are we?"

In 1954 our son was born and although he was four years younger than Margaret they developed together and he even got her playing cricket and other games in the garden. When he grew up and entered the business world he always thought of her and was one of the first to visit her when she was having treatment in hospital. He was profoundly grieved when she died. Because Margaret was the middle child, he was eight years younger than his older sister but after a few years the difference levelled out. We know some parents with a handicapped child, who were hesitant in taking a further risk. One mother, when she saw our son as a toddler, said, "He's all right, isn't he?" We felt then that we may have given other parents some reassurance.

The doctors were certainly right when they said Margaret would be a loveable person. To quote a touching example: in 1972 her elder sister had recently married and her brother had gone to college in Nottingham. While assisting Margaret to bathe, Vi said, "I wonder what Jean and Alan are doing now?" Margaret said, "You've still got me." This amazed Vi very much because Margaret thought very quickly that her Mum was upset, when Vi was really only commenting.

Margaret was always very helpful. Nearly every year we took her to see an uncle and aunt in Devon. She used to 'help' him going up hill and it was amusing to watch because he was over six feet tall and she was only a little over four feet. We occasionally experienced unwelcome help when, not having much idea of time, Margaret brought us tea about five or six o'clock in the morning. It was a difficult task for her because she was not very steady, but we responded by drinking a weak and lukewarm cup of tea at that early hour.

The local Mencap Society

In 1955 we saw a letter in the local paper about the Cambridge Society for Mentally Handicapped Children. We later became members and got quite involved. It helped, because we could talk to other parents and they understood. It was very much based in the community – looking after the children, comforting their mothers and fathers, and giving the children fun.

In 1960 Vi became Honorary Treasurer just before Edmund House, the society's residential home, was purchased. She dealt with the money collected from two public appeals. Edmund House was purchased in 1961. When we bought it, it was a derelict house on three and a half acres of land, so we all had to work hard on both the house and the gardens to get it ready. The first three residents went there in August 1964, looked after by a married couple, following the old idea of 'houseparents'. By the year 2000, the new Edmund House Group of Homes had 42 residents. I became Honorary Secretary in 1965 just before the official opening by Sir David Renton in September 1966. The Cambridge Society was the first in the country to open a residential home. There used to be a bazaar each year from 1960 to 1992 which would raise between £1,500 and £1,700 at peak periods. Vi dealt with the cash arrangements from 1960 to 1990. There are also fewer helpers to sell flags on the annual city collection day. However, there are some members who continue to do their best and we still have the weekly club, the annual pantomime trip, the annual dance/party and the services of a welfare visitor and a newsletter.

The later years

We thought Margaret might survive us, so we let her go to live in the bungalow in Edmund House Group of Homes in 1989. We didn't want her to go at first, but I realised it was the right thing for her and that she would be safe there. She was very happy there and often came home for a few days. She also came on holiday with us.

We learned later that some Down's Syndrome children developed spinal troubles and Margaret was one of these. In 1980 she had a repair to her spine and she loved being in hospital because they were so kind to her. In November 1960 a Social Club had been formed for the Cambridge Society by medical students and one of them, later a doctor, recognised Margaret while she was in hospital. Later in 1994 she was operated on again. She was in hospital for three weeks under observation and when the surgeon suggested she had a weekend at home, she was reluctant to leave and the staff nurse said, "Your bed will still be here for you, Margaret." Once again she was very happy and the surgeon told us that she was the only patient who had given him a kiss. The success of this second operation could not be completely guaranteed, but it did prevent her from being less mobile until 1996 when she relied more on a wheelchair.

Margaret died from a bleeding duodenal ulcer in March 1996 when she was 46. The hospital consultant thought this was due to painkillers. We were very sad to lose her, but we did not wish her to continue life in a wheelchair. All her life she did very fine drawings – we have over 50 or 100 of them. Recently some of these formed part of an exhibition about the history of local Mencap societies – and we feel that was a lovely memorial to her.

Chapter 3
I don't think I'll ever give up till I die

Rene Harris

Rene Harris, 1919–2000

I met Rene in 1991 in the course of my PhD research. I'd been pointed towards her by a contact in Luton who said she was the person to help me reconstruct the history of services for people with learning difficulties in Bedfordshire, and that she knew everyone. I formally interviewed her twice, to gather oral history data for my research, but we became friends, and I visited her in her home in Sharpenhoe on a number of occasions subsequently, each time gleaning more information. She was immensely generous with her time, memories, her store of historical treasures, and her contacts. If I can point to one person who made my PhD possible, and who brought my enduring interest in the history of learning disability to life, it was Rene. To me, she typifies the redoubtable energy and determination of the founder members of Mencap, 'the Society'.

I last saw her a few weeks before her death in March 2000.

This account is drawn from her own words, recorded at our interviews.

Jan Walmsley

Colin – how it started

Colin was born in 1941. I didn't know he was backward until he was three years old. He was admitted to hospital for medical tests. During that visit, the sister said to me, "He's very backward, isn't he?" That was the first I knew there might be something wrong. I was referred to a paediatrician who told me, in effect, to stop protecting him and put him down to walk. By the time he was five it was clear to me that he would not cope with school. They sent the attendance officer round, though it should have been clear to them that I'm not the sort to keep my children off school for no reason. My first son had an excellent record of attendance.

I had to look round for alternatives. There was very little. I was told by a friend about Osborne Road School. I said, "But that's the 'silly school'." My friend took me to show me around. It was in an old farmhouse with four rooms. There was no special transport, but the caretaker came on an ordinary service bus to collect the children from the Town Hall. Colin went there for two years, but he wasn't happy. At Osborne Road they were supposed to be getting the rudiments of the three Rs into them, and he just couldn't cope with that. He left after I received a letter from the education authorities telling me he was 'ineducable' and should be excluded from school. I still have that very hurtful letter. Ineducable. It's a terrible blow. I tried to fight it but I knew I didn't have a leg to stand on. I knew he was terribly backward.

I was confused. I was indignant, I suppose. How dare they say my child was ineducable? And yet basically, I knew, though I did try to take it further. I had discussions with my MP, I had discussions with the Education Department in Luton, and they said, "Well, you have this avenue of appeal", and I said to my husband, "I don't think we have grounds for appeal." But nobody said what could be done, you see.

I was at a very low ebb then, and I opened my heart to a woman I met on a park bench. She said to me, "Well, there is another place, I don't know where it is, but I know there is another place because the coach comes round and picks up those poor little souls." That was how I heard about the Occupation Centre, in a lovely old house in Church Street – all been swept away now by the Arndale Centre – and in the garden was the most wonderful walnut tree. It was the first time I'd ever seen a walnut tree. The lady who was there, a very, very kind secretary, did all the work of the Department. It amazes me now when I go into Bedford House and see all these social workers, and then there are more at Dunstable. But this lady had it all on her shoulders. My experience with her was very kind. She told me about the Occupation Centre, and we went there. Colin went there, and he was a lot happier.

I went to Hitchin to hear Judy Fryd after I read about her in the paper. The first that I knew of her they had an article, '40,000 lame chicks', in the *Sunday People*. That was the headline, and I thought, "These children are like mine." Wonderful woman. I was absolutely inspired by her. Oh, I was so moved because she said everything that was in my mind. She said everything in her talks and in her groups that was in my heart and that I hadn't been able to say.

You see, you don't think it happens to anyone else. It wasn't uncommon, before there was so much publicity, for people to hide the fact they'd got a handicapped child. The only other people I knew were Mr and Mrs A. who were very friendly with my sister-in-law, and they had a Down's boy, Stephen. He never went out except in a car, nobody knew of his existence, and the neighbours used to say, "That little boy, he's like a monkey", because they used to see him looking out of the window for Daddy coming home.

It was the woman at Church Street who helped me form the Society, really, because she couldn't reveal any names because of confidentiality.

We had actually started the Society in 1955, and the way we did it was, we wrote invitations to a party in the old St Mary's Hall in Church Street and gave them to her, and she passed them on to people. I'll never forget that first party because I didn't know anything about mentally handicapped people except my own, but I was very good at catering. And all these people came, children of all ages, and they were very amused because, as they said, "How did you know about us, how did you know?" Well, we didn't, you see, and that was how our membership started.

We had lots of battles. When they opened the Dunstable Occupation Centre they wanted to make it small, they said they couldn't provide for a nebulous group, not knowing how many there were going to be. So we produced the facts, lots of people we knew about and they'd never heard about, and so we got a reasonably sized Centre, but within six months they'd had to take back their site at Kirby Road and start the adult workshop.

In and out of Bromham Hospital

"Put him away and forget all about him" – that used to be the advice – "Put him away and have another child." It's taken me years to persuade parents that it's not 'putting away'; it's 'letting go'. I had the decision forced on me, really, by my other children because I had a son doing A levels and a daughter doing O levels and this very disruptive element in the middle which you just couldn't cope with, and I realised it was either him or me, one of us would have to go away. I actually did go away, to a convalescent home in Brighton by the racecourse to think it out – because I had a total breakdown. I spent days walking the hills out at the back of Brighton, and I realised things weren't going to be any different when I came back so I had to sit on my hands and take a fresh hold of the dear old soul, and pull myself out of it, and cope. And I think that was when I decided we'd have to. And this was the time when the first surge out of hospitals was taking place. There were such a lot of people – I'm sure it was the same all over the country – a lot of people that had been there for years, and only because of some sort of misdemeanour. They did go out to work, they went out of the hospital to work, so it was obvious they could go out and live a life in the community. Some actually married and came back to the hospital to show the staff their babies. And so there were vacancies in Bromham Hospital then, and this was the time I was at my lowest ebb. Colin was then under the mental welfare officer, probably Mr. French, and he said, "Well, there is a vacancy", and I thought, "Well, I'll have to take it." And the staff there – he hadn't been there very long – said, "We should have had him years ago. You've spoilt him." It was probably true. He did settle down very well – I was quite surprised really.

It is a very, very hard decision. I should think for 18 months after that I cried myself to sleep. I felt like a murderess. I really felt I'd condemned him to death. And that was when I threw myself into Mencap, heart and soul. I thought, "I must fight for all those who are in the community because perhaps parents won't have to undergo this trauma in the future if we can improve services in the community." There really were not many alternatives, you know. There was no adult training centre. I think I told you this before, that he was at Kirby Road, and there he was, this great six-foot boy. Mrs Bewes used to let him do all the humping of the furniture you know, he used to do all the moving of tables and chairs, things like that. But there was a party at St Mary's Hall, and all these little ones came to it, and I realised there was never going to be room in that school if great big boys, six feet tall, were occupying all the places, and Colin was one of them.

Throughout the 1950s and 1960s, the one fear of my parents was that their child would have to go to Bromham – they couldn't bear the thought of it. I tried hard to persuade them that it wasn't a fearful place; it was quite marvellous in those days. It perhaps wasn't ideal because they had those huge dormitories, but the surroundings were so lovely, and the staff were wonderful, really dedicated caring people, lovely people. You had your upsets, for example, clothes going missing and the fact they didn't want them to have their own clothes; they wanted them to have hospital issue, which was pretty awful. I used to keep a spare set of clothes for him. And there was the other upset: the masturbation by some used to upset mine, who knew it was not nice. So it wasn't ideal; but it wasn't as dreadful as most of my parents regarded it. I visited him twice a week, Thursdays and Saturdays. We had to get our own transport then. Before that we used to cycle, because if you went by public service it took all day. I knew a wonderful little lady from Hatfield, a Catholic – she used to go to Mass at seven or eight, and then straight on to public transport to get to Bromham.

When we parted with Colin, when he went to Bromham, I thought that was it; that was the end. I was absolutely amazed when we got back from holiday one Christmas and Mr Marsden, the mental welfare officer, was waiting to ask me if I would agree to him coming out of Bromham to be one of the first residents at Wauluds Hostel when it opened. I was absolutely amazed, because I'd been given to believe that they had to go about in the community and care for themselves, and I didn't think he could do that because of his lack of speech and he hasn't got a lot of confidence to go out. Anyway, I was very pleased, because he improved beyond belief when he came out; he was very much more aware and was making himself understood.

People

I doubt if Brian remembers his father. His mother is a dear little soul. In her garden a weed daren't grow. She's very, very nice but she's practically illiterate. If she gets a form, she panics; she's on the phone, saying, "I've had this letter; can you come?" But what I'm sorry about is, I've known him since he was about eight. I suppose the Society took him on the first holiday. I think I told you about Mrs Messenger being the first home teacher in the county, and she realised what a terrible waste of time it was going from one end of the county in her car, just for an hour here, then driving back across the county, so she started groups, you see, and the first one was in Barton in the village hall. Brian never went to school because they wouldn't have him at Barton because he wasn't clean and he had tantrums. So, because his mother didn't have enough about her to find out what she could do, he didn't do anything until Mrs Messenger came on the scene. I'm so sorry about Brian because I did hear about him through Muriel Messenger, but I didn't really realise – I was so busy with everything else, and I didn't realise that his mother didn't have enough up there to become a member, and therefore she wasn't on my list. She didn't get letters or, if she did, she couldn't read them, and so she slipped through the net. At the time she would definitely have got attendance allowance, and related benefits, but she didn't have the savvy to apply and I didn't realise she hadn't applied. When we did, of course, it was too late; they'd started tightening up on things, not giving them as freely as they earlier did.

He's now got a job at Homebase. One of the reasons parents are afraid to let them go into full-time work is the fact that if they do not make the grade and people sack them you've got to go through all the channels again to get it back. I mean he would be earning £100 a week if he worked there full time, which is far more than his benefit.

I wouldn't say there were many middle-class children, not very many; the majority were from feeble-minded parents. I knew quite a lot of middle-class people who would not let their children go, even when the new centres opened. I know that Mr Marsden – who was at that time the Chief Mental Welfare Officer in Luton, and before that he was one of Mr French's boys from Bedford – he went to several of these people personally and told them that the Centre was open. They said, "He couldn't get on that coach with them", and one wonders what's going to happen. I mean some of these parents are now in their eighties, and the child is at home, a middle-aged man or woman. And I know that the parents' prayer is that their children will die before them – they definitely have this deathwish, and several of them are so poorly themselves, they are only hanging on because the child is alive.

There's a very lower-class family up the road here. Kathleen has Down's Syndrome and was one of Mrs Messenger's group at Barton – she was a contemporary of Brian's. There are two sons at home who are very peculiar. There's another son who is married and who has turns, and there's Kathleen, the youngest, and then there's Dorothy – well Dorothy's unbelievable. She looks like a witch; she is absolutely filthy, her teeth are black, like black tombstones, and she sits by the roadside all day long. She has a bicycle and now she's developed a pram, but she has had a bicycle all these years, which she never rides, but pushes into Barton and back, and on the handlebars are six plastic bags – no one knows what's in them. Absolutely terrible; but will they part with Kathleen? No, she is at home with them all the time.

Opinions

I really do think our children need a family atmosphere, a mum and dad. That's why I quite like what Roy and Ann are doing. They are private homeowners and they are keeping the home small and as a family unit. Though I think Ann has got to learn that when you've got a family of five or six children they do not always agree. Of course, Ann hasn't got any children herself. I don't know if she's got brothers and sisters, but not having children she probably doesn't realise that life isn't always sunny. The authorities wanted Colin to go to Ann and Roy. I said no. The long and short of it is I am against private care. Nothing against Roy and Ann; they are doing a splendid job there, but personally I don't think it should be done for private profit. It ought to be done by the state. And the smaller the group the more difficult, because they can't get away from each other, whereas if they are in a house with 20 others they can go and join another group.

I liked Wauluds Hostel very much when Mr and Mrs Hills were in charge, with Mr and Mrs Bond as deputies. Mother and father. Then Mr and Mrs Bond moved on to open a home in Dunstable, and the Hills retired. That was it. No more joint appointments. I'm still in touch with them. Wonderful couple. They remembered every one of their residents, they remembered their little peculiarities, they remembered their relatives. Now there are so many workers at Wauluds doing part time and shifts …

I don't think the younger parents are the same at all because we did so much spadework. There has been so much publicity through the media that they know at once as soon as the child is born whether it's a Down's or a spastic. They know immediately that they can get help, and they go all out for it, their children go into respite care from the word go, and they get all the allowances. They get the allowances now before the age of two. I always thought it was ridiculous to pay them Attendance Allowance at the age of two, because a child of two is a child of two.

I've been going through these Mencap *Yearbooks*, and it's awful really; way back in the 1960s we were talking about community care and better day services and we haven't really progressed very much, have we? I'm in the process of collating a letter to go to the Director of Social Services pointing out how many 70- or 80-year-olds we know of in the community who are looking after a 50-year-old child, and there will have to be provision very soon for these older men and women. As ever, the people who are most deprived are the people who stayed at home because they never make any demands. The young ones now are making the demands and are taking all the time of social workers. Yes, while you carry on, you can. Oh yes, it's always been that way. There were people for whom it was such a blow; they just curled up inside and closed the door to the world.

I don't think I'll ever give up till I die. No.

Chapter 4
April showers

Jo Wain

I have known Jo since childhood, and I knew her sister April also. April was the first person with Down's syndrome I ever met. When Jo told me she had been doing some creative writing around her sister's life, I thought of it as an opportunity to include it in the book. It is also a memorial to April who died, sadly, in her forties.

Jan Walmsley

To tell such a tale as this is a tall order. The making of memories is a process I can no longer recall. But past memories, ones already made, these are fresh and green in my mind. Sometimes there are so many images that I lose track of them. Like yesterday, I forgot my name. I could see it blowing softly down the wind, but I chased after it and snatched it back, just in time. I could not tell you what day it is today. I am lost in the present, but embossed on my mind are the landscapes of times past. Tracing over familiar mounds and hollows, I can keep in view memories that stretch to near and distant horizons. *You see I am not like they say.* I am not empty. I am full. I am bursting with colour.

The rays of the sun are thinning to the first shadows of the night, and I realise my moment of telling is to hand. *So trust me, and remember that it all happened long ago.*

Imagine it is the month of April and the year is 1949. My birth is quick and relatively easy, if the event of a firstborn can be described in such simple terms. I am cleaned and tightly wrapped in white winceyette. The matron is composed, functional and unhurried. She hears and sees no cause for alarm. My mother's sore and cleanly shaven lower body is washed slowly and thoroughly and covered, as if all signs of my bloody birth must be erased. I am placed in her outstretched arms. A daughter. A disappointment? Maybe, for one fleeting moment. My father, proud and excited, enters the room. *So, for the moment, compose from this scene an image that is yet unspoiled.*

The next day is one of flowers and visitors. Two of these visitors will be my grandmothers. Picture them arriving, arm in arm, grey-haired and both small in stature. My father's mother, Ellen Raine is strong and vibrant for her 68 years. But then again, no one expected anything less from Mrs Raine.

April

Always energetic, a workaholic by nature, Ellen Raine has succeeded in bearing 15 children during her lifetime (two were stillborn) and has helped to build a thriving family business in the meantime. Apart from allowing herself the indulgence of two weeks' bed-rest after each birth, she has cooked and baked daily for her string of grocery stores. It is not surprising that Ellen Raine has an excessive, puffed-up pride. She sails confidently in and out of her children's lives, lowering the boom when she chooses. See how she beams proudly at her youngest son, Harry, and opens her arms for his embrace.

I should perhaps explain that my two grandmothers were sisters, and you would be forgiven for not making this connection, as they were not at all alike. But surely the most common genetic resemblance is this unaccountable difference between siblings. The same parent, the same genes, or to put it plainly, out of the same pot, but you just never can tell what is going to be dished out.

My maternal grandmother, then, is Flora Treadwell. See Flora kiss her youngest child and lower herself gingerly into a chair. Flora Treadwell is of a nervous disposition, worn out by the endless verbal battering of her husband, William Treadwell. But everyone loves Flora. Gentle and sweet-natured, her love is of that rare and generous kind, a virtue that allows her to see the good in everyone. Flora's only downfall is that she would rather turn the other cheek than retaliate in anger. Downtrodden by a discontented husband and five sons of a sullen nature, the only thing Flora had ever really desired was peace. But just as a clearing in her life had begun to emerge, as her sons, one by one, fled the homestead, that space was filled again. Flora was tired and 45 years of age when she discovered she was with child. Rocking her swollen body, Flora wondered what explanation God would give her, if she happened to ask the reason why. And 24 years later my grandmother looking down at her newborn granddaughter, wondered again what that same mysterious God would reply.

She questioned why my hands did not grip her fingers the way that babies usually do, and why my arms seemed limp and floppy. Flora shut her eyes and held me tightly to her bosom as a sharp twist of fear made her stomach churn.

But these were her unspoken thoughts, and she had a lifetime of practice in the keeping of her countenance. Instead she smiled at my mother and asked, "Jenny, what are you going to call the dear little thing?" My father gave my mother's hand a squeeze and answered for her. "We want to call her April, no second name or anything, short and sweet – it seems to suit her." Ellen Raine came forward to take me in her arms. "Little April Raine, it's a lovely name, Harry." And as my grandmother cradled me in her arms, for one unnoticed and transient moment she too was quiet.

See Ellen Raine straightening her hat, picking up her leather bag, saying her goodbyes and taking her sister's arm. Observe that my two grandmothers uttered not one word until they were outside the hospital doors.

Only then did Ellen gently take Flora's hand and say, "Flora, what did you think of the baby?" Flora sighed and looked at her sister, "Oh Ellen, the baby's not right, just not right." Whether it was the combined experience of 21 births or two pairs of eyes which saw more than most, I could not say. But my grandmothers were the only two living souls who recognised my defect. They took the trolleybus home, silent and thoughtful, as they travelled through the busy streets.

My grandmothers kept a silent vigil for six months. They noted my difficulty in sucking the milk from my mother's breast and her subsequent disappointment when the milk ran dry. They watched my mother become tired and frustrated by the time it took to feed me by bottle. They observed anxiously my delayed development of movement. They would vigorously shake my rattle in the hope that I would reach out and pull it from their hand. Ellen purchased the most expensive teddy bear she could find, but even the soft caramel fur could not tempt me. They watched with dismay as it tumbled hopelessly to the floor. But then, suddenly, I would grasp a finger, or hold my head up for a few seconds, and lull them back into a restrained silence.

It was fear of the unknown, of unspeakable things, which sustained this silence. *Regard my grandparents speaking in guilty whispers.*

"We should never have allowed it to happen," Ellen said accusingly, "It's your fault, Flora, you've always been too soft with that girl, you should have had more control over her, sent her away somewhere."

Flora sighed at Ellen's criticism as she methodically folded the white napkins into neat piles. She knew from experience that Ellen would never blame one of her own children, whatever they might do. Ellen snapped open her bag and took out a packet of Craven As. She puffed hungrily on the cigarette; she loved the rush of nicotine in her veins when she was angry. "She manipulated my Harry, I saw what she …" Flora touched her sister's arm, "Ellen, stop. That's not fair, you know there was nothing that I could have done. They were both deeply in love, and the war … ". Ellen exhaled in an irritated hiss, "Poppycock! You've lived in a dream world all your life, Flora. The reality is that daughter of yours has always been difficult, and you never did know when to say no to her and this is the result. I told you, too much mixing of the same blood always leads to bad things. You mark my words, Flora, I know I'm not wrong and something has to be said soon!" Flora Treadwell made no reply. She had already retreated to a familiar and integral space.

So imagine the inevitable breaking of silence and in that utterance the close relationship between my mother and father became the root of all evil.

The doctor shifts comfortably in his chair and momentarily peers at the papers on his desk. He then looks directly at the persons opposite. "Mr and Mrs Raine, I've examined your daughter and she is mentally defective, to be more exact, she comes under the classification of a Mongol." The doctor pauses to let his words sink in before he continues. Nothing seems real to Jenny – the doctor's words resonate around the brown and dingy office walls.

See Jenny twisting the gold band round and round on her finger while Harry, in a broken voice, says, "Can anything be done? I don't care how much it costs, I want her to have all the medical help available, I'll … " "Mr Raine, please, you must listen to me. There is absolutely nothing that can be done.

Believe me, I know what I'm saying. You can get a second opinion by all means, but you will be only told the same thing."

Jenny suddenly leans forward and her voice is surprisingly strong and level as she demands, "I want to know exactly what has caused her to be like this, and why it's taken six months for anyone to tell me." Harry can't look at Jenny; he knows what she is thinking. The doctor looks sharply at Jenny, and the slight edge to his voice is discernible as he replies, "Mrs Raine, I'm afraid the answer to your question is not that simple. There are only theories rather than proven evidence as to the cause of Mongolism. The only aetiological fact that has been so far discovered is the maternal age at the time of conception. Mongolism seems to occur more frequently in older mothers, but naturally this doesn't apply in your case. So … my other suggestion would be that it's due to an unhealthy condition of the uterine mucosa at the time of conception, or it's a throwback to a previous ancestral type, in that it occurs in stock with an infusion of Mongolian blood. Now, has that helped?"

Jenny interrupts impatiently, "What I mean Doctor, is that my husband and I are first cousins and I want you to tell me if this is the reason for her condition." The doctor sighs and glances pointedly at his wristwatch. "Look, it's a very remarkable fact that defectives such as your daughter (who have such strikingly similar physical characteristics) can be born into such varied families, often quite devoid of any neuropathic predisposition. In other words, there's no rhyme nor reason for such births, so I'm sorry, I can't answer yes or no to your question, only that it's a possibility. Now …"

See the distress and anger on Jenny's face and the quick movement of body as she leans forward to speak once more, but also see her husband gently touch her arm as he says, "Jenny, just leave it. What good will it do now?" The doctor, seizing the opportunity, intervenes in a deliberate and patronising manner: "Mrs Raine, I suggest that you listen to your husband. The evidence is that your child is defective and it is your child. If this is too much for you to deal with then I can arrange for it to be institutionalised as soon as possible … "

Jenny becomes still, rigid, as if she is trapped in time, as the doctor continues, "However, you are not in any position to make any decision until you have heard all the facts." The doctor pauses to open a file on his desk. "Now, I'm going to read to you the clinical description of Mongolism, which is the most recent information I can give you. It comes from the latest amended Mental Deficiency Act of 1913, as issued by the National Health Service Act of 1946. There are pictures, which I will show you, so you know what to expect as … April, isn't it? … as April progresses. It's important that you're not under any false impression about your daughter's capabilities."

Harry nods his head in agreement. The doctor reads from his file. "'Mentally, Mongols are cheerful, good-tempered and appear bright and interested, but their attention is mostly of a passive nature with so little retention that response to training is very slow and limited and they are usually of the idiot or imbecile grade.' Now that means that your daughter will at the most only be able to perform simple routine tasks and that she'll need constant care and attention either from yourselves or an institution." The doctor pauses once again, but receiving no responses from either of the couple, he continues, "'A characteristic of Mongols is that they often display a marked interest in rhythm and are often good mimics. The principal features are stunted growth, a small, round head – of ten as wide as it is long – obliquely set eyelids, an extra fold of upper eyelid at the inner margins, together with squint, nystagmus, cataract or other eye defects. The ears and facial bones are small and poorly formed and the nose is stubby and depressed. The hair on the scalp is coarse. The tongue is usually protruded, rough and fissured (often not marked for a year from birth). The neck is short and relatively thick.' These photographs will help you to visualise what April will look like." The doctor hands Harry and Jenny some photographs. "As you can see, the palms of the hands are square and crossed by a transverse crease. The fingers are short, particularly the little finger, which curves inwards, and the thumb is short and broad. The feet also are short; there is a wide cleft between the big toe and the second toe and often a crease runs from this cleft down the sole. Sometimes the fingers and toes are webbed. Muscles generally are toneless and ligaments lax, with abnormal range of movements of the joints. I'm sure you've noticed some of these characteristics in your daughter already. As far as her health is concerned, bronchial catarrh and congenital heart abnormalities with poor peripheral circulation are frequently present. It is rare for Mongols to reproduce, but a case has been reported in which a Mongol girl gave birth to a Mongol baby."

Jenny is refusing to speak. It is Harry who asks the questions, "But I don't understand. April doesn't look like this. She's a pretty baby, I can't believe what you're saying." The doctor nods in agreement: "Yes, she is at the moment, but she will alter as she grows older and this is what you must prepare yourself for. However, it may be a blessing for you to know that it's unlikely she'll live beyond the age of 14. Very few Mongols survive for longer. So my advice is an institution or you do the best you can for her. Give her a tin can to bang on and she'll be fine. I'll be arranging for an officer from the Local Health Authority to pay you a visit in a few weeks to ascertain what you have decided to do. Now are there any other questions?"

See my parents mutter a negative reply.

The doctor stands to shake their hands as a means of ending the interview.

So, my physical characteristics have been defined, my mental capabilities labelled and my death has been predicted.

Afterword

The above is indeed a piece of fiction. April survived the predicted childhood illnesses by receiving homeopathic treatment from Dr Foobester at Guy's Hospital, London. She received an ordinary education through the acceptance of a local Catholic school – a situation unheard of at the time – and was able to read and write fluently. She was encouraged to partake in every social occasion available to her. Through the extraordinary love, tenacity and vision of her parents, April developed a vibrant and strong personality that allowed her to survive in the outside world. She lived a full and happy life until she died in 1998 from Alzheimer's disease at the age of 49.

Little April Showers
Drip, drip, drop little April Showers,
Beating a tune as you fall all around
Drip, drip, drop little April Showers
What can make with beautiful sound?

Drip, drip, drop when the sky is cloudy,
Your pretty music will brighten the day.
Drip, drip, drop when the sky is cloudy,
You come along with a song right away.

Drip, drip, drop little April Showers,
Come with your beautiful music,
As you fall all around,
Drip, drip, drop, your beautiful sound.

Bambi (Walt Disney)

Chapter 5
An advocate's story

Marion Hicks

I met Marion Hicks and interviewed her for this chapter in 2001. This account is drawn from her own words, recorded at our interview. Marion has been a long-term friend and advocate to Maureen Westwood, a deaf woman with learning disabilities. Marion originally met Maureen when she began her first job as a keyworker in a health authority unit set up to bring people back to a London borough from long-stay hospitals. Maureen is now in her sixties and the two have maintained close contact over the years.

Sue Ledger

Transitions

Maureen and I first met in November 1988. She was the first person I ever keyworked. It was my first proper job. Kingsbridge Road was set up by the health authority at that time as kind of training house to give people who had been in long-stay hospitals the chance to lean new skills and to get used to living in the community.

Maureen at my son's christening, 1988

Maureen and I met when I was very young, as you can see from the photo. I had just left college, and Kingsbridge Road was my first full-time job. I saw it advertised in the local paper and I applied and I got the job. I was asked to keywork Maureen. Everyone who had moved into the training flat had come from long-stay hospitals apart from Nigel[3], who had come from children's services. Maureen had been there a few months when we met and the task was to teach people skills – it was very training-orientated. It was very much run on an NHS model. The managers were qualified nurses – they dispensed drugs with senior staff. It was always intended to be a temporary home for people to be taught new skills and to be settled back into the borough so

3 Some of the names of places and people in this story have been changed to protect the confidentiality of service users, agencies and other involved parties

they could then move on to new more permanent homes when these were found. It was always thought we would have more people coming in after this original group.

Maureen came with Amy from a long-stay hospital in south London. They needed to experience living in a smaller group. Although Maureen and Amy had not really known each other very well they were moved to Kingsbridge Road together because of their links with the borough. Maureen herself had not lived in the borough for many years so the area was very strange to her.

When Maureen came there were no photos or any life book or anything else that came with her. The hospital she came from closed but there was no talk of any visits. When she moved she had a few clothes in her bag but only some of them were hers. The clothes she came with from the hospital were Bri-nylon or velour. At that stage there was no clear guidance on how best to support people moving from long-stay hospitals. I suppose it was all so new. There was no active care-management involvement, and psychologists themselves didn't always seem sure what to do. The local learning disability community team were great if you made referrals, though, and the speech therapists and nurses were very helpful. There was no resettlement manager involved and it was basically just us and the day service. No advocacy, of course. I think it was new to everyone.

Not a lot is known about Maureen's earlier history. We know that she had family at one stage but it was decided not to try to trace them as it was so uncertain how they may feel about contact with Maureen. Maybe it was wrong, but at the time it was deemed that it would be best not to search for them.

Maureen was the only person on the unit who had no family contact. She had no visitors. Most people had at least a little family contact. That did stand out on a Sunday lunchtime when people came to visit. Also on Maureen's birthday and at Christmas you were conscious there was no one there for Mo. B's father and uncle would come over, N's mother did, A's family did occasionally, B's mother did – so I always felt Maureen needed a bit more. So when it was decided that Kingsbridge Road was going to close I then became involved in resettling Maureen to Colville Road, the residential home where she still lives.

We had moved A. first to Colville Road and there were concerns that Maureen was too old for Colville, as she was already in her fifties and most of the other people were in their thirties and forties. So we tried to jazz Maureen up. We bought her some quite funky clothing to wear so that people wouldn't see her as being old, because we knew that Maureen was very lively and young at heart and we were worried that she was going to lose the chance to move to this new unit. But it has worked. It was a good decision at the time. So I was involved in lots of meetings about the move: I came to a staff meeting with

Maureen; I discussed her likes and dislikes. I was still employed at Kingsbridge then. Then Maureen moved to Colville after a series of tea visits, overnight stays and a resettlement meeting. It was not as in-depth as it is now. It was a bit more 'try this and then just go'! We did seem to do things slightly more on the hoof then. Although it was still very professional in the way people were treated, it was very different. There wasn't the policy and practice guidance there is now – it was very much more ad hoc. On the day she moved, Maureen wouldn't go in the cab. She got very distressed and very upset. So GH took her in the cab later on, and two of us came over with her stuff first. That was a Saturday morning. We just took things bit by bit and Maureen settled in very quickly, from what I remember. I kept in contact through the initial resettlement period, which I said I would, and just kept coming back.

Friend and advocate

By then I was working further away in Hammersmith, as I'd transferred to another house through the health authority, but I kept in contact. It's been easy just to pop in. Over the years people have just accepted me as someone Maureen knows, and gradually my role has become one of advocate as well as friend, because I kept coming back. I used to take Maureen out and used to bring her back to my house for Sunday dinner, so she knew my mum, my dad and my sister.

It was her keyworker in Colville who first asked me if I would be an advocate for Maureen as she had no one and the staff could not find an advocate who could work with someone who did not communicate in a conventional way. Then when a placements manager from social services talked to me more about my role as Maureen's friend and advocate, and the fact there were no independent advocates available for someone like Maureen at the time, I agreed to do it and I started to do it more formally by coming to reviews to support Maureen. Before that I hadn't come to any reviews or meetings. I was just someone who would just pop in and take Maureen out.

Maureen then started to come and stay with me and my husband – that began after we moved in 1995 when we got a house. She'd come over by herself in a taxi or go back in a taxi after I've picked her up. She was at my wedding reception, dancing on video; she's been to both my children's christenings. We go shopping together. It's changed a lot over the years. Now, as I have my own children, I can't see Maureen as often as I used to, and when my job changed and I became a manager it was harder to find the time to visit, but I've stayed in touch at Christmas, Easter and birthdays and special occasions. I feel that now we will always be in touch. I think I would feel guilty if I wasn't – I think Maureen would make me feel guilty as well. Every time I've felt, "Oh, I need to cut back", something has happened to make me feel I want to be involved again – like Maureen moving, or her eczema is playing up again, or hearing-aid issues, or feet issues, and also because staff in supported living or residential situations can be very transient. They don't tend to stay around people for more than about two or three years, so a lot of information gets lost: things like people's likes and dislikes, and what they have done in the past. Swimming, for example. There were issues about whether Maureen could go swimming, and I was able to say, "I used to take her swimming in the past – Friday evenings were swimming evenings from Kingsbridge Road. We'd go down to Kensington new pool." It's very important, that knowledge that you build up over the years with someone – it's the kind of information usually held by a person's family – but of course Maureen has no family, and it could so easily get lost.

When Maureen moved to Colville, people couldn't believe it when I said, "Maureen can have a temper. She will do the things she likes to do." I think they thought, "Oh no, she's a sweet old dear. Surely not." The first night they supported Maureen, I had a phone call saying they weren't expecting it, and I said, "I did warn you, this is the reality." I think it's more to do with frustration for Maureen, partly jealousy as well. In our relationship she gets jealous if there is anyone intruding on our time, like my husband or my oldest child. She was fine when they were babies, but she seems not so sure now that they are a bit older. But I still think it's important that she has some time and some links with others away from her home. I think she gets a lot out of it, even though sometimes she will ignore me for the whole outing or visit – especially when I have to leave or she has to leave.

Sometimes her behaviour can be a bit surprising, unless you are used to working with people with learning disabilities. I remember once when I was in Hammersmith going shopping with her around Christmas time, and she went running up to this 3-year-old and I had to go chasing after her to get her back. I think they were one of twins and that confused her. She couldn't understand why there were two children who looked the same – that really seemed to upset her. Sometimes you don't know if it's triggered off something that happened earlier in her past, and that's making her behaviour hard to manage or it's just upsetting for her.

Within my family and friends this is not an issue. My mum loved her, and she has learned to accept my husband – though always on her terms. She was great with my oldest child when he was a baby. She used to give him his bottle and she would quite like to push the pram. It supported her physically and she's always been so baby-orientated. As he has got older and demanded more time they have not really got on that well. The last visit was a bit tense so I have to stop those for a while, especially as we have a new baby now. But she was fine at the christening and the baby came to visit her at Colville. She was quite excited – she held him and gave him a cuddle. That was nice because it was a visit for her and no one else. Everyone else in the house saw this. They all wanted to join in but I was clear and I said hello to everyone but also made the point that I was Maureen's visitor and that Connor and I had come to see Maureen especially. And then, as I said, she was at the christening. She got a lift with one of my friends in their car and they got lost and there was all sorts of traumatic excitement. They were following us and they got lost in between the church and the reception. My sister was there and she was talking to Maureen because she has known her for years and my dad, and the neighbours, too, whom Maureen has seen. I don't know if Maureen remembers them but they remember Maureen and make a point of saying hello.

I have always been treated well by the staff at Maureen's home. They know that I'm here for Maureen. Although I'm not here all the time, they know I'm involved. I've always wondered what would happen if Maureen was to become very ill – it would be a real wrench for Maureen and the staff too if she was to have to leave. There was one time I was thinking of moving away from London, maybe to Devon, and although I was worried about Maureen I thought, "Well, she can come for visits." I'm sure we would have got round it somehow. But I found myself wondering whether she could manage coaches and trains. So the contact is very important to me.

Maureen at my son's christening party, 2001

Tracing old friends

Maureen has known so many people, like May Rodgers, whom she used to talk about for years and years. For years I didn't know who 'May' was, and then one day I found a doll and it had her full name on it, 'May Rodgers', with a ward number. I'm sure I moved this here with Maureen but I don't know where it is now – I haven't seen it for years. I spoke to a psychologist and we

Maureen with my son

got notes from the hospital that had closed and traced some records back to the former long-stay hospital and I spoke to someone in their office and then spoke to one of the nurses who remembered Maureen and May. I phoned up the local community team where May was known and managed to trace her address. We then managed to arrange some visits. I went with Maureen to look at where May was living, as Kingsbridge Road was closing down and we had nowhere to place Maureen. We visited, but Maureen didn't move there and sadly the contact between Maureen and May wasn't kept up. When they met up they seemed to know each other, but I think I had been watching too many films and was expecting them to run into each other's arms with tears, but it wasn't like that at all. I was really disappointed. Also, being so young at the time, I think I had a really idealistic view of the world, so I thought it was a bit strange. But they exchanged presents and Maureen stayed there overnight and May came to stay at Kingsbridge Road overnight. It was a nice piece of Maureen's history because before that, people who didn't know Maureen well thought she was talking about me when she said 'May'. They thought she must mean me, 'Marion', but she didn't, and it was good for other people to know this and to realise who May was. She had always said 'May' – it was one of the few words she ever said clearly: 'May', 'baby', 'aeroplane' – but May was always her clearest word. They were obviously very important for each other at the time – but they may have just sat next to each other in a hospital ward for ten years. We had no way of knowing – but I'm glad I found her. I had to turn into Miss Marple to do that, though, tracing names and contacting various resource teams around London. It was interesting – it also gave me something new to do in terms of my job.

At Kingsbridge we were good at holidays, trips out – these were things Maureen hadn't done before – going on holiday, going out, going to church – there was an evangelical church nearby and Maureen started to go and she seemed to like that. There were other things we noticed Maureen could do – she could crack an egg open with one hand perfectly. I thought she had probably worked in the kitchens – it's quite a skill. I couldn't do it and Maureen could! I remember she used to like cooking and doing the laundry.

Changes

In terms of how services have changed over the years I think they are now much more client-orientated. People seem to have a sense of professionalism that wasn't there. It was much more *ad hoc*. We didn't keep notes in the way we have to now by law – which is better, as people now should have much fuller information. We didn't put the same effort in as you would need to do now. People listen to clients much more now. I never knew the term 'advocacy' when I started at Kingsbridge 13 years ago – it never came up – there wasn't advocacy, there wasn't support. If people didn't have family they didn't seem to have anyone. In some places at that time they had visitors – lay visitors or volunteers from the hospital-visiting services. Kingsbridge as a health resource was never inspected by Social Services Registration and Inspection Unit so people didn't even get a visit once a year through that process. We never had that outside scrutiny in the house. In fact, Kingsbridge was very nice – it was only five-bedded, all ground floor. There was respite care next door and it was a good staff team. I think for me it was a very nice introduction to the job. We had waking night-staff. When Maureen's epilepsy started again, she had her first fit in ten years and I was on the waking night-duty and it really worried me. I had to race to get the sleeping-in member of staff. I was terrified – I had never seen anything like it and I was very worried for Maureen.

All these memories. I suppose in many ways I have really grown up with Maureen, as I was only 20 when I left Kingsbridge. There's a lot of history there between us.

My earliest memory of Maureen is when she came back from her day centre on my first day – I think I was on a middle shift and Maureen walked in and threw her bag down and stormed off. She was still settling into St Mark's (local day service) then. That was hard for her. People had had very little daytime occupation in the hospital, it seemed, and we were expecting them to get on the coach, go off to a day service with lots of other people and then come back and prepare dinner. I think sometimes we over-challenged her, but she will only do the things she wants to do. She has changed a lot over the years, too. She is much more self-assured now and she won't let people push her around. Still a bit of a collector! But only for the things she wants, and I think this comes from her having so little in hospital for so long.

I am very proud of Maureen and what she has done. She has met every challenge that has been thrown at her through the process of leaving Kingsbridge, coming to terms with getting older, people she knows – residents and staff – leaving. And now I hope to be involved in Maureen's next move – on to bigger and better things. But Maureen has not stood still and the services have changed with her. My role has changed, too, from a paid member of staff to an advocate. I think the fact that I have worked in a supported living and residential setting as a member of staff and as a manager has helped me as an advocate. I can appreciate what staff are up against at times and I try to appreciate this when supporting Maureen.

At Colville Road she has always been very lucky and had really good key workers, and staff who have taken the time to get to know her and supported her – in particular with her art which she enjoys so much. And that led to her art exhibition which she was really proud of. The exhibition was great for Maureen as a lot of people she knew came – a lot of people she hadn't seen for a long time came. The exhibition wasn't done in a tokenistic way but was very professionally organised in a proper gallery. To have the opportunity to exhibit their paintings is something that a lot of people would love to do – and Maureen has done it. She was selling her paintings in beautiful surroundings. The evening boosted her confidence no end, and she was so proud.

Maureen is still a very young-at-heart person. She now has a local network of people she knows and likes and the future looks good for her.

One of Maureen's paintings

Chapter 6
Daughter Anne

Van Brunning

I met with Van Brunning in July 2001 to talk about her experiences of bringing up her daughter Anne. The interview has been transformed into the following account, told in Van's own words.

Lindsay Brigham

A bonny baby

At her birth on 19 August 1956, it was apparent to everyone else except me that her head was bigger than it should have been. Both my husband and I knew very little about babies, but we did know that babies' heads always look bigger compared to the rest of their bodies. I think that we did have an X-ray at the hospital before we left, but I can't remember – it was such a long time ago. But it was evident that there were some concerns, because each time we went to the specialist, or so it seemed to me, he always had a tape measure in his hand ready to measure to see whether or not her head had increased in size. The specialist didn't give me much idea of the extent of the problem because he didn't know the degree of it – looking back, you can understand that.

Friends and family didn't mean to be unkind but they would say things like, "Well, she should be doing this now", or "She should be doing that now. My son or my daughter, you know, did it at …". I don't know whether mothers keep a calendar of when their offspring do things, but it seemed at the time that everybody knew when they did things. They would say, "Well, isn't she doing this or the other" and I used to cry. It upset me, because although she was a sickly baby, she walked at about 18 months and that surprised me and I was sort of very proud of the fact and would say to people, "Anne is walking now." Some would say that she wouldn't walk for a while and people would say that boys were more adventurous and they walked quicker. And I would say, "Oh well, perhaps that's why." I would find all kinds of excuses as to why she wasn't doing things. I didn't like to think that she wasn't doing things because she had a disability, but I must have been blind. I think my husband was hiding it from me. We had to go constantly down to Great Ormond Street to see one of these paediatricians, one of the specialist hydrocephalics at the time, but even then I thought they were just being sure.

Also, you always have the very kind person who would come and say, "Don't worry, my daughter didn't do something … oh, and she's lovely", and so she was. She was a bonny baby. She had dark, curly hair – she was born in August and I remember for the first few months it was very warm, and she looked liked a little Negro – all of these little tight, black curls – oh, she was pretty. My husband used to say, "They'll think we had a milkman in." We used to laugh about it. I think we used to hide our feelings from each other really.

But we used to talk about Anne, and I would constantly watch her to see what she was doing, when she gripped things and when she touched her toes, more or less. She didn't sit up, and when I would take her out in the pram I would prop her up so people couldn't see she couldn't sit up of her own accord. Looking back, it was the wrong thing to do, as her spine would have been injured in some way. It was rather nice for people to see a nice, bonny baby sitting up in her pram. When I'd got her propped up with her lovely black curly hair, and brown with the sun, it wasn't so evident. Mothers are very silly people, well not silly, but they are very sensitive, they get disappointed and they get hurt. On the whole we plodded along. We went regularly to Great Ormond Street and I always felt better afterwards because I thought they would pick out anything wrong. Had there been anything that urgently needed attention, they would have seen to that.

As she got older it became evident that she was acting at four years old perhaps what one expected an 18-month-old child to do. When we moved to Newcastle, I think that it was a relief in one way because I didn't have to hide the fact that Anne was a bit backward. I devoted the whole of my time to seeing to Anne. She has been my life's work. I am not saying that in a 'pity me' sort of way; it's because I wanted it to be. So I don't think the move affected us – we were transferred from Great Ormond Street to see a very nice paediatrician in the Royal Victoria Infirmary and he took over where the professor in Great Ormond Street left off, and he was very nice. He introduced us to various places and people that would help us and it started off in that way.

Anne's education

She went to a nursery for a couple of years, until she was about seven, and then she was admitted to a Children's Training Centre and from there she progressed to an Adult Training Centre. At the Children's Training Centre they did very little, but I think they did their best. It was an occupation centre. I doubt if the staff at the time had any qualifications or any training at all; they were there rather as carers and I don't think they had any idea of stimulation or progression and of progress at all, and I was so pleased when she was sent to a different Centre, hoping that things would be different. I don't know whether they did more at the second Centre because Anne was older and was able to do more. I don't know whether it was the Centre or whether Anne would have progressed as she did without going there. I taught her on hands and knees on this floor. I found that she had a great interest in books and liked looking at pictures and it progressed from there. I think now they do a certain amount of simple reading and writing at Centres, but once they can do that they progress to special units and colleges – which Anne herself has.

She has been at college for quite a few years now, and one of the highlights was last Christmas when she won the Newcastle College Christmas card competition and her card was used by the college staff to send to other places – and I thought that was very nice.

Anne

She had to go down and some bigwig was there to give her the presentation – I think she had a voucher. But she had won this competition between all the art students – dozens or maybe more – it's quite a big department. The Art Department alone is very big so I was very pleased about that. Yes, I am proud of her but I didn't like to say that I was. I am very proud of her academic prowess really and she's very, very artistic – she has this GCSE in Art – with a B grade – which is not to be laughed at. She likes to be top of the class, you know, and she often is, or so she'll tell me, "I did best at this today" and I'll say "very nice". And she has certificates for computing, one with the lady from *Coronation Street* with Anne – Denise Welch.

Denise was doing the presentation for some of the people there and Anne was one of the lucky ones – and that particular certificate was for French conversation and I was so proud when she went to pick it up and everyone else said "thank you" but Anne said "merci" – possibly the only word she could remember – and Denise Welch very nicely said "très bien" – oh yes, loads of little incidents like that which have pleased me.

Second Prize
'My Mum'
by
Ann Brunning

Prizewinning painting 'My Mum' by Anne

Anne on the catering course

And now she's doing just the NVQ in catering, which she is completing tomorrow with hygiene. But she's done the course and the tutor was saying that she will eventually get the certificate, so that's an NVQ. But that's still a qualification. Oh yes, she doesn't sit around doing nothing. She has progressed. Wonderful progress, isn't there? When I was told that she wouldn't be able to do a great deal, I would like some of the people that told me that to see her now. Now she is absolutely wonderful. From a very bad beginning she is a wonderful lady.

I think the best thing that happened to Anne was her acceptance at Newcastle College because she didn't really fit in to the Adult Training Centres (ATCs). They are all right for some people, other people maybe, but she needs stimulation and she didn't have enough. At Newcastle College they understood that, and all the people and all the lecturers were there to stimulate Anne, to increase her ability to the best of their own ability. I am sure that was the turning point for Anne. I don't think that the ATCs were to blame; that was how ATCs were. They were there just as carers rather than teachers. Anne has been going to college for six or seven years and I don't think she would fit into the background of an ATC any more. Going to the college is a new thing that has only happened in the last ten years or so. Until then there wasn't anything else but the ATCs. We had the Special Schools for up to 16-year-olds and then you had to go from the Special Schools to the ATCs. College suits Anne. She didn't like the ATCs; she was very unhappy there and I used to really have a bit of a battle some mornings to even get her to go there. I'm sure that going to the Newcastle College was a good move for her.

Continuing education

But it is always a struggle to make sure Anne gets what she needs and it's still continuing. We are in July now and Anne's courses for last year have finished, and they have two-year courses, and they talk about continuing education and Tomlinson.[4] But Tomlinson never spoke of two-year courses, and I think, "Well how did they think that one out?" So every other year you'd come in the middle of it and you'd have to start all over again to get some sort of programme. As Anne has been an established member there they are very helpful, but the courses are getting fewer and fewer. There isn't a kitchen there any more so

4 The Tomlinson Report for the Further Education Funding Council on inclusive learning.

there's no catering. All being well, next September, she will have two and a half days, but what about the other two and a half days – there's nothing. People like 'Skills for People', the advocacy group at Newcastle; they have various courses, but whether she'll be able to fit in the days there rather depends which days of the week they are on. What is she going to do for the two and a half days? That I do not know. It's a bit worrying. She regresses, like we all do. If we don't do a thing for a while we forget how to do it. It means more or less starting again from scratch. I know that this will happen with the catering because she doesn't have the opportunity at home – I haven't got the facilities.

There has always been this problem of keeping Anne occupied. When I say occupied, I mean a *meaningful* occupation, not just something to pass the time away. She may as well just stop at home and watch the telly. There should be something more stimulating – it doesn't have to be educational but most occupations are educational. She, like everyone else, is pleased when she has certificates – she has loads of them in the other room. It's rather nice, it shows some achievement. I don't know what else there is really – in day-to-day living, we cope like mother and daughter do. We sometimes get fed up with each other. She'll say, "I'm sick of you" and I'll say, "I'm sick of you too"! It wears off after a few minutes.

Changing attitudes

I think with people's attitudes there is more acceptance now; there is not so much of a stigma as there was a few years ago. There was a time when they were hidden – they weren't taken out of the house unless they were taken out by their families – but now you see them walking the street and doing things as we all do. They are not completely integrated into the community. I think the attitude still has a way to go but it has improved tremendously I would think, as far as Anne is concerned.

I think that the main change that is needed is more money. It's difficult in a city as big as Newcastle to allot the right amount of money to different sources. I have a person with a learning disability and of course I am biased in that way and I think that they should have this much and that much for resources, especially for people like my daughter. People's attitudes should also be slightly different, I think. People like my daughter, they are still segregated and they are not wholly integrated into the community. She knows people – she has had friends for years and it's almost as if they are in a community of their own. They all know each other because of their background, and most of my friends are people like myself with people with disability in the family. Yes, the attitudes – we need to educate other people – I know that's a stupid sort of corny way of saying things – but they do need to learn more. I don't know how that's going to happen. Not in my lifetime I suppose, but it is improving.

Anne's future

Well she is able to travel independently on the bus, and I don't think she'll starve as she has a certain amount of catering skills. She's just done this NVQ. She always has liked cooking and messing about – she uses a tin opener very well so I don't think she'll starve. She is not particularly good with using money. I often tell her that she thinks money grows on trees. I think there's something wrong here – she should be more informed about the worth of things. This is my house, and I hope that when I am no longer here, she will be able to manage to live here with some sort of social service support. I think she'll manage that quite well. I think she will be happier living in this area where she knows most people. I am working towards that end. The money ... well, I don't know whether she doesn't want to learn or she just can't learn. I am told that whereas many are literate they are not numerate. She manages to write and she manages to read up to a certain level, quite well really. She looks at the paper and says, "Oh, so and so has happened" – very good. She's wonderful, when you consider they don't get the help they should have.

My main support

Oh, my main support is my church, my faith. I think that God is looking down on us – I mean that very sincerely. I think if I didn't have any faith I wouldn't go very far. I've met an awful lot of nice people so we've been helped tremendously on the way. I've met more nice than nasty people, who have all tried to help, so it hasn't been all down. Do I sound 'pity me'? ... as I'm not at all sorry for myself, I'm a very happy person. You know there are some awful things happening, and I thank the Lord that I had a girl like Anne, because she hasn't been a ha'porth of bother all her life. Isn't it nice to be able to say that? It horrifies me what is going on in this world.

Chapter 7
Never take no for an answer

Brenda Nickson

This chapter is an account derived from an interview conducted with Brenda in 2000. The interview was recorded as part of an Open University course, 'Care, Welfare and Community', and Brenda has kindly agreed to our re-editing it for publication in the book. Brenda and her husband were founder members of the Bedford local Mencap society.

Jan Walmsley

Early days – Roger's birth and the beginnings of the Society

I had my son in 1955. I was just told that he was a 'Mongol', as they were called in those days, and there would be no future for him, and that he'd probably not live longer than five. They said the best thing for us to do was to put him in an institution. Needless to say my husband and I were so horrified we just picked up our bags and left. I had a good weep, of course. I think I spent the first two years crying.

We were just left then. At that time nobody acknowledged you. My mother-in-law, for instance, wouldn't acknowledge that there was anything different with Roger except he had a bad heart. Of course, he did have a bad heart, he had what they called then holes in his heart. But that wasn't his basic problem, that was the plus problem. She didn't want to accept that. My own mother was marvellous but she was away down in Devon so she couldn't do that much. And when you went out with the baby you just felt you were pushing an empty pram because people didn't know what to say to you. So life was very traumatic, because you felt so lonely.

In those days the baby clinic was once a month in the village, and the health visitor at the baby clinic suggested that I met a parent of a Down's syndrome (I'll call them 'Down's syndromes' now but they were 'Mongols' then), who lived in Kempston. This girl, Mary, she was already five or six, but I said it would be nice to meet her, and that's how I met the first person – live person – who had a child in similar circumstances – and that was the beginning of any contact at all with anybody. She came to see me quite a lot, and she brought her daughter with her. She was a quite bright Down's girl, she could talk, which is more than my son can do, he can't talk at all.

But then I discovered the Society. I think it was through a person called Mrs Crouch who somehow knew there were people that had handicapped children in the town. She notified my husband and I that there was going to be a meeting in the town of people interested in setting up a branch of the Society for the Parents of Backward and Handicapped Children. I think my son was four months old then, it was very early in his life. And we went to this meeting. It was headed by some people from the St Albans society, including Judy Fryd. I can't remember exactly how many people were there but it was amazing how many. I was the only one with a baby, all the others had practically grown-up children, so I couldn't converse with them. They were all talking about their children but mine was a baby that did nothing at all. Anyway, as a result of that meeting they decided to form the Bedford branch of the society, and that was the beginning of it.

They were trying to get support and recognition as much as anything, to try and get people to treat our people as though there was at least a certain amount of normality. They were all human beings. All the parents are proud of their children whether they're handicapped or not. But if you're not a parent it was of no interest to anybody else to help you, and that's why the Society was needed. Some of those parents of the children that we took on those first holidays – they weren't children, they were adults by this time – had never had one day's relief from looking after them. There was no such thing as respite care or carers then. And so the aim was to see about that, helping each other. We were a self-help society, of course. And also to try and get the children, although they weren't children all of them, recognised as people.

They weren't all Down's syndrome like Roger by a long chalk. There were a great variety. And that's the biggest tragedy of all. At least with the Down's they're not going to be a normal person, but it's these that look perfectly normal that are so heartbreaking. I hadn't got a situation to compare, because mine was a baby, but the people I was meeting had families say up to adult age, and it was quite amazing to see that they'd lived with their handicapped offspring with no help, no financial help, no help of any sort. It had tied them entirely and ruled their lives – it rules your life in any case – but they had had nothing to support them, and of course that was what we were aiming to get, recognition and support from someone from the health authority. Of course, we didn't get education till 1971, which was a long, long time to wait. But they did get what they called occupation centres which were run by the social services. So the branch of the social services for mental health was the one we contacted, and the mental health officer, to try and push and get something done.

I didn't know what the other families had gone through, because what they were talking about was all news to me. I didn't know what I was heading for because my baby was only three months old, so I couldn't compare my circumstances with them, because they'd gone through so much without any help and support at all, and that was what we were trying in those early days to put right.

My son had holes in his heart, and it caused him to have very bad chest problems as a baby. He'd go down with pneumonia probably three times a year, and I never knew whether it was going to get better. It was touch and go whether his heart would stand the pneumonia, and one thing triggered the other off. I asked for further consultation to go to a heart specialist because I'd heard they'd just started doing heart treatment, mending holes in the heart, I don't know what they called it in those days. And I was referred to Hammersmith. Roger went in for the investigation to X-ray the heart, see what holes were in it. Then we went to collect him. The specialist said that he was very sorry but he couldn't do anything for Roger. He had three holes in his heart and it was a fifty-fifty chance that he would survive. That would mean a death on the table which we all know is a thing that surgeons will do anything to avoid. And in any case, he said, "It would still be a Mongol." It was the last remark that really shook us because we knew perfectly well he was going to be a Mongol. That could never be repaired. So we went off, and the registrar took us back to the ward. He said, "This is very interesting. I've never had anything to do with children like this. How do you manage at home?" And I said, "Well, just like a family." I said, "He's got an older brother, and we're a family of four and we do everything together as a family. I've got two children and that's the end of it." And he was most interested to have that opinion of something that he had never come personally into contact with.

When we started the Society, people just thought, "They're just mentally retarded, probably idiots." They were referred to as 'idiots' in the old days. Nobody expected you could do anything with them. We always took Roger with us everywhere the same as Paul, we never left him behind at parties and visits to relatives and friends, we never excluded him. And the little remarks would come out, "Oh, he can do that." And I'd say, "Yes, of course he can do that." They'd ask things like, "Can he dress himself?" – silly things like that. It was in the lap of the gods how far you got, but you treated them just exactly the same as you treated your other child, and hoped that eventually things would work out. But it really was quite surprising, that sort of attitude, nobody expected to see that he could do things. Of course he didn't walk, my son, until he was four, which meant that he was still incontinent. He wasn't toilet-trained until he could walk – once he walked, both things fell into place. Once he walked he'd come along with me just like any other four- or five-year-old child. I can remember when Roger first walked. Until he was four he used to crawl round on his bottom. When he walked his first steps my other son Paul, who was six at the time, couldn't get to school quickly enough to tell the teacher that

Roger had walked. And it was so exciting, and we all had to know about it, and that was the family feeling, that's how it affected the family, when things like that happened. We made people aware because we didn't hide it, we made ourselves noticeable.

Nowadays you see the handicapped people about, which you never used to, and nobody takes any cruel unkind notice. People don't turn away in the way that says, "Oh, you, we don't want to know." If they turn away I think it's because they don't want to show embarrassment by not knowing what to do, that's the big thing. The embarrassment is because they don't know how to cope with it.

Respite care

It took a long time, took a long time. But things started working as soon as the Society got going. We had very enthusiastic members, who'd suffered for so long they were only too glad to get going. And then of course my husband was the right sort of person to boost it up. So really I had the benefits of that. Roger was ten, the first time I had any respite, any respite care at all. There were no respite places anywhere, except Bromham Hospital. By this time he was ten years old, and we were very involved with Bromham Hospital. We knew all the staff. My husband went to see them (not behindhand, because he was also involved in it through the Mental Health Department) to see if they couldn't give some sort of respite care if they had spare beds at Bromham. It was 1965 and Roger went there. In those days they had a school there for them, it was very different from now – well of course it doesn't exist now – but even compared to what it was latterly, it was a very happy place. And, they were very well cared-for, and he was quite happy there. He went three times there eventually. He was ten before I had a night off or a day off.

When my husband said to other parents, "Try and get some respite care by going to Bromham", people were very wary. It was very difficult. These parents had been the only ones looking after their offspring the whole of their lives, and like any parent, they thought nobody else knows how to do it. So they were very wary about letting their child go to somebody else to be under their care. I know. I had a good old week. I was supposed to be going on my first holiday abroad in my life when Roger went into Bromham for this fortnight. He couldn't speak so he couldn't articulate what he wanted. I just had to hope that he could make himself understood enough with the people. We'd taken him to meet them all and show him where he was going so that it wasn't going to be a shock.

Then Brookside was opened, which was a hostel. Even then there wasn't truly respite care. But through the Society we put forward the idea that it should be used as a respite if it was possible to fit it in, so that when any of the residents were away on holiday that space could be used by somebody for respite care. And so my Roger went to Brookside several years for respite: when we went on holiday, he went to Brookside for *his* holiday.

I don't think anyone had thought of having respite care except the parents. I don't think anyone thought they needed it. This is where the parents came in. It was through the parents who knew that they'd never had a break. They put forward the idea that they needed a break – all the parents needed a break after being with their offspring say 10, 20 or 30 years. And so respite care was very much to the forefront of the Society's agenda. Respite care was the culmination of, as I say, a long effort, because the first respite was having a night out at a club, one night a week or a fortnight. And that was one evening that the parents had without their offspring. That was the first respite for the parents, to get initiated into letting their children go somewhere where they weren't in charge of them.

That was another thing. The Society, or the members that ran the Society, were adamant that there's no reason for their offspring not to have a club to go to and meet other children like other people did, and have activities of their own. It didn't matter whether it was thumping a drum, or just scribbling on a piece of paper, they could all do it together with somebody to look after them, and have some music. And those were the beginnings.

My husband, Jim, was one of the prime movers. People had no option. When he said he wanted to see somebody, he wouldn't ever take no for an answer – shall I put it that way. If he wanted to see the mental health people, well, he went to see the mental health people.

Barkers Lane Occupation Centre

Barkers Lane was for the over-16-year-olds, and it was called the Training Centre. When we wanted to get Barkers Lane built, Jim organised a trip to the Parliament to see our MP to get it aired, and that was the first centre in the town built for them. It must have worked because eventually they did get it. We did go to the top, and if you ever want to get something done, that's the way to do it, to go to the top.

It was a large area. They had a garden area where they grew vegetables and flowers and plants. Of course it was a big organisation because you don't just have to build a thing, you've got to get the staff, you've got to get the transport, because none of them could go on their own. So there would be a gardening group, then there was a woodwork group – and they had lathes and made wooden things and they chopped up firewood and they sold that. They had contract work from small firms like Crayola. And the residents or the trainees did the packing. Now they can't count, so they had a pegboard with 12 pegs, and one person would fill the pegboard with 12 crayons, and the next would put the crayons in a box. And the next one would put a label on the box, and the next one would put them in another box to go in a package – and that was the sort of conveyor belt, and they were marvellously happy. I can remember Roger used to come home covered with chalk. But, oh, he thought it was marvellous. Another thing, they did hairpins, on the same principle, rollers with pins in them for the hairdressing people. And although they couldn't count, everything was done. And they also had some plastic toys they would put together – like a teapot had a handle and a spout and a lid – and they put those together. And that was contract work. They got paid for it. I don't think the money was the ultimate aim so much as the occupation. What else did they do? They also had work from the RSPB making wooden boxes. Oh, and there was also a social corner where they learned how to cook, how to look after a room, make a bed and do things like that.

Spreading the word
There was another thing that Jim did. We couldn't get the names of people who needed our support because it was confidential: the authorities felt that they would be breaking confidences to give us names. So Jim had leaflets printed to put round in all the doctors' surgeries. I don't know how much good they did, but it was an effort and it was done. And that's the sort of thing that he did.

So eventually there were the holidays, and then no less than three clubs. A general club; another one for the more able-bodied people; and a junior club. I think they've got another club now, because the need is never any less. We had a swimming club, and of course the holidays and outings, so all these things were what normal children and growing adolescents had the opportunities to indulge in. We started our clubs before the Gateway Clubs were inaugurated. And then Barkers Lane also had sports so that those who were able to could partake in football and cricket and running races and whatever they were capable of. There was somebody that would do it with them, so that they were no longer different to the extent that they were originally looked on as being different. I think that was the biggest aim that the Society was trying to achieve.

To start with it was very difficult to get publicity, because we had to be very circumspect. A lot of the parents at the very beginning didn't want publicity. That's going back 40 years. They'd lived with it so long in seclusion that they didn't want it broadcast, they didn't mind getting help, but publicity's a different thing. And I can remember the first holiday that they went on, and we had this coach going from St Peter's, and I said, "Have you had the press there for it to go in the local paper?", and they said, "Oh no, no, they can't give their permission to have photographs taken." And of course that changed gradually, because why shouldn't they have their photographs taken? They'd be delighted to see their photographs in the paper when they were going on holiday. But that was how it was with the publicity at the beginning, it was very, very difficult. Gradually, the work the Society did, and all the various openings that went with the clubs and the parties and outings and things like that, broke down the barrier of being averse to publicity. When we had a bazaar or a party or anything like that Jim always invited the press and the mayor, always. He hoped they'd come. Sometimes they wouldn't bother because they didn't think it was worth the mayor, at first – it wasn't regarded as interesting news for the paper. But they did come, gradually. Because in the same way as anything that has been brushed under the carpet and then brought out, *there was no question about it.*

Living with a Mencap activist

I saw all this grow and I was terribly involved with it, because I was Jim's wife and it all went on from home. But I didn't actually go on committees or anything like that because he did it and I felt that was enough, enough's enough. And I suppose really he felt that for all we achieved and all the things that are better, there was still an awful long way to go. He would never give up, there was always another project to do, and when he died he was doing a workshop programme for them.

He went up to London and heard that there were places where they could go to work. Well that was it. My husband came home determined that they were going to have it. This was what he wanted. (Of course now they recognise a certain amount of work has to be given to handicapped people). But unfortunately at that time it didn't materialise because we didn't have the money. There were plenty of empty places that we could have applied for to use as a café or a drop-in coffee place, that was it, nothing elaborate, just a coffee place, run by Mencap people. But of course the rates were too high. You had to have trained people there to be supervising, and you've got to pay their wages. So it needed an awful lot of money, which of course we didn't have at the time, and it fell through. But now, which he won't have seen, it has happened, and it's in a church hall in St Peter's. They have this two mornings a week, and it's supervised, and it's just got off the ground this year. And they are supervised and when I visited I said, "Oh, if only Jim was alive to see this, he'd be so thrilled" – because it was another project and it was the last one that he was thinking of before he was taken ill, and went.

Mind you, Jim just could not let it rest. He was fluent in Spanish because he was brought up in the Argentine so they were bilingual. And we had this holiday in Spain, and it was a lovely holiday, too. I don't know who we wrote to, but he got in touch with somebody to see what the circumstances were like in Spain. And at Burgos he contacted this person and it was very interesting.

But this was what used to get me down. We took it away with us, it was as though he couldn't leave it alone. And we met this head of the Society who also had a Down's syndrome son about the same age, and we didn't know this until we met him in Spain, and his other son was a doctor, it was so strange. And he took us round their workshops that they had. My husband was so keen to see how other people approached the problem and what they gave their handicapped people to do. And we went round these workshops where they did a lot of pottery and the girls did a lot of very fancy sewing and needlework and it was sold. He did the same in Brittany. He went over to Spain, Brittany and France, to see how they were approaching the problem and what new ideas could be brought over here. Now things like pottery and fancy sewing and that sort of thing I'm afraid have not materialised in these circumstances. I think there must have been a lot of private money that went in with these sort of things, and I suppose if you went to some of the private set-ups in this country, that are for handicapped, you would find like facilities. Rudolph Steiner and Camp Hill Village do an awful lot of this and there are various other places that do it.

Making contact. Making contact. Never said 'no', made wonderful contacts. Jim used to just make a nuisance of himself until he got noticed. And he either got it because they wanted to shut him up or they had to put up with him bothering them. He never ever gave up. It didn't matter, he didn't ever take no for an answer. If they said 'no' well then that was that, but he didn't forget it, it would always be there to be brought up again if he thought that it was a viable proposition, if it had been taken in the right way, that was the point.

A lot of the services that are there really have developed from the fact that they started as voluntary services. Who would have thought of them putting a swimming pool in St John's School! We used to take the boys on holidays and they went swimming and naturally Jim thought, "Why can't we go swimming with them?" And he got permission to have a swimming session at the college on the Saturday morning 12pm to 1pm when nobody else wanted it, providing we had to supply our own supervision. And we got two professional life-savers, swimmers who volunteered to come. He could get people to come and work for him – it was absolutely amazing. We did say that people would not have to supervise their own children, but they had to bring them as we couldn't run transport. But when it was first mentioned, I can remember, they said, "Good heavens, you're not thinking of taking these sort of children swimming?" – that was the attitude. "Who on earth do you think will go to look after them?" It went like a bomb. We got them in, and some of them were lovely swimmers, and of course now they all go swimming, don't they. Those are the sort of things that really happened here. Whether they were the same in other towns and cities I don't know. At the time you just worked damned hard and hoped for the best and hoped you could do it.

In my day there was no such thing as welfare rights or anything like that. And this is another thing my husband used to go in for – all sorts of things, getting the rights we used to put in for. I know we got things that he would put in for as test cases. One thing we went to a tribunal for. We'd been refused something, so we went to a tribunal. He didn't think he'd win but it was publicity. And it made people think.

Thoughts on the present

Now they talk about them as people with learning difficulties. I think everybody's got learning difficulties. You and I have got learning difficulties, haven't we, before we start. It's a euphemism, isn't it really. Yes they've got learning difficulties, but they haven't the power of reasoning, and it's this reasoning power that makes them vulnerable and incapable. Some may have a certain amount, but how many of them when you give them a choice, which is reasoning power, know what the heck choice is? They tried to do this with my Roger and you go and you hand them a plate of cakes and say, "Which one would you like?" – he'd like them all. It's the same even with people that can really look after themselves, it's very hard to get the reasoning in. So it's the reasoning, having to work things out logically that they can't learn. You give money to pay for something and then somebody gives half of it back to you. What's logical about that? We'd say it's logic. "We can't go swimming today, it's raining." You can't say that to a child, to somebody like that, because you're going to get wet anyway when you go swimming, so why can't you go out because it's raining? Everything is very logical, everything's very basic, and literal. I've got what I call a 'low grade'. I get told off about this, but even the higher-mentality ones that have got much more sense, you've got to be very careful, it's very literal. I can remember on holiday, one of the children, lasses, she was frightened of thunder and she said, "Look at that dreadful big black cloud!" I said, "You don't want to look that way," I said, "look over there, the sun's shining." And she said, "Oh, yes", and she forgot all about the black cloud.

I'll tell you something that I do get a little bit frustrated with is when I hear people complaining about what there is now, when there is so much more, and no one now can go – unless it's of their own volition – without having respite. I only went ten years, most of the people I was with at that time had gone 20, 30 years without a day off. And now they get it, it's an acceptable thing that you get this break and everything is put in.

I do think sometimes when I see some of them complaining, and there are plenty still complaining, about not getting their rights – and I don't dispute the fact that probably they should perhaps get more help – but I think they should be thankful for what they've got, sometimes.

I think they take it for granted that it's what they deserve, which is what we hoped for. The aim was that parents should think of their children as being capable and being accepted as people that could do, in as far as their ability was, what any other person of their age was doing, and I do think that the parents accept that.

I think the parents are rather sitting back and waiting. I should be very careful about what I'm saying here because I have now really retired from it all, I'm really an outsider, because I'm not with the current situation enough, but there's a very small number of dedicated people who we try to keep roped-in to carry on with the work, and of course they're all parents because they know what it is that's wanted. But it is hard to find enthusiasm to do this sort of thing on a voluntary basis now, because it appears to me, and I could be very wrong, that parents expect everything on a plate without them doing anything to do it. The majority want, and will take, but don't give. They use the help, and I expect you find this in all self-help societies whether it's Mencap whether it's Alzheimer's, MS and all those arthritis societies – they are all people that know what they want and the ones that are involved, and they'll all see what they require.

I hope the Society carries on doing all that it can do. And as new ideas come, I hope that they will be accepted. It rather shakes me when I see things like computers in the centres when I haven't a clue what a computer's doing, and I see several of them playing a computer game I think, "Well it's me that's mentally handicapped, not them"! The whole attitude of the world has jumped so much that I just hope that it goes on. Because I think, money shouldn't be necessary really, but it is necessary. And without it, I think it's only the people involved in the problems that can see ways ahead much more than the outside people like yourself. You're willing to learn about it, but you're only learning from the experience of people that have gone through it. Nobody knows what the pain of a broken leg is until they've broken their own – "Oh dear, that must be awful; have you got to use a stick?" – but it's not until you're in the same boat that you realise the complications, and I think that the parents need to keep themselves to the fore with ideas, because as modern things come along, there must be lots of things that they see that could be beneficial.

And I think quite honestly the biggest thing we had to fight was the professional people who approached us with the idea, "You don't know anything about it because you're not trained professional people." If you've had the problem to deal with 24 hours of every day for about ten or 20 years, then if you don't know something about it you jolly well ought to.

I think what we achieved is the fact that you're not ashamed of admitting that you have a handicapped family, which of course nobody would have admitted at one time. This was what happened with my mother-in-law. She wouldn't admit it: "Nothing like that in our family." And now it's different, isn't it?

Chapter 8
Why us?

Lilian Fisher

I first met Lilian Fisher in 2000 when she agreed to be interviewed for a project I was doing on the history of local Mencap societies. She and her husband Roy were most generous with their time, and talked to me many times about their family and their daughter, Wendy. Lilian was a founder member of Lowestoft and District Mencap Society in 1962 and she had many insights to give and experiences to recount. For this book, she chose to start at the beginning and write the chapter herself.

Sheena Rolph

When our elder daughter, Denise, was about two years old, we were visiting my mother in Blackpool from our home in Grimsby, where we had moved just before Denise was born. As we walked along the road leading to the shops, I saw a young, pretty lady adjusting the covers of her baby's pram. I spoke to her and peeped in the pram, and saw a Down's syndrome baby, although in those days such children were referred to as 'mongoloid'. No one then considered the term derogatory. The young mother gazed with anguish at her baby and at me, and I felt her pain. What a cruel fate to have a mentally handicapped child, I thought. I never dreamt I was to suffer the same fate, although not so obviously recognisable.

On deaf ears
When our elder daughter was aged four, our second daughter was born in January 1955. Instead of the large hospital where Denise was born, I went into a private and somewhat inefficient nursing home for our second baby, Wendy. There seemed to be nothing untoward about the birth, although there was blood in the baby's mouth and nose, but surely that is not usual. However, right from the start there were difficulties with feeding, and I noticed that my baby had a strange mewing cry. I sensed that something was wrong, yet my anxious questions seemed to fall on deaf ears. Once home, we soon realised something was seriously amiss with our baby. Although pretty – quite doll-like, in fact – Wendy didn't feed, didn't sleep, didn't respond to affection, attention or stimulus. Each feed took hours, and then the milk shot right back again. We learned that this was called projectile vomiting. Our doctor did not seem to share our fears, and whether this was to soothe and alleviate our distress I have never been sure. There was a 'wait and see' attitude at the baby clinic, too.

A family group, with Wendy on her father's knee

We moved to Lowestoft when Wendy was ten months old, and once more we were among strangers. Our new neighbours tried to be helpful, otherwise there was no respite from the endless struggle to feed and the sleepless nights.

Visits to doctors and specialists began in earnest, and we were referred to a consultant at the Jenny Lind Hospital in Norwich, who suggested there could have been brain damage at the time of birth. Whether this was so we shall never know. We were told there were no tests to carry out – and even if there had been, what good would they have done?

My days were spent trying to feed Wendy, always hoping that she would respond to the affection and close contact we all tried to give her. But she did not respond, and this really struck fear in my heart. She took no comfort in being hugged and kissed or in any human contact. I was conscious, too, that our elder daughter was being pushed into the background. How could we devote time to Denise, who had been so looking forward to a baby sister to play with? Even so, Denise did her best to help. It was a daily problem – how to give Wendy the constant attention she needed and to make sure Denise was not neglected. We worked out a system whereby when my husband, Roy, came home from work in the evening, he would take over Wendy's bathtime while I spent time with Denise, who, we realised, seemed to do far too many tasks for her years, but who never grumbled, and was always loving and kind. Then, when Wendy was three years old, we had another baby – our son Michael. How we wished our families lived nearer. Our mothers came to stay for a time during the summer months, and we looked forward to the assistance they gave, although my mother was often choked with tears, and my husband's mother prayed loudly over Wendy, which only increased our despair, yet we knew they meant well. They never really came to terms with Wendy's handicap.

Our doctor in Lowestoft was very kind and attentive when I was expecting Michael, and when the time of the birth arrived (a home birth this time), he told my husband to ring him as soon as I went into labour. When this happened our doctor came and stayed with me throughout the birth. He had cancelled his surgery so that he could be with me. We were very grateful for his attention, and only later discovered that he, too, had a handicapped child – a son.

One good thing about our move to Lowestoft was that we now had a small car, and at weekends we could have a few trips into the countryside. We tried to make life seem as normal as possible, but we could never manage the beach, for Wendy seemed to be afraid of the sand, which she rubbed into her eyes, and screamed with pain, and yet the water attracted her. A large, plastic paddling pool in the garden turned out to be a really good idea, and this is mainly where we spent the school holidays. Wendy developed a very infectious laugh, which was quite a joy to hear. Any sudden movement would trigger this – someone tripping or something falling – so we all encouraged her laughter by doing these things.

Our older daughter, Denise, cuddling Wendy

We had faced the fact that Wendy had very little understanding, and my husband and I read as many books and articles on the subject of mental handicap as we could. We learnt about the extra chromosome which causes Down's syndrome; the terrible effect which German measles can have; and of course, brain damage during birth. Then, when we read about phenylketenuria,[5] we thought that might be Wendy's trouble, and I went to the doctor, carrying the article to show him. Of course, we were wrong, and we realised there was no cure. Only training could help. We read, too, that a handicapped child meant a handicapped family, and we soon learnt how true this was.

5 Severe impairments of brain development in untreated babies are clinical features of Phenylketenuria (PKU). It is the most frequent disorder of amino acid metabolism, and is caused by a lack of vital chemicals. Research still continues into the underlying causes and processes of PKU.

First steps – Wendy growing up

When quite small, Wendy began to have small fits – referred to then as *petit mal* (an outdated term not now used). They happened quite without warning, and medication seemed to have little effect. She would just crash to the ground wherever she was.

In the early years, when Wendy was small, we could manage to take her in our newly acquired car to visit our families – my mother in Blackpool and Roy's mother in Barrow-in-Furness. There were no car seats then. We took the top part of her wooden high chair and propped it on the back seat with Wendy on a cushion, tied in with scarves. We stopped frequently, and the journey took over eight hours. How we managed seems a miracle to us now.

We also had to hire a cot and take masses of bedding, waterproof sheets and nappies. It was hard work, but we thought it was worth it, for Denise and Michael really enjoyed the change, and we had our families around us.

A family picnic, with Wendy, Denise and Michael

When we look back, we often wonder how we coped. Each day was a hurdle to be overcome. Wendy did not walk until she was five years old. She shuffled about on her bottom, getting along quite quickly. What a joyful occasion it was when she took her first steps. Also, we all of us worked hard to try to train Wendy to use a spoon to feed herself and to use a potty, for she was still in nappies at five years old. What a blessing disposable nappies would have been. All the family was involved with this training. Even Michael, not yet two, was engaged in looking after Wendy. He would hurry to bring her potty, and he confided in me, "We have to help Wendy. She is just a baby." We must have had some success, for we were able to apply for Wendy to attend a Special School, where potty training was a necessary requirement, and Wendy was eventually, but not immediately, accepted. A bus came for her around 9.30am each weekday morning and brought her home around 3pm. We felt this was a real achievement.

Wendy, on a family picnic

And what a tremendous difference it made to our lives. Denise was at school, but for a few hours I could give my full attention to Michael. I took him, in his pushchair, for walks on the sea front, and in the early afternoon, as we waited for the bus to bring Wendy home, we would spend the time doing puzzles and I would read to him. There were no playgroups then, of course, and during the school holidays, this respite ended.

Some help was on hand from social services, however. We found that it was possible to have a two-week care break during the school holidays to enable us to take our other children on holiday. We took Wendy to the recommended private home where she had been booked in. It was a large house in a small village, and we fully expected to be shown round to see where she would be sleeping and cared for generally. But this was not allowed. We had to remain in the hall, and we wondered why. What was being hidden? But what were we to do? We were not happy with the arrangement, but we looked at our other two children, excited and looking forward to a holiday, and, with misgivings, we left Wendy and went on our way. Fortunately, all was well on our return. We need not have worried, but it seemed bad practice on the part of the Home.

The local Society
It was the formation of a local branch of the Society for the Mentally Handicapped, which made the greatest difference to our lives. The branch was launched in 1962, and I remember the inaugural meeting. I walked into the room (I had

left my husband babysitting) and felt quite nervous. Who would be there? Who would I meet? Yet I felt this was the way forward. There was a coming-together of parents with a handicapped child with the aim of helping ourselves and each other. How wonderful it was to meet them and to know we were not alone! I met families with not one but two handicapped children – an even crueller fate than ours. We determined never to refer to the society as Mencap. We always gave it the full title, for we thought then that the abbreviation trivialised and demeaned the handicapped, and feel the same about the current expression 'learning difficulties'.

We founder members formed a committee, and decided what our greatest need was – and that was a little respite, an opportunity to take our other children to all the usual dental or doctor's appointments – the things families usually take for granted. Then we began to organise fund-raising events. I look back now and see what a release this all was. We could use other skills – not just parenting. We could advertise our cause and bring our children into social contact, and by the standard of our events, encourage attendance by those in a position to help us. The Social Services department (a very small outfit then; only three social workers, I remember) were our allies. Our MP, Jim Prior, also lent his support to our cause. We formed a committee, and the head of the then Grammar School became our Chairman. Over the years I took various roles, including Minute Secretary, then Secretary. I, as did others on the Committee, prepared notes and gave talks to schools and women's groups to alert as many people as possible to the plight of these previously forgotten children, and to try to enrol their help.

We organised many fund-raising events. Apart from the usual jumble sales, we arranged cheese and wine parties; we also held rather splendid dinner dances (they were very fashionable then); and as the funds began to accumulate, we first hired a lady to babysit (yes, that is what we called it) to enable mothers to go out for a while. Some of the mothers had never been out on their own and at first didn't quite know what to do. They were just glad of a visit and a friendly chat. Then we started a baby unit in a newly built church hall – I do believe we called it a crèche in those early days – and a tremendously popular youth club, which is still in existence. As we went on, we became more ambitious, and confident. We organised a sponsored swim which raised £500, which seemed a miraculous sum to us. We were then able to buy our own minibus. Now outings for the whole family could be arranged – sometimes the first they had experienced.

In 1965, our next project was to start a Training Centre for the over-16s who had nowhere to go after leaving the Occupation Centre. This was held in the premises of a youth club on two days per week, increasing to three as soon as funds would allow. About 25 young people attended – all ages and abilities.

Various ideas were sought to keep everyone happily occupied, and then we had a great coup. A local television factory found the young people some work to do – folding guarantee cards and sorting nuts and bolts, and for this work they were paid a small amount. It was referred to as their 'wages'.

In 1967, a special care unit for very young children was launched using a modern church hall, where we were charged a nominal rent, and were allowed to use all their facilities. Later, we received a donation from the church, which more than covered the amount we had paid. We employed two supervisors, backed up by voluntary help from our members. All the children were collected from their homes by minibus. Fundraising events continued to finance all these activities, and by then we also had help from the County Council, who were perhaps conscious that we were taking on a huge responsibility and helping the Council, except we didn't see it that way. We were helping our children and ourselves to a better life.

At about this time, Wendy went into care. It was an agonising decision. We felt guilty, and yet life became so much better for us and our other children. But we never ever neglected Wendy. We always visited her each week and brought her home. She is still part of our family. I have heard of families who say their handicapped child enriched their lives. This may be so if the handicap is not so great, where there is an ability to communicate and to give love as well as receive it. That, unhappily, was not our experience. Even now, at 46, Wendy is not much different from when she was a small child, and has never spoken. I realise now that it would probably have been better if Wendy had been a Down's syndrome baby, for I see groups of such young people at our local college, and discovered they were taking part in courses to learn various life skills and were involved in what is called a Life Long Learning Programme. This seemed real progress to me.

Our activities on behalf of the society did not cease, but as the years went by, there was a gradual handing-over of our enterprises to the local authority, who were by this time able to offer more services, such as a full-time Adult Training Centre, and in 1973 a hostel for the handicapped was built and equipped.

We all realised that it was a good thing that the services we had launched and worked so hard to provide should be taken over and enhanced by the County Council, but we also knew that it was through our initiative and enterprise that the handicapped and their parents had been helped over the past years.

Reflections

Did Wendy's handicap have any good effect? We have often wondered. Her condition certainly made us, as a family, pull together, but wouldn't we have done that anyway? Our son tells me that he knew, as a baby, that Wendy was 'different'. It puzzled him, but he cannot remember that it ever worried or alarmed him. Our elder daughter found her experiences more upsetting, and prefers not to recall her memories. Certainly, our own experiences and the contact with other families in a similar position alerted us to the need for further facilities for the handicapped and their families and this is what we worked for.

Wendy in the garden

Chapter 9
Just an ordinary life

Margaret Littlewood

Margaret Littlewood had long wanted to tell the story of her daughter Moira and had originally arranged to talk to the late social researcher and writer Maureen Oswin for inclusion in this book. Unfortunately, Maureen's final illness precluded this, but Mrs Littlewood agreed instead to talk to me. We spent a whole day together at her home in Leeds in August 2001, tape recording the story, stopping only for lunch at the local pub. The account here is told entirely in Mrs Littlewood's own words. As she has now outlived her daughter, this story is told in memory of Moira.

Dorothy Atkinson

Margaret Littlewood

Early days – is it bronchitis?

Well, Moira was born in the local maternity hospital in 1949. And, as far as we knew at the time it was a normal birth, but her birthweight was very low and she didn't really feed properly; we were having difficulties with breast-feeding. Anyway, she was looked after by our own GP and I also used to take her to what they called in Leeds 'the baby's welcome', which was like a little welfare place where there were nurses, and they would weigh her and keep a note of her progress and this and that. And as far as we knew she was normal until she was about five months. And she was in the bath one day, just a little tin bath because, as I say, she was only a little baby, and I suddenly saw that she was acting in a peculiar fashion, and her eyes began to roll upwards in her head and her face went peculiar, I didn't really know what was happening; it was foreign to

95

me, I had never seen anything like it before, and it was all over in about a minute, maybe less than a minute, and I didn't know what had happened but I knew something had happened which shouldn't have.

So, when my husband came home from work I told him and he said, "Well, I really think we ought to go and see the doctor and tell him", which we did, and he said, "Oh, she is cutting teeth, it is probably a little convulsion or something of that description, and we will put her on some calming medicine." I think they put her on bromide medicine, and he insisted it was teething. Anyway, this went on and some days it would happen again, other days it wouldn't, but eventually it became more frequent and she was having it every day after a few weeks' time. But the doctor still insisted that this bromide medicine was the right thing to give her, so we just carried on with things and we never found out what it was, but it was happening.

And then after she was – I should think she would be about six months, possibly – she suddenly started to have a very high temperature. She had awful perspiration at night, everything in the bed was wet through, not just urine wet, but sweat, her hair would be ringing with this perspiration, and so we approached the doctor again. But it wasn't the doctor we had approached originally because there were six in this practice that we went to and it was another doctor the second time, and we told him what the other doctor had prescribed and what had been happening, and so he said, "Oh well, I think this is a bronchitis that she has got now", so he gave her some medicine for her chest, I think. So, we continued and these little convulsions were still happening and he told me to take her down on a certain date to see him.

I took her down and she seemed a lot better, she was still having this sweating in the night but she had no cough or anything left and I think she was a bit better, so he said, "Well, we really think it is time you had a vaccine", and I said to him, "Well do you think she is fit to be vaccinated?" I said, "Do you think she is better?" and he said, "Well, we will leave it a week or two, but I really think you should be thinking about it." She was about just over six months. She was very young. So, I came home and my mother came over regularly and when I told her what this second doctor had said, my mother said, "Please don't have her vaccinated", and I said, "Why?" And she said, "Well I don't know, but I have an awful feeling about it." My father never would let me be vaccinated because he was worried about it, and she said, "I have got the same worry now for my granddaughter." And I said, "Well, I think we are going to have to have her vaccinated." This was because my husband was a true believer, having been in the army and having all the vaccinations that they gave them in the army, he was a true believer in all these immunisations, vaccinations, whatever they were. He would insist that she be vaccinated for smallpox, I knew that. And my mother said, "Well, I don't like it at all", and she was very worried.

And it all turned out as I said, my husband said, "Oh yes, she has got to be vaccinated", and she was vaccinated. She would perhaps be going on for about seven months by this time, and this second doctor we had seen vaccinated her, and told me to take her back I think it was in a fortnight, so that he could see if the scab that would form was OK, or whatever it was that he wanted to look at. So, anyway on the day I should have taken her she woke up that particular morning and she was really poorly, she was vomiting and really sick, and she looked poorly, she had still been having all this perspiration. So, I rang this doctor up and said, "Look, I should be bringing Moira in to see you this morning, but I am afraid she is not fit to be coming out. She is running a very high temperature." I said, "Really, I think you should come and see her", which he did. And he said, "No, it is what I said, she has just got this very high temperature because she has had some kind of bronchitis."

He still thought it was bronchitis, so he continued with some other medicine but it wasn't antibiotic, and I mention that because I have learned a lot about this since, and she should have been on antibiotics ever since she started with these little convulsions. I have been told this by the Vaccine Damage Commission, I have talked it through with everybody. And she never got the antibiotics, and she got worse, and it was definitely not full-blown epilepsy. And she got to about nine months and it was still going on and I was still taking Moira to this 'baby's welcome'. I told the nurse there everything that was happening to her, because I still kept up my fortnightly appointments, I think they were. So this nurse said to me, "Well look, Mrs Littlewood, go back to your doctor and tell him that you want a second opinion." She said, "I know you have had two doctors but they both belong to the same practice", she said. "Now I want you to see a consultant and you have my permission to tell them that it is my advice to you that it is imperative you see a consultant."

I went back to my GP and it was the first doctor who was seeing me again, so I told him all this, told him what had happened with the second doctor. So he said to me, "Well, I will find the best consultant I can for you, and I will make an appointment for you to see him", he said, "that is the best thing for me to do."

Weekly visits to the clinic
So, this was as it was left, and eventually my doctor got a note from this consultant that he would like Moira to go to his clinic where she would see a doctor (though not the consultant). It was one of his junior doctors, you see. And he would see Moira and he would examine her and I could have a chat to him. This was at Leeds Infirmary. The doctor examined Moira and said, "Well, I really can't tell you at this moment", he said, "I shall have to see her a few more times than this before I can come to any conclusion as to what has

been going wrong." However, he did notice by this time that she wasn't using her right arm, though we had pointed this out to our own doctor. Anyway, he noticed it and said, "Well, I have noticed that", he said, "and I have tested her reflexes as you have seen in her legs and in her feet." He said, "She is also not using her right leg properly, and I am afraid that her right foot is going to be deformed eventually unless we can find out what to do with it for the best."

So, this was his advice to me, but I was to go and see him every week and I did, faithfully, every week. And it was the most awful thing I have ever had to do because I had no transport to take her down, I had to carry her. I had to go on the tram and it went all around Leeds and up Cookridge Street, and she was absolutely terrified of this tram, she really was. She used to scream all the time we were on it and the other people would be saying to me, "She wants a good hiding, that is what she wants", you see. This was the sort of thing you had to put up with.

This was every week. I used to dread going. Anyway I saw this doctor every week and Moira got to be 11 months old. She was still having these fits and they were getting more frequent. She lost the use of her arm altogether and her leg was going funny. You couldn't tell there were anything wrong with the foot then, but he said she wasn't using it properly and she wasn't responding to when he tested her reflexes with a feather on the foot you know, this sort of thing. Anyway, we saw him until she was about 11 months old, and then one day when I went, he said, "Mrs Littlewood, I am afraid I am going to give you what I think will be bad news for you." So I said, "Oh, what is that?" And he said, "Well, I am leaving the Infirmary, I am going to Canada." I had every faith in this doctor, I really did. I don't know why, but we got on well together and he talked sense to me, which a lot of them didn't, they talked to me as if I was mentally handicapped – and I liked him. He said, "The reason I am going to Canada is because I have got interested in people like your daughter, but I am not able to do anything much for them, I don't know enough about it. I just can't feel that I am any use at all. So I am going to Canada because there is a course there for spastic children." He said, "I have a feeling that your daughter has spastic tendencies, and I hope that when I come back to the Infirmary I shall know a lot more than what I know now, and I might be able to advise you." And I really was upset, I was very upset that he was going because he was so nice. I said, "Well, when you do come back you will see her again, won't you?" "Oh yes, definitely", he said. By the time the doctor left Moira was well over 12 months old. I was still going every week, but every week that I went I never saw the same person twice. It was always a different doctor and I wasn't getting anywhere, but we were still carrying on with it. On one particular occasion, a doctor said, "I would like you to take Moira to physiotherapy, we will arrange it with the physiotherapist for you to come every week."

So I was going on Wednesdays to the physio, and I was going on Fridays to the doctor. This was twice a week I was going and on the tram again, and Moira was going mad all the time.

Two left shoes – advice from the consultant

So, this was how we went on. Well I got fed up with this, and I was going to my GP as well and I said to him one day, "Doctor, I am not getting anywhere at all with Moira, they stopped the physio but she is not normal, she is not behaving normally, there is something that should be being done for her that is not being done." And I didn't know what it was. I told him about this doctor leaving and I said, "This was the worst thing that could have happened as far as I was concerned."

In the end we paid the consultant to see her privately and he agreed to see her. He wanted to see me and also my husband, as well as Moira. We were to go to his private consulting rooms in Leeds and he would see Moira, so we went. I have never been treated like it in my life, I have never had such treatment in my life. He wasn't friendly. He had a big, posh desk so he said to me, "You sit there, Mrs Littlewood." That was opposite him at this big desk, and all around this consulting room there were chairs, ordinary wooden chairs. And he said to my husband, "And you, you can sit over there" – on one of these uncomfortable wooden chairs. He said 'you', like that, not 'Mr Littlewood', you know. And I thought, "Oh God!" because my husband wasn't the most patient man. He was never rude to anybody but he wouldn't stand such treatment as this was you see, and then he said to me, "And as for her!" 'Her'!

I had plopped 'her' down on the floor, you see. And he said, "As for her, just sit her down here near me and I will have a talk to her." I thought to myself, "You don't look as though you can talk to her at all!" I was quite sure. Moira sat there, and he turned around in his chair, and he said to her, "Hello Moira, look at man." She looked at him, and she was absolutely bewildered. She didn't know what he meant by 'look at man'. I was just going to say, "She won't understand what you mean, you will have to say, 'Look at me', or 'I am Dr Alton, look at Dr Alton', not 'Look at man'." I was just going to interrupt him and then he said to me, "Be quiet, be quiet, I am talking to her." So I thought, "Right, well get on with it, she won't understand what you are talking about." She didn't look at him, she just ignored him and he kept saying, 'Look at man' 'Look at man', so my husband chipped in from over there. He said, "I am very sorry to interrupt you doctor, but she won't have a clue as to what you are saying to her. She doesn't understand what you mean when you say 'Look at man'. If you said 'Look at me' or 'I am Dr Alton', she might take notice of you, but she just doesn't understand what you mean when you say 'Look at man'."

Well, I thought, "Fancy a paediatrician, who is supposed to be a child's doctor, addressing a child of five like that!" Anyway, after that he kept me going to the clinic but we were not getting anywhere with her. By this time her fits were worse, they weren't epilepsy but they were getting on that way. Anyway, she was five, and we had to go to the clinic at the infirmary every two weeks, I think it was, and he would see her there. But I had to go at 8.30 am every fortnight because that was the time his clinic was due to start. So, we started to go into the infirmary again, every fortnight on a Friday.

I told him I had difficulty, I said I had no transport or anything and the conditions, and he wasn't interested, no, no. One day, Moira starts crying as soon as she sees him. She didn't like him! She never did like him [laughs], neither did I. Anyway, this day she starts crying so he said, "Is she going to cry all the time?" and I said, "I don't know." So he said, "Well, if she is you can take her home." And I looked at him and said, "Are you serious?" So he said, "Yes" and I said, "No, I am not going to take her home until you have had a look at her foot." I said, "I want to talk to you about that foot and I am not going home until you have given me your opinion." So he looked and he said, "Can she walk?" and I said "No." He said, "How are we to do anything about it then, if she can't walk?" And I said, "Well, that is just what I want her to do, I want her to walk. Can you tell me how I can get her to walk with her foot like that?" And it was obvious she couldn't put it flat on the floor.

He said, "The only advice I can give you", and I looked at him, "is to tell you to go and buy two left shoes and put her left shoe on her right foot and her other left shoe on her left foot." I said, "Is she supposed to be able to walk with her left shoe on? Because she can't walk in any case, even if I put her shoe on she will still not be able to walk, because she can't balance." He said, "Well, that is all I can tell you. Buy two left shoes and put them on." And I said to him, "Will you tell me something else then, doctor, where am I going to get two left shoes?" [laughs]. He looked at me and he said, "I can't tell you, I can't answer that" [laughs]. I thought I had gone to a madhouse, I did really.

Well, I said to Ernest, my husband, "How am I going to walk in the shop and ask them if I can buy two left shoes? They will think I am mad, won't they?" So, I had to keep going to the doctor and keep going to the Infirmary. I kept going for the physiotherapy and the physiotherapist said, "It is doing Moira no good whatsoever." I told her what Doctor Alton said about putting two left shoes on and she ridiculed it altogether. She said, "That won't cure her foot." She was trying to do exercises with it. This was the story of my life from then on, I never saw anybody who could do anything for Moira.

Fighting every inch of the way – in and out of the occupation centre

I felt as though I had to fight every inch of the way, and yet I was getting nowhere.

And then, it was time Moira got to school because she was five. And I think I had to go to see Dr Maxwell. She said, "Well, I think if we send her to the occupation centre I think that will be the best thing, and then we might be able to find one of the school doctors who might be able to suggest something." But there were no school doctors at the occupation centre; we never saw a doctor up there either.

She went there but nothing was being done to help me or to help Moira. Then they sent her home from the centre, asked me to keep her at home and not to send her again. She was six by this time. She was five when she started at the occupation centre, just turned five. Then one day, Liz Coogan was in the bus, she was a parent of a child at the same occupation centre. And she said, "I have some bad news for you, Mrs Littlewood. Mrs Tomkins says you are not to send Moira any more." Mrs Tomkins was the headmistress, and she was a qualified headmistress, she wasn't a social worker or anything, just a headmistress. "You are not to send her any more because Moira disrupts all the other children and they will not do as they are told while Moira is there." Then she gave me a letter and said, "Mrs Taylor has sent you this letter, what is in this letter she has told me exactly what she has told me to tell you." So she gave me the letter and I opened it, and I read it after they had gone with the transport. I read this letter and it was exactly as this lady had told me, that Moira was nothing but a nuisance. She upsets all the other children, they couldn't get anything done with them because of Moira.

Well, in a way, I wasn't bothered really, because she wasn't doing anything at the centre, and she wasn't happy. I stopped sending her, but I went to see the headmistress. I thought, "This isn't good enough, I ought to have a reason for this, something other than in this letter." But, when my husband came home that teatime, I gave him the letter and he read it, and before I could say, 'Jack Robinson' he had put it on the fire. And that did it for me, because I had no proof then, of all the nasty things she had said about Moira I had no proof at all, only this lady who knew what she had told me. So, I went to see this headmistress and I said to her, "I was very upset by the letter you sent me, and I am not going to hide anything at all, my intention was to take that letter down to Simon Holms." He was the man in charge of the mental handicap things in the public health department, he was the mental health officer. And I was going to take this letter to him and ask for his advice, I wasn't going to be nasty, I was just going to ask him what, in view of that letter, was my next step with Moira.

Of course, then my husband put it on the fire! And I said to Ernest, "Oh Ernest, whatever have you burnt that letter for? That was the only proof I had, why did you do it?" And he said, "Well, I wasn't thinking, but my idea is this; obviously nobody wants to look after Moira, there is nobody at all, the paediatrician doesn't want her, they don't want her on the ward, they don't want her at the occupation centre, so what does that leave us? Who is going to look after her in future?" So my husband says that we will look after her in future and we will see what is to be done for her, because nobody else wants to know her at all. I was upset, I really was upset. Well from that day onwards, I was a prisoner in my own home.

I couldn't take Moira on a tram, she was afraid of cars in the street, she was afraid of dogs and it was all because of this sort of treatment she had been having. I couldn't settle her at all, we couldn't go out with her, she couldn't go out in her wheelchair, she would not go out in anybody's car. She was terrified, she was terrified of everything. And this is what had been done to her, it was nothing we had done, I am sure. And I never went near them again, and I kept her at home, I couldn't go out, I couldn't go shopping until my husband came home from work at night, I had to dash down to the shops before they closed. I couldn't do anything at all, I was confined to the house for a full 12 months and I never went out, only at weekends, and then I had to go into town to do the shopping that I wanted in town.

Mrs Fortune, the welfare officer, used to come. She used to come and see her, but she never gave me any advice, she had nothing to offer, you see, she agreed with me, there was nothing that they could do. No, it really was hopeless. Moira was 49 when she died and she had been going to another training centre in Leeds three years when she died. So she would be 46 when she next went to a training centre. In 40 years I never had any help, never. Nobody came to bother about her, only Mrs Fortune. I was very friendly with her, we were bosom pals eventually because she was sorry for me and she could see I was doing the best I could. I had no experience really, I learned by experience – by letting nature take its course, and never being cross with Moira or upsetting her, or making her angry. She would fight anybody, though we managed to stop all this nastiness. She would go for people's hair, you see, she would even go for mine sometimes. If I wasn't doing something that she thought I should have been doing, oh yes. And she used to bite all her clothes, in a temper. It was frustration, I think.

Life at home – with *Mrs Dale's Diary*
She had a dreadful life until she was about nine or ten I think, because she had these bouts of behaviour and nobody could understand why. And it was only when I met this lady, Brenda, that I began to understand Moira. She came to talk to another lady at Mencap about autism. I could feel she was talking

about Moira, and these moods that Moira had and these bouts of temper and frustration, and not recognising herself. Moira didn't know who she was, you know, it must have been a dreadful life for her, now I realise this, but I didn't know what to do. I had nobody to tell me what to do, you know. Brenda was a nice lady, she really was, I liked her very much, and I went and talked to her after and told her the situation I was in. She said, "Look I will come and see her. I am writing a book, I will come and see you and I will come and see Moira, and I will tell you all I can tell you as to how she can best be handled." She said "I will put her in my book, and we will draw the authorities' attention if we have to do, I will do whatever I can to help you." And she did, and we corresponded for about a year, I think. Her husband was a doctor in a mental handicap hospital, so I presume he knew something about it because he was working in that place. And even if he didn't know anything when he went there, I should think he knew something at the end of it anyway [laughs].

Anyway, Brenda did as she said and she was lovely, and she really helped me, and between us I am sure we saved Moira from autism, because she really wasn't all that bad. She wasn't as bad as some that Brenda told me about, you know. And I had seen them in Mencap in Leeds, I think I could pick them out, you know. So that was that, and I managed to get Moira out of this autism. So, Brenda, when she came to see me she told me exactly what could happen and what to look out for, and asked me what Moira did and what was she interested in, or did she write various things or whatever. Now the only interest which Moira had in those days was that she loved to listen to the wireless, and her wheelchair was right next to the wireless, it was on a set of drawers. Her favourite thing that she listened to was *Mrs Dale's Diary*.

Well she loved it, she loved Mrs Dale, but the person she liked best was Mrs Dale's mother [laughs] and she used to say – she was talking by this time – 'Mrs Freeman'. Oh she loved Mrs Freeman really, and she was a really old fussy woman was Mrs Freeman on the programme, but Moira liked her, and if Mrs Freeman was on Moira was as good as gold. So we had this on every day and Moira would talk about "What would Mrs Freeman say?" and I would say, "Now don't do that, Moira, because I don't think Mrs Freeman would like it, you see." Then she would say to me, "Well what would Mrs Freeman say?", you see, and so we got on, and she was no longer like she used to be. She would sometimes say 'I' and I used to say to her, "Well we will have to call you 'I' in future because Mrs Freeman wouldn't know who 'she' was, so you are 'I' now." So she started this 'I' this and 'I' that.

Well we had this on every day, and then Moira would try and stand up, she still couldn't walk much but she could manage a bit better. However, her foot was still crooked, so she had a job to stand up. Anyway she managed to stand up and balance somehow, and I would sometimes, if I could, take her to the window. And then she said to me one day, she was just standing there shaking the curtain and she said, "Mrs Freeman said I shouldn't do this." I looked at her, and I said "Mrs Freeman?" and she said, "Yes." So I said, "Why? Is Mrs Freeman behind that curtain?" and she said, "Yes." And she thought Mrs Freeman was behind that curtain, that was why she wanted to play with it. She must have had an imagination, you see, which I didn't think she had. Well, always then, oh we were going to see Mrs Freeman behind the curtain, you know. Then she would do things only because Mrs Freeman wanted her to do them, you see. So, eventually it was Mrs Freeman who was ruling the roost, it wasn't me. I was just saying, "Oh Mrs Freeman wouldn't like that", you know [laughs].

Well, as I say Moira's life was *Mrs Dale's Diary*, and everything that was happening Moira thought was happening to her, she was still autistic in a way, but there were other people as well, she wasn't alone in this world, she was with these other people. Also Moira loved poetry, when they all rhymed at the end of the line she thought it was lovely, and she started to try and talk in rhyming words, actually. I was trying to expand her vocabulary, you know, and if she wouldn't do something sometimes I would think to myself, "I will say it in rhyme." And she loved music, her second best thing was music. She could sing anything, she would only need to hear a tune once and all her life she could sing it. And she was even singing opera before she died, she could just pick it up like that.

Anyway, she was going through a phase when she wouldn't eat much. I also wanted to expand her vocabulary and make her understand things. So I began to sing to her when it was dinnertime. I would get a tune and I would put these words in: "If you don't eat your dinner, you will be getting thinner" – something like that. And that was what she liked, the dinner and the thinner, and so I would do it to a tune, you see, not a tune that she knew or anything, just a tune I made up. And then if she had been looking at a book and we had been talking about anything, such as, she had one book where there was a big green pig in it, and it was always eating its dinner. So I would tell her about this pig eating its dinner and that if she didn't eat her dinner then she would be thinner, and this, that and the other. And it was only through experiences like this and through singing and rhyming things with her that I got through to her in the end.

So, this is how we were progressing, and as she improved her behaviour improved and the things she did became more sensible. And you couldn't think she was really mentally handicapped because in some ways she was quite clever, and I could never reconcile the two in a way. Still, I was so relieved that at least I had managed to unlock something, you know. And I always felt after that, that these autistic people needed a one-to-one relationship to get them into the proper world.

Unfortunately Moira could never read. She couldn't concentrate long enough, that was her trouble. If she had been able to concentrate for any length of time I would have got her reading, I think. She could recognise letters but she couldn't put them together to make words to read, you know. But she could recognise them, and if you said to her, "How do you spell 'Moira'?" she would say 'm, o, i, r, a', but she couldn't read it. She just knew how to spell it. But we were achieving something with her, you see, but I mean nobody else did because she wasn't going anywhere.

Forty years on – a new training centre
The community nurse had been coming, she had been coming quite a while and this was when we came to this house. Moira liked her very much, and they got on very well together. And Angela, the community nurse, tried to persuade me to try a training centre again, but with my experience of the other training centre, I think she knew she was going to have a job to persuade me. And anyway, she kept on and she kept saying to me, "Well you are going to have to make your mind up one of these days because Moira is going to have to go somewhere when anything happens to you or your husband." She was trying to get me to think in those terms after 40-odd years, you see, and of course I was thinking in those terms. It is every parent's nightmare as to what is going to happen to their child, isn't it?

And I think Angela thought perhaps that I was being a bit awkward about it, but it wasn't that at all, it was just the experience that I had had, and the experience that nobody had bothered to do anything for Moira. Also Ernest had said, "We will look after her" and we had done, you know, that is all it was. But she kept on at me and in the end I said, "Look, if you take me to a training centre that you think I would like and where Moira could be catered for, and where the people were sympathetic and not autocratic – like the woman who had been at the other centre – then I wouldn't say no. I would go and I would agree with you possibly. However, I don't know if my husband would agree or not." My husband had really taken it to heart about nobody wanting her and had made up his mind that we were going to do it, you know.

Anyway, Angela said, "Well I think she should go to Hillcrest Centre", and I agreed with her that it was the best one that I could think of. And they took us up and the staff were so nice, and it was so obvious that they knew what they were doing with these people. I mean, the other centre I had been to, they hadn't a clue what they were doing with them, there was no sitting on potties and things like this, they were all being helped, you know. And they had three nurses on the staff, and this special care unit with only 25 in. There was a big clientele in any case, but there were only 25 in Moira's lot and there were three nurses among them. The other staff were experienced people too who knew just what to do with them, and they all loved one another, it was obvious, you know. And I thought, "Oh how marvellous in comparison", and I said to Angela, "Oh if only Ernest will agree, I will agree any day to Moira going, providing she settles down." Anyway we decided to try it and Ernest liked it as well, and he liked the people and he agreed, so she started going. And she loved it, she did really, and they were marvellous with her, they did all the things that she liked them to do, they got her painting. She could have had a marvellous life, especially when we got her out of this autism business. And I have always regretted that she never got the chance to go until she was 46, you know. And they loved her and she loved them. I never had a minute's worry about her, you know.

Moira in the garden at home, about 1977

Outside the home – working for change

For years, Moira was afraid of cars and wouldn't go out. Well all that was resolved gradually. That was through finding certain bits of information from other people, you know, and really that is the way I mostly learned – from other folks, you know. Well when I used to go and visit other parents in their homes, a lot of them had the same problems that I had, you know. Especially with getting people in the right frame of mind to listen to what you have to say, because otherwise they don't know what people's attitude was. Often it was to think that the whole family was a bit mental, you know [laughs]. There wasn't much respect for mental handicap or the people associated with it. That's when I was with Mencap, on the welfare side.

I worked very hard for Mencap for 20 years, when I did the welfare work. And yet Mencap never did one thing for Moira, except I could take her on my welfare trips because I was in charge of her. But they never invited her to anything, never came to see her. I knew some of the officials and they were always very friendly with me, but they never bothered about Moira. In fact, there was no difference between the people at Mencap than any of the professionals I had met in the health service or the social services. They are all about as helpful as one another, and that was nil [laughs]. So, I just don't go to Mencap now, I have no need to go, and I go to the health committee called 'the equal access', and this is to see that mentally handicapped people get a fair crack of the whip and equal access to all the facilities and all the equipment that they provide. And I have to be on this committee to make sure that they are going to get the crack of the whip. And every time they ask me why I am going I always say, "Well, I didn't finish my job with Moira", which I didn't. So I am trying my best for her. I wouldn't like anybody to be in the position I was in, at any time in my life, you know. I mean, my life wasn't a misery, don't get me wrong, we were very happy, yes. But Moira's life could have been a lot better. So that has changed a lot too.

It was through Mencap, I think, that the information was passed on that these councils were going to be set up and that volunteers were needed as well as so many local government representatives and a certain number of regional appointments. This was going to be a watchdog for the National Health Service and it was going to be run by the people, as it were, and they were people who were elected, not like the chairman of the Health Authority who is appointed still. They were going to be elected by people who knew them who could do the job and this type of thing. Well how I got on first I was nominated by Leeds Mencap, and that was my place and I had to go to a meeting, and we all had to speak and say our piece.

Certain names were put forth and that was how I got on it. That was for the first four years, we were only allowed to be on for four years at the beginning, but you could be re-elected after you had served one four years. Anyway I served my four years. And then there was a ruling that came out that if you had done what was termed a satisfactory spell of work for the CHC but you lost your place in the four-yearly elections, that they could co-opt you. So, they co-opted me back on. So, that was how I got back on. And then I was on eight years then, two fours, you see. And because I had been in charge of mental handicap for eight years as it were, they wrote to me and asked if I would like to be the regional representative. I jumped at that because it gave me a bit more standing to do what I wanted for people with the mental handicap. And so I represented them for about 14 years altogether.

And for about six of those years I was a regional rep, you see, through the Regional Health Authority. I was chairman of the regional Mencap then. And I think that was possibly how my name got to the authorities.

Changes at home – deaths in the family

It was hard to be on the CHC because it really did take a lot of your time. But by that time my husband had had a heart attack and he got over it, he was 51, I think. He retired then. His doctor told him to give up work, you see. And he was only 50-something, so he had a very good retirement because he was 85 when he died. We had not had a lovely life because we couldn't go anywhere with Moira but we used to take her out every day and we used to walk miles with her. I was so glad Ernest retired when the doctor advised him, because we all enjoyed it, it wasn't just him who enjoyed his retirement, you know. And Moira loved to be out especially down in the woods, you know, because it is nice in the woods and she used to love the birds and things like that.

He died suddenly when he was 85, from his second heart attack. It was all over in a quarter of an hour. And Audrey next door was ringing for an ambulance while Mavis was trying to give him the resuscitation. She told me to get ready to go with him, you know, I think she just wanted to get me out of the way. She said, "You go and get ready and get a bag ready to take with you when the ambulance comes and then you can go with him, and we will stay and look after Moira", which they did. I went with him and all the time in the ambulance the ambulance men were trying to resuscitate him.

I asked my two neighbours not to say anything to Moira. I said to them, "Don't mention it to Moira, leave her in bed until I come home, she will be all right, give her a cup of tea." I was home by about 10.30am, I think, so it wasn't too bad for Moira, you know. And I didn't tell her anything, I just said that Mavis and Audrey had come to sit with her because I had to take her dad in the ambulance to the hospital, and that I had left him with all the doctors and they were all looking after him and giving him tests. You see she was familiar herself with hospitals, with being in and out. She knew what the procedure was, and she always liked to watch the nurses, she loved to watch them, what they were doing. It was something that was familiar to her, you see, and she understood. So when I told her this, it seemed to pacify her that the doctors were looking after him. Then she went to the centre one morning very early. They arranged to come for her that morning before 7.30am, because the funeral was at 10am. So we got the funeral over and everybody had gone home by the time it was all over and she never knew about that. And then one day she said to me, "When I was in hospital mummy and daddy used to come and see me", and I thought, "Oh heck, she has been thinking this over." It took her quite a bit to piece things together, but she did it in the end. She knew he had a bad heart you see, she knew that. And she accepted it, and then she began to worry about it and then I realised it wasn't really what I had told her, and so I told her.

I was sorry I had told her when I had to go to hospital because I knew she would be putting two and two together. She managed it, she survived, but I think she gave up, I am sure she did. The community nurse who came to see me in the hospital was trying to get Moira placed in a home somewhere, but she couldn't. I don't know really where she went, I can't remember, I don't think I know half the places she went to. And then occasionally just for a day or so they would take her into St Mary's but she could only stay the day and they would have to find a place to sleep at night. And I mean that was upsetting for her and she couldn't understand why she couldn't sleep there, you see. And they brought her to see me at St James and I knew she was poorly, I didn't know what was the matter with her, but I knew there was something sadly wrong.

This was when I had the stroke, you see. And I was in eight weeks altogether, but I had been in five weeks when Moira died, and my consultant had said he wasn't going to send me home. He said, "I shall never send you home, you will have to ask me when you want to go home, because I won't ever send you, you can stay here", and I suppose he was taking a firm line because the beds were in such demand, you know. I had been there five weeks, then one Saturday night the charge nurse came in and he said, "Mrs Littlewood, will you come into my office?" and so I said, "Yes." I went in and he said, "I have just got a message from the infirmary", and Moira had only gone in the infirmary on the Friday, and he said, "I just got a message from the infirmary asking you to go down, they want you to go and see Moira." He didn't tell me anything else, he didn't need to because I had been in the afternoon, he had let me go in the afternoon. And he had sent a nurse with me to look after me! [laughs] So, I understood, I knew Moira was very poorly then and I knew that. She went in because she had a shocking cough, she couldn't speak, she was hoarse, and she wasn't interested in me, she knew who I was but she wasn't interested, she was too poorly. And I had been with her in the afternoon and I knew she was too poorly. And I got there about 8.15pm and she didn't know me, she could hardly breathe, oh, it was awful to watch her. They were really good though, they left me on my own with her so I could talk to her, she wasn't answering, but I think she understood. I was telling her she was coming home, and I knew she wasn't. And it was obvious to me when I got into the ward that she was dying then, and she knew who I was but she didn't speak to me. But I was just telling her that she was going home.

Anyway, she died and after about a week at home on my own I thought, "Well, I really ought to be getting Ernest's will done." I had this probate to get done, and then I thought, "How am I going to manage it?", because I wasn't walking very well. Anyway, two of Ernest's cousins came and stayed three or four days with me and took me into town, and I managed to get walking and I just went on my own in the end and it was all right, it was a bit of a job walking but I managed it. I saw this probate clerk who was so nice. She said there was about £300 and I thought, "I have done the right thing, you know" [laughs]. But I am not over Moira's death yet, not really, I don't think I ever will be. I could accept my husband, he was 85, I could accept that but Moira was only 49 when she died. She would have been 52 now.

I don't regret it in a way because I had her all those years, and I had her to myself, I wasn't dependent on anybody else, I couldn't be, could I? Because there was nobody there, only my husband, and of course I was dependent on him. We had a very good life together. He couldn't have been better as a dad, you know, he took his share of the burden, more of his share, because he allowed me to go and do what I wanted to do.

Was it vaccine damage after all?

Well, I saw it in the paper, about the Vaccine Damage Commission. I didn't know anything about vaccine damage, but it said in the paper that anybody who felt that it might apply to their son or daughter should get in touch. They explained that it could be through vaccination, you see, and they said if you wanted you could get in touch with the commission they were setting up. You were at liberty to write and give them your point of view. So, I did this, I just told them what the position was, what Moira could do, what she couldn't do, what she had suffered, anything I could think of, really. And I got a letter back from them asking if I could put together in a document as much as I could possibly remember from when Moira started with her problems. If I could put down as much as I could remember and anything which I thought was relevant at all, they would be very interested to receive it and they would keep in touch. So I just wrote up as much as I knew.

And then I should think at least six months after that we got a reply, and this reply said that they were very interested in the news that I had been able to give them. They could see a pattern, from which they could deduce what had happened to Moira. They couldn't definitely say that it was through the vaccine that she had had. But on the other hand, they couldn't say that it wasn't. And that was in black and white. Could I think of any way in which I could let them have a better idea, even though the information had been very helpful in that they had been able to see a pattern, which evidently I could not see? So I wrote back and I discussed this with Ernest and Ernest said, "Well look, I have got all my diaries here." He always kept a diary, never missed, all the years of Moira's life he had got this diary, all the way up to his death anyway, day-by-day account. And so we looked at the diary to where she had that first attack and we sent a copy of every day's entry for that year. And this was as the attacks got worse and worse.

About three months after that we got a letter back from them saying that they had been very, very pleased to receive the daily account of Moira's life and her happenings and were very impressed by the evidence which the diaries had given. Because it conformed exactly to the sort of pattern they would have been able to interpret for Moira. It wasn't a definite agreement that it was the vaccine damage that had caused it, but it certainly did not say that it couldn't have caused it. So, it was just the same reply in a way. Well anyway, it ended up that they had decided with the information which we had got and all the trouble we had taken to let them have it, they had decided that she was worthy to receive the £10,000 which it was, and she got the £10,000.

When Moira was six, after they had sacked her from the occupation centre, her life just went on with us, just an ordinary life. She went out every day of the year if it was possible, because she loved to be out. And she never went short of anything. She had her music, anything she wanted. We were never poor as you might say, nor were we ever really wealthy, I am wealthier now than I have ever been. But that is nothing to do with Moira now. But, she had everything that she needed and she was happy. She could have had a happier life if somebody was interested and just taken over and just given us a bit of help and that sort of thing. And Moira's interests in her life, she had certain interests which we tried to foster and her music and such as that.

But I mean, she never had the companionship of people like herself until she was 46, you might say. She met one or two that she knew, people we met in the street, you know, she met one or two of them. But she never had any friends as you might say, she never had a special friend until she went to the centre. Oh, she had a little girl there called Sharon. Oh Sharon, I had to kiss Sharon before I kissed Moira when I went up to the centre, you know, and Moira thought she was lovely, she wasn't jealous or anything like that. But she could have had all those nice little things you know, which she never had until then. But the last three years of Moira's life were at the centre and they were the best three years really, for her.

Conclusion: emerging themes

Several themes emerged from the stories told by the 'witnesses' in Part 1, and we discuss these in the following section, setting each one in historical context. The themes we have highlighted are:

- silences and denials

- pressures from professionals

- challenging professionals and fighting for rights

- progress and achievements

Silences and denials – pushing an empty pram

Most of the stories focus on the moment of birth and the following weeks and months. Instead of certainty and direction from medical professionals, parents were very often met with silence, delay and obfuscation. As Lilian Fisher says, "My anxious questions seemed to fall on deaf ears … Our doctor did not seem to share our fears", and Gladys Abbs recalls that "even the doctors didn't know, couldn't diagnose". Some families, though anxious, were reassured by this silence and continued to believe that all was well. Far from the doctors diagnosing quickly and preparing to take some control over the children, in line with the legislation, in some cases it took many months, sometimes even years, before families were told that anything was wrong with their child. Rene Harris was not told that her son was 'backward' until he was three years old; Gladys Abbs waited to be told until her son was 11 months old, and Jo Wain, the author of 'April Showers', told a similar story. Van Brunning was reassured by her frequent visits to Great Ormond Street Hospital with her daughter "because I thought they would pick out anything, had there been anything that urgently needed attention, they would have seen to that". In the case of Margaret Littlewood's daughter, the misdiagnosis and complacency of the doctors led to a compounding of the initial problems when Margaret was advised to go ahead with vaccinations, despite Moira's increasingly frequent convulsions.

There were also silences within families, as some members of the family suspected that something was wrong with the baby, but did not speak to one another or voice any fears. Van Brunning and her husband hid their feelings from one another; while in 'April Showers' the two grandmothers 'kept a silent vigil for six months'. The author says that "it was fear of the unknown, of unspeakable things, which sustained this silence".

Other forms of long-term silence and denial took place within the extended family. As Brenda Nickson said, "It was brushed under the carpet." Her mother-in-law never would admit the truth: "'there's nothing like that in our family' … she would never acknowledge there was anything different with Roger except he had a bad heart". Grandparents' grief and disappointment was sometimes expressed in ways that were not always helpful to the struggling family. According to Lilian Fisher, "My mother was often choked with tears, and my husband's mother prayed loudly over Wendy which only increased our despair, yet we knew they meant well. They never really came to terms with Wendy's handicap."

When the silence was eventually broken by the doctor or specialist, sometimes the news and diagnosis gave rise to a twofold continuation of silence outside the home. In the first place, the initial silences within the family were now echoed by the need to hide from the outside world. Rene Harris talks about families she knew for whom "it was such a blow they just curled up inside and closed the door to the world"; nobody knew of the existence of their children who remained hidden indoors, or were only taken out in the car or after dark. This self-imposed silence sometimes meant that any help forthcoming from outside the family – for example after 1946 from the newly formed local societies associated with the National Association of the Parents of Backward Children (NAPBC) – was often not welcome, and publicity for the societies was frowned on: "A lot of the parents at the beginning didn't want publicity. That's going back 40 years – they'd lived with it so long in seclusion, that they didn't want it broadcast" (Brenda Nickson).

In the second place, the outside world did not know how to react, and the silence and isolation were continued and compounded. Reaction from other mothers or people in the street was often ambiguous or worse. According to Brenda Nickson, "At that time, no one acknowledged you … When you went out with the baby, you just felt you were pushing an empty pram because people didn't know what to say to you. So life was very traumatic, because you felt so lonely." In order to avoid this kind of public denial, Van Brunning, still in denial herself, took steps to cover up the fact that her baby was in any way different: "She didn't sit up and when I would take her out in the pram I would prop her up so people couldn't see she couldn't sit up of her own accord … It was rather nice for people to see a nice bonny baby sitting up in her pram. When I'd got her propped up with her lovely black hair and brown with the sun, it wasn't so evident."

Once the child was home from hospital, being cared for by the family, there was also silence from many of those whose role was to support and/or monitor families in the community. According to the life stories, the support for some families was in fact almost non-existent. Vi and Don Hardy were visited on one occasion by a mental welfare officer who brought their daughter a game – 'pegs in holes'. According to Don, "The Visitor said, 'I will call to see Margaret in about a fortnight.' Vi next saw her in eleven months' time. She was really useless." It was the District Nurse who stepped into the breach and who encouraged Don and Vi to believe in the abilities of their daughter. According to Gladys Abbs, on a day-to-day basis, "Nobody came. We didn't have anybody. We just did it ourselves", though she was supported by a very helpful family doctor; and Brenda Nickson, having been sent home from hospital, said, "We were just left then." Some forms of community care were concerned to control as well as provide care, with control and supervision of people with learning difficulties being called for by the eugenicists in the 1920s and 1930s (Thomson, 1998; Fennell, 1996). However, the surveillance of families, intended to be so strict when the legislation was first in place in 1913, on the evidence of these stories was in fact a hit-and-miss affair. It could be said, therefore, that the neglect of many families at least spared them from the controlling gaze of professionals, and that in such cases 'silence' was sometimes preferable.

As regards the professional silence of officers whose role was to visit all those families on their lists, several reasons for this have been put forward by former mental welfare officers themselves (Rolph, Atkinson and Walmsley 2002, 2003). Chief among these are: the huge lists (as a result of a push on 'ascertainment' after the war) given to only the relatively few duly authorised officers, who already had large workloads which tended to prioritise those with mental health problems; the lack of interest of some medical officers of health; and little in terms of resources to back up any support the officers could offer. A mental welfare officer working in Norfolk in the 1940s recalled that his statutory duty to visit those with learning difficulties every three months was necessarily carried out in a most cursory manner, inspecting and supervising rather than supporting: "We did very little work with people with learning difficulties in those days. We kept a register, but we were run off our feet, and the mentally handicapped people very sadly were on the back boiler … most of my work was emergency psychiatric … We did do some after-care, but looking back it was pretty primitive. (Rolph, Walmsley, and Atkinson, 2003).

Many officers did devote much energy to finding extra resources and filling the gaps, but the service differed widely from county to county and according to the interests of the officers and their superiors. This explains in part at least, Don and Vi Hardy's unsatisfactory experience of help from the officer in Cambridge in the 1940s.

Evidence for another silence comes from 'The advocate's story'. There we learn that there are few remaining records of Maureen's early life. It would seem paramount that records should have been kept of her family – who had lost contact with her – her friends, her activities, her likes and dislikes. When, however, she moved from the long-stay hospital where she had spent most of her life, "there were no photos or any life-book, or anything that came with her", and Maureen was "the only person on the [new] unit who had no family contact".

Pressures from professionals

When the professional silence was broken and the doctors at last made a diagnosis, they then often put pressure on the families to place their children in an institution. In 1939, Gladys Abbs was advised to write her son off 'as just one of those things', and place him in the local colony: "Don't come and visit him and don't enquire anything about him, just acknowledge that that was that." In 1955, according to Brenda Nickson, doctors were still giving the same advice: "I was just told that he was a Mongol as they were called in those days, and there would be no future for him, and that he'd probably not live longer than five. They said the best thing was for us to put him in an institution."

Even when the doctors did not try and persuade the family to part with their child, they often placed parents under other kinds of pressure. For example, by giving a very negative diagnosis, they gave parents anxieties and fears which sometimes ruled their lives. Don and Vi Hardy were told by the doctors that "they thought Margaret was a Mongol … The paediatrician said that she would be a loveable child who might only live to about the age of ten and would never be able to do very much. This of course was a shock to us …"

Another kind of pressure was ongoing surveillance, although as we have said, it was not carried out consistently. Only one of the families we spoke to experienced this, possibly because their son was the oldest in the group, born in 1939 at a time when monitoring was still being carried out with some degree of regularity, though still only once or twice a year. As their son grew up, Gladys Abbs's family was visited on several occasions by the Medical Superintendent of the comparatively new local colony in Norwich, opened in 1930. He saw his role as filling up the hospital, in particular with those people or children with mild learning difficulties, who looked 'normal' and who therefore were thought to pose a greater threat to the community. His role was also to check on families in the community to see that they were both caring for and controlling their children. He visited the family in 1947 when Rodney was eight years old, and urged them to place Rodney in the hospital. He made several return visits in the following years to check on the family and see that Rodney was well cared for and not out of control, eventually, however, admitting to Gladys that the family had after all done a good job of parenting.

The background to the pressure on families to give up their children to institutions lay in the segregation policy of the time, and the opening of large colonies and (after 1946) hospitals throughout this period. Medical superintendents would themselves go out into the community to visit families on their lists, checking their home circumstances, and urging admittance where they felt it was necessary (Barron, 1996; Potts and Fido, 1991). In particular this was the case if there was felt to be a risk of the person with learning difficulties starting a relationship or getting married. It was often very difficult to resist this pressure and local archives tell the stories of mothers writing to mental deficiency committees asking for their children to be allowed home again (Rolph, 2000).

The work of the medical professionals was backed up in the 1940s and early 1950s by the community officers who were also on the lookout for 'dangers' to the local community. Harry Orme, a former Mental Welfare Officer, recalled that in Ipswich in 1948, "it must be admitted that, effective as supervision for 'mental defectives' was, the effectiveness was often a form of control. We … were constantly advised to nip any budding romances off very firmly before they had time to ripen … the geneticist movement still had a powerful influence" (Rolph, Walmsley and Atkinson, 2003). Some families were able, however, to start resisting the professionals, and, like Gladys Abbs, to build a new life through their individual efforts and struggles.

Challenging pressures and fighting for rights

Weaving through all the life stories was the twofold theme of challenging professional dictates and fighting for rights.

The most fundamental way in which families challenged professionals often took place when they were at their most vulnerable, the mother having recently given birth. Brenda Nickson, for example, refused to comply with the paediatrician's advice to place her baby in an institution. She said that when they had the interview with the paediatrician, "needless to say, my husband and I were so horrified we just picked up our bags and left. I had a good weep of course. I think I spent the first two years crying." Gladys Abbs remembered that, on receiving similar advice, "I couldn't believe it. My husband and I talked it over, and Rodney belonged to us and we were going to see it through, which we have done." The fictionalised autobiography, 'April Showers' includes a detailed interview scene in which the doctor says, "Give her to an institution , or do the best you can for her. Give her a tin can to bang on and she'll be fine." This represented the advice given to her parents, and ignored by them to the extent that the 'fiction' was indeed a fiction and bore no resemblance to the truth of April's later development towards acquiring skills and abilities, and a "full and happy life".

After the initial shock and consequent loneliness and isolation, families began in the late 1940s and 1950s individually to challenge professional and public attitudes and the actions (or inaction) of local authorities, and to take steps towards change. This resulted in the formation of local NAPBC societies, one of the largest grass-roots voluntary movements to be formed in post-war Britain.

Struggles began in small ways, within the family, and the arena was often the issue of education. Vi and Don Hardy decided to ignore the predictions of the paediatrician, and follow the advice instead of Vi's sister who advised them not to 'take any notice of what they say: you teach her to read'. Their daughter Margaret defied predictions and learned to read and write. When Rene Harris received a letter from the education authorities telling her her son was 'ineducable' and must be withdrawn from the special school he attended, she took the matter to her MP as well as the local authority in Luton, "I still have that very hurtful letter. Ineducable. It's a terrible blow. I tried to fight it … I was confused. I was indignant. How dare they say my child was ineducable?" As a result of her own experiences, and the lack of help forthcoming from any of the official bodies she consulted, Rene founded the local society in 1955, whose first aim was to ensure suitable education for children like her son. Three of the other mothers in this section, Gladys Abbs, Lilian Fisher and Brenda Nickson, were also founder members of the Norwich, Lowestoft and Bedford local (Mencap) societies, respectively, which they used as a springboard to challenge professional views and lack of local authority interest; and Vi and Don Hardy became Treasurer and Secretary of their local Cambridge society, with their daughter also involved in some of the work.

Gradually, the damaging silences began to be broken as a result of the confidence given to parents by their association with the local societies. Positive and campaigning articles even started appearing in the press. Rene Harris describes how she felt when she read the article written by Judy Fryd, the instigator of the National Society, in the *Sunday People*: "Wonderful woman. I was absolutely inspired by her. Oh, I was so moved because she said everything that was in my heart, *and I couldn't say.*"

Being a founder member of her local society also gave Brenda Nickson the opportunity to begin the process of breaking taboos and stereotypes, and challenging some of the silences. She said, "When we started the society, people just thought, 'they're mentally retarded, probably idiots'. They were referred to as 'idiots' in the old days, weren't they? Nobody expected you to do anything with them." Instead, Brenda took her son everywhere with the family, he was never excluded. As she said, "We made people aware because we didn't hide it, we made ourselves noticeable." Families who challenged their doctor's advice or predictions showed great bravery, especially in the face of the entrenched attitudes we have highlighted in the previous pages. There was, however, after the war, a gradually changing climate which contributed to the growing success of these challenges and made it possible for families to emerge from all the hiding, denial and silences, make a stand and change attitudes.

The education policy in particular caused great resentment among parents. The Education Act of 1944 "laid down an arbitrary quotient of 50 as the lowest assessment at which education could be considered. Those who were assessed as possessing an IQ of 50 or above could be admitted to state education as 'educationally sub-normal' and attend special schools. Children below this assessment were designated 'ineducable' and unless spaces were found for them at occupation centres the parents had to find private education for their children or were left with nothing" (Shennan, 1982). Mental welfare officers have spoken about the great difficulty they had with this policy and the requirement on them to write letters like the one received by Rene Harris. Some refused to write them, but instead made a home visit to tell the parents face to face. Some teachers refused to comply, and, where they could get away with it, allowed children to attend their schools. Rene's experience – having no alternative offered to her by the authorities, and with several other children at home also needing her attention – caused her to have a breakdown and in the end to have her son admitted to Bromham Hospital. It was this experience above all that convinced her of the need for action: "It was a very, very hard decision. I should think that for 18 months I cried myself to sleep. I felt like a murderess. I really felt I'd condemned him to death. And that was when I really threw myself into Mencap heart and soul. I thought you know I must fight for all those who are in the community because perhaps parents won't have to undergo this trauma if we can improve things in the community." The exclusion of their children from education and from the benefits of the Welfare State was a catalyst which inspired parents to fight for the rights of their children.

Set against the hardships and difficulties of this period, therefore, are the enormous achievements not only of the families, but also of their children.

Progress and achievements

On a personal level, the stories tell of progress against the odds; of achievements by many of the daughters and sons with learning difficulties; of huge change but some continuity in the pattern of the battles fought by the parents between 1946 and 1959.

Though some of these achievements relate to a later period – the children's teens and adulthood – it is appropriate to mention them here because they were made possible by the parents' efforts towards change during the period covered by this section. Margaret Hardy, as we have seen, learned to read and was eventually able to help her parents with the local society newsletters, as a result of her parents' teaching. Van Brunning taught her daughter, Anne, "on hands and knees on this floor really ... I found that she had a great interest in books and liked looking at pictures and it progressed from there really".

Anne went on to college and to win numerous certificates and prizes for her work, and to gain a GCSE B-grade in Art. April, whose parents had been told by the paediatrician to give her 'a tin can to bang', went to an ordinary school, and learned to read and write fluently. By learning about autism, Margaret Littlewood was able to connect with her daughter and introduce her to music, poetry and radio: "She could sing anything, she would only need to hear a tune once and all her life she could sing it. And she was even singing opera before she died, she could just pick it up like that." In later life Maureen, encouraged by her advocate, has taken up painting and has held an exhibition of her work.

Parents of children with very severe difficulties were equally tireless, and their children also made progress beyond the early predictions. Lilian Fisher remembered 'what a joyful occasion it was when she (Wendy) took her first steps' at five years old. The whole family, including siblings, worked hard to help Wendy to become toilet-trained, the vital requirement for acceptance at a special school. On a momentous day, the school bus came for Wendy and took her to school: "We felt this was a real achievement." Brenda Nickson's whole family also took joy from her son's achievements: "I can remember when Roger first walked. Until he was four he used to crawl around on his bottom. When he walked his first steps, my other son, Paul, who was six at the time, couldn't get to school quickly enough to tell the teacher that Roger had walked. And it was so exciting."

As regards the more public achievements of the parents themselves, many of the stories tell of the new services which the local societies either provided themselves or persuaded local authorities to establish. These were often plans for respite care, residential homes, welfare visitors, holidays and employment opportunities. But above all in this early period they pushed for more and better education in the form of local society (as opposed to local authority) occupation centres and industrial centres (later adult training centres). They often raised the funds to buy and run their own centres. They made representations to central government concerning the serious lack of educational facilities. Some of their plans came to fruition in the period after 1959, so we will talk about them in more detail in Part 2. We feel it is important, however, to highlight the fact that many of them had their origins in the early difficult struggles of families in the 1940s and 1950s, and in families' unswerving belief in the abilities, educability and rights of their children.

Summary

Families had to wait many more years for the education policy to change: it was not until 1971 that education was accepted as a right for all children. However, attitudes were changing, partly as a result of the work of parents and societies, and partly as a result of the revelations of the National Council for Civil Liberties of the ill treatment of people with learning difficulties in some of the large hospitals.

The Mental Health Act was passed in 1959. In the lead-up to the Act, the National Association of Parents of Backward Children (NAPBC) was asked to participate in discussions and to make proposals to the Royal Commission: families were, it seemed, going to be listened to at last – the official silence well and truly broken, neglect at an end. The NAPBC pleaded for mandatory powers for local authorities to provide education and training facilities and hostel accommodation for all who needed them. In the event, the Act was a major disappointment. Although it paid lip service to a greater development of community care, it was permissive rather than prescriptive, offering little more in terms of resources, and so ensuring that the situation within local authorities remained largely unchanged. The families and advocate in Part 1 have borne witness to change, heroic progress and better services provided at their own instigation in the 1940s and 1950s. However, as we move into the 1960s in Part 2, family stories record that many of the same battles still remained to be fought, and that invisibility and the 'wall of silence' often remained intact.

References

Barron, David (1996) *A Price to be Born*. Huddersfield: H. Charlesworth & Co.

Fennell, Phillip (1996) *Treatment Without Consent: Law, Psychiatry and the Treatment of Mentally Disordered People Since 1845*. London: Routledge

Fox, Evelyn (1930) Community schemes for the social control of mental defectives. *Mental Welfare*, 11(3), 15 July, pp.61–74

Potts, Margaret and Fido, Rebecca (1991) *A Fit Person to be Removed. Personal Accounts of Life in a Mental Deficiency Institution*. Plymouth: Northcote Press

Rolph, Sheena, Walmsley, Jan and Atkinson, Dorothy (2002) 'A Man's Job'?: Gender Issues and the Role of Mental Welfare Officers, 1948–1970. *Oral History*, 28–41

Rolph, Sheena, Walmsley, Jan and Atkinson, Dorothy (2003) 'A Pair of Stout Shoes and an Umbrella': The Role of the Mental Welfare Officer in Delivering Community Care in East Anglia, 1946–1970. *British Journal of Social Work*, 33, 3, 339–359

Shennan, Victoria (1980) *Our Concern. The Story of the National Society for Mentally Handicapped Children and Adults 1946–1980*. London: Mencap

Thomson, Matthew (1998) *The Problem of Mental Deficiency: Eugenics, Democracy and Social Policy in Britain c.1870–1959*. Oxford: Clarendon Press

Walmsley, Jan and Rolph, Sheena (2001) The development of community care for people with learning difficulties 1913 to 1946. *Critical Social Policy*, 21(1), 59–80

Poems by Tom Hulley

tears

you burst into tears
unexpectedly
for the smallest reason
but also for
every reason

the difficulty of change
this bombardment
of trying to cope
against the odds

for a short time
when you are inconsolable
the pain of it
turns and twists inside me
probably reflecting
how you feel

what you cannot express
the frustration
the endless sense
of being short changed
which life delivers
with a deceptive grin

wood nymphs

smoked daughters
a rare delicacy
evoking woods
in springtime
open air fires
crackling with
the last dampness
of seasoned trees
making sparks fly
scents of barbecue
bonfire and burning
smell the smoke
in their scented hair
on their brightly
patterned woollies
on their gloves
their fleecy coats
and thermal trousers
all women are daughters
but the smoked ones
so much more stylish
than the rest

age of consent

the college sent a form today asking for consent
"we know your daughter is old enough but
we are caring and prefer the parental nod"
it is strange how discrimination is spelled
c-a-r-i-n-g and risk protection dressed
as some deep concern for us
tonight she did not want the beer I brought
while she ignored the asking busy with her friends
decided that she did not drink beer
did not desire a dark brown mild however named
but sent me for a fizzy drink instead
and after this she tried the 'panther' found it good
enjoyed the taste of coffee with a ruby kick
was tempted by a sip of bobby's 'galaxy'
becoming starry eyed attuned to the jazz
and the ethos of tasting at a festival
she liked the sound of 'classic blonde'
— a beer not a slinky smoke voiced singer —
but don't we all?
the disputations carried on as she devoured
the biggest burger seen this year
and then demolished as I turned away
my prize choice my glass of 'tower pale'
the strongest in the show
dismissing my consent my first decision
that low strength mild insisting girls prefer
something golden stronger something wild

Part 2

Change ...
and continuity
1959–71

*Edited by Dorothy Atkinson, Nigel Ingham
and John Welshman*

Introduction

A sense of challenge and resistance to the old order pervades the stories in the middle section of the book. At the same time, families recount the price they paid for resistance, and the losses they experienced through the migration, separation and exclusion of their sons and daughters because of the continuing segregationist policies of the period 1959–71. The timeframe for the stories is marked at its outset by the 1959 Mental Health Act. This repealed the Mental Deficiency Acts, introduced the terminology of 'mental subnormality' and heralded an increasing shift towards care in the community (though without the compulsion – and the resources – to implement it). Further attempts to support the switch to community care came with the 1963 *Health and Welfare* White Paper. The period was also a critical one for the further development of Mencap and for the birth of the advocacy movement.

The period 1959–71 ends with the major changes brought about by the 1968 Seebohm Report (and the introduction of social services departments in 1971), the 1970 Education Act and the 1971 White Paper, *Better Services for the Mentally Handicapped*. This was a period of transition. The stories reflect this, capturing the sense of isolation, exclusion and oppression that characterised some of the stories of the earlier period, but also witnessing the widespread changes that came in the wake of major shifts in policy and practice. The stories capture the changes and reflect on what they have meant for families.

Part 2 Timeline   1959–71

Year	Legislation	Social policies
1959	Mental Health Act	Younghusband Report highlighted shortage of PSWs
1960		
1961		Enoch Powell's 'Water Towers' speech: mental hospitals to close in 15 years
1962		Ministry of Health report: *A Hospital Plan for England and Wales*: 10-year plan included development of hostels
1963		Publication of White Paper *Health and Welfare: The Development of Community Care*
1964		
1965		Seebohm Committee established to review Local Authority health and welfare services
1966		
1967		
1968		Seebohm Committee report
1969		Howe Report: inquiry into ill-treatment at Ely Hospital
1970	Education (Handicapped Children) Act made education universal. Local Authority Social Services Act: new Social Services Departments to take over Local Authority health and welfare services	
1971		White Paper: *Better Services for the Mentally Handicapped.* UN Declaration of the Rights of Mentally Retarded Persons

Publications	World events
	Plane crash kills Buddy Holly. Singapore gains independence from Britain. Fidel Castro gains control of Cuba
Erving Goffman's *Asylums* critiques institutions	First American in space. Chubby Checker introduced the 'Twist'
	American spy plane identified long-range missiles in Cuba
	President Kennedy assassinated. Martin Luther King delivers his 'I have a dream' speech.
Jack Tizard's *Community Services for the Mentally Handicapped* makes the case for small residential units	
	Vietnam War starts
	England wins football World Cup. Hindley and Brady gaoled for Moors murders
Stanley Segal's 'No Child is Ineducable' paved the way for education for all	
	Martin Luther King assassinated. Russian tanks enter Prague
Nirje's 'The Normalization Principle'. Pauline Morris's *Put Away* puts the case against hospitals	Richard Nixon becomes US President
	Four students killed by US National Guardsmen during anti-war demonstrations
Maureen Oswin's *The Empty Hours* showed the deprived lives led by children in long-stay hospitals	Decimalisation in Britain

Chapter 10
In Trident Booksellers and Café, Boston, USA

Michael's sister

A sister's story – 25 May 2001

I have been reading the Writer's Yearbook 2001 *and one of the tips for budding writers inspired me to write about the following experience. The article in question encouraged one to try to consider oneself from a variety of different angles – this evidently helps with character development. I had no intention of writing about my relationship with my brother, but found myself doing so when trying to consider a time when I had behaved in what I perceived to be a cruel and selfish manner. My brother had suffered severe brain damage from epilepsy and had an estimated mental age of 'under three' for the majority of his 38 years. The text that follows will surprise no one more than it surprised me.*

As a child I can recall the jealousy I felt towards my disabled brother. I felt guilty at these feelings, but I was young and I didn't understand why I felt how I felt.

Michael screamed often, and he received attention. It didn't seem fair. I didn't scream and shout to get attention and I was probably only six or seven years old. He yelled and my mother would run to him. I wanted her attention. I wanted him to shut up. Mum said he couldn't help it. He was just trying to express himself, but I suppose that didn't matter to me. The noise was just driving me mad. The noise was pervading the house, high-pitched screaming. "Be quiet! Be quiet, please be quiet", I would think to myself. I willed Michael to be silent. He wasn't. My mum went out of the room, asking me to keep an eye on Michael to make sure he was OK. I forget where she went. Maybe she went outside to hang out the washing.

I went into the back room, the room my parents had converted to a bedroom for themselves and Michael. He was too weak physically and too heavy now for them to get him upstairs to bed. This meant that it was always difficult to have friends over. Sure, we could go into the front room, but there was always the danger of interruption from Michael's screaming. I suppose this didn't matter so much when I was six or seven but, as a teenager, it became acutely embarrassing – as did the untidy house. My mother never had the energy, or the will I suppose, to tidy up – I think her environment was a reflection of her inner feelings of defeat. Of course, I realised none of this when I was six or seven, or, indeed, later, when I was a teenager.

Anyway, while my mother was outside, out of the way, I crept into the back room and I pinched Michael hard. Still, he didn't stop screaming. He was excited. I pinched him again. God, I wanted him to stop screaming. He didn't, so I slapped him. My mother came back into the room and caught me.

With an unusual passion, she smacked my bare leg – the school dress hung just above my knee and offered no protection. A big red hand mark appeared and I ran upstairs sobbing and shut myself into my bedroom.

For years afterwards, my mother brought up that incident – saying how selfish I'd been to inflict pain on my defenceless brother. I think the guilt I felt, together with my mother's disapproval, coloured my whole attitude towards my brother. I look back now and wonder why I could never share time with my parents without the shadow of my unfortunate sibling. My mother refused to accept any respite care for Michael if, indeed, any was ever offered – Social Services weren't so good then as they are now.

Many was the time after this that Michael was given as the excuse for either one or both of my parents not to come to my speech days, my wedding, my graduation … Was Michael also the reason why my parents were happy for me to spend so much time at the stables? (I was a keen horsewoman from the age of nine throughout my youth and teenage years.) Was it, as I thought, 'because they didn't have time to spend with me because Michael needed them more than I did'? I'm not complaining. I loved horses and sought solace in their silent, non-judgemental company and in the camaraderie of my horsey childhood chums.

I look back now and I see why I pinched Michael. Yes, I was cruel and selfish, but I hadn't chosen to live a life that appeared so different from that of my schoolmates. Perhaps I wasn't cruel and selfish, perhaps I was just a kid who was angry and frustrated, who didn't understand the whole picture. I wanted the perfect family that my friends seemed to have.

Of course, I know now that their lives weren't perfect, but they at least fell superficially within accepted norms, beyond the stigma of 'abnormality', with which society labelled my family.

My feelings of love, pain, jealousy and grief were never stronger than when my brother died. This is the poem I wrote when I woke during the night before his funeral.

For Michael

Dear brother
Special and needy
Our mother loved you
More than life itself —
We loved you too
But didn't understand
Circumstances too tragic
For childhood hearts

Jealous of our mother's love
Greedy for attention
We gave you less
Than you deserved
Now, wracked with guilt
And loss and pain
We mourn your
Absence from our lives

Wrapped in self
Too little time
Trapped in the everyday —
Our grief now the product
Of actions too little, too late
Of wishing we'd
Done more
When we could.

Chapter 11
You do as well as you can for them

Emma Atkinson

Emma was interviewed in Carlisle, at her home, in March 2002. Stewart was in his early thirties and I had known the family for around eight years. The family never received a diagnosis for Stewart and spent many years unsure of what to do for the best. When he was 32, Stewart was tested for 'Williams syndrome', which proved positive. Emma felt relieved that there was now a 'reason' to explain Stewart's difficulties.

Rohhss Chapman

It was a normal birth

Stewart was a late baby; I don't know whether or not that has any bearing on his condition. It was a normal and a quick birth, in the end. Nothing was said when he was born; as far as we were concerned we thought it was a normal birth and he was a healthy baby. We noticed when he was about six or seven months that he was slightly nervous at everything, like sounds, and he got shocked a lot if he were to do anything. As he got older he was late in walking, late in talking, and he cried a lot. Basically, I think we had an idea that there was something wrong, we kept thinking he was a little bit slow, but that he would catch up on things, which every parent does.

As he progressed and got older we kind of realised, there's something wrong here. He cried a lot, even when he was about 2½. I realised he wasn't walking very well, he was struggling. He wouldn't walk anywhere, actually; we had to take him in pushchairs mostly, right up to when he went to school because he refused to walk – he just used to stand there screaming. When he got to about two or three, I told the doctor that I wasn't happy with his progress and I got an appointment with the paediatrician at the hospital, Dr Eversley.

He made it as if it was our fault

Everybody knows Dr Eversley – he has quite a reputation. Anyway, we went. He was abrupt, he examined his heart, measured his head – I don't know what he measured his head for. We weren't told anything at all; we never got any information from him to say what was wrong with him. He made it as if it was our fault – we were worrying parents, and we were worrying for nothing, that he would come on, and we felt absolutely terrible. As Stewart got older, things progressed from there. He had a bowel condition, he was either constipated or the other way, and I wasn't happy so I went to see the doctor again, and he sent us back to the paediatrician. I told him I refused to go to Dr Eversley because we got no information, we didn't know what was what, it was absolutely dismal. So we changed to Dr Cooper and he was just the opposite, he was a really nice man, and he got a consultant from Newcastle to come and see Stewart. I think he had a prolapsed back passage at four or five, but the doctor kept in touch, we kept going there regularly for a while.

Stewart starts school

Stewart started school, in the mainstream school. He wasn't doing anything there, he was getting smacked a lot and the teachers were ignoring him. They never told me that he had a problem, although he used to scream all the way there and all the way back and he wasn't very happy at all. It was a health visitor who knew me who actually said he was getting smacked all the time because he was breaking his pencils, ripping his papers, and she said, "I think he's got a problem, I don't think he's coping with it."

He's an awkward child

I went to see the headmistress and again we didn't seem to get very far. She said, "Oh, come on, he's just an awkward child", and all the rest of it. And I said, 'No, I believe he can't do the work and it's upsetting him.' I said, "Surely there's somewhere where he can go, where he can get help to bring him up to standard?" She said, "We've nowhere, we just have York School." So I said, "In that case I want him taken out and put in York School." So we more or less had to fight for a place for him in the special school.

York School was for children who couldn't cope in mainstream schools, where they had a learning difficulty, but were physically able. There weren't any disabled people there. Within a few months of going there, it was completely different; he loved to go to school. They didn't teach him a lot, and I didn't expect a lot, so long as he could learn what he could learn, and I think their philosophy was they just brought them to what they could do, and they worked with them really hard, and they were really good teachers. Unfortunately, that's shut down now, government policy, but it was a really good school. But his personality changed, he settled down, he would go to school, in fact he wouldn't miss a day, it was completely different.

And I think really, the first school should have picked up on Stewart's difficulties. They never did, they could have come to me and said, 'Look he's not a happy child, he can't do the work.' We got psychologists in to give him tests and things, and they found that he was well behind. He had a condition where he looked at the board, but by the time he got it down on paper it had gone out of his mind, he couldn't concentrate, it had just gone completely.

Surely teachers, experienced teachers, should have picked up on that, and they didn't, which was disappointing. We thought he might have been at York School for a couple of years, caught up, gone back to mainstream school, but it didn't work out that way, he stopped there till he left school actually. But he was happy, and I wasn't bothered.

Options after school

I think he did have an extra year at school, but I had two options. I was told that he could go on this course at technical college, or he could go to the adult training centre. I asked about the course at the technical college, and the tutor said it was a course where people who get into trouble go on as well. That wasn't for Stewart because he is very easily led and as soon as they said that I thought no way. I would have had to take him, pick him up, make sure he didn't go anywhere afterwards or get into trouble. It took too much looking after really to go on a course like that, so I plumped for the adult training centre.

The first day we went to the adult training centre to see round it. It was a shock to the system, because it was the first time me or Stewart had been near anybody disabled, or who had physical features that could be threatening when you don't really know the person. It's a real shock the first time you go and you hear all this noise, and see everybody rushing at you, so friendly, and Stewart kind of pulled back with alarm and I thought, "Oh gosh, I hope I've done the right thing here." Anyway, he settled in, no bother, and they all said he would help anybody who was less fortunate than him, anybody that needed help, Stewart was there helping them. In the long run it's turned out to be better for Stewart because they've had a lot of patience. I've had an outside job. Stewart's actually been out on job release, and it's not worked. Every time he goes out, for some reason, something happens, so obviously he can't cope.

He's happy where he is and we just decided to leave him. He keeps saying he wants a proper job outside; he did work in the offices at People First and he did manage that really well for a long time. He's had other jobs where he didn't manage it so well, or something's gone wrong and he's been pulled back. But that's Stewart's fault, its no fault of the place where he's working, you know, he just can't really cope in some of the jobs that they've put him in. Some of the jobs haven't been that nice really. He was at the abattoir, cleaning and so on … it's not nice … I don't think he cared for that. Later he went to a bible firm, and he was going to be sweeping up, and they promised him a machine. He didn't get the machine though, he just got a brush and a shovel.

I think it's awful that they can't actually go back to an Employment Liaison Officer and say, "I'm not happy, I want out." They should be able to do that without getting shouted at and told, "It's your last chance! If you don't settle at this, that's it." And it shouldn't be the last chance, because a job's like everything else, you either like it or you don't, and when you've got learning difficulties and you're unhappy there, there's all sorts that can go wrong.

At the adult training centre he was in the woodwork section. Then the training centre closed down and was dispersed, so they've got a smaller unit. They haven't got as much work, they haven't got as many machines, they don't do a lot of work. He's a bit bored, whereas before he used to love it. This is government policy of course, I suppose, and lack of money that they're making smaller units but it doesn't always work. He's lost a lot of contact with his friends that he used to have at the big training centre. Basically they are walking the streets most of the time, at the baths or the pictures or walking round the town. I think they're pretty bored, either doing that or sitting watching videos, because the work isn't there for them.

I think they want work because they like to be kept busy and they like to know they're being useful, to see a product at the end of it. Unfortunately for Stewart he might be there for a while, you know, the chances of him going into mainstream jobs are low. He's capable of going if he could settle down and not get into trouble. But when you've got to be right behind him, or things go wrong, you just can't afford to let that happen.

Life at home

Basically, Stewart's problems at home were very difficult for the rest of the family. He had behavioural problems, I won't go any further than that, but it upset the whole family. We've got an older boy who didn't get as much attention as he could have. We couldn't go away with him, spend a night away, so we never really got holidays. It disrupted the family, constantly being on your guard to watch him, to make sure he didn't go away with anybody. He was very friendly, too friendly really, very trusting of people. I never, ever left him with my parents, not overnight, because I didn't think they could cope until he was older, and then he kind of settled down a little bit. But we always had social workers.

Help from services

He was doubly incontinent, and I think it started because of that. We were trying to help him over that. He was about 11 or 12 when the social worker made arrangements for him to go into Arnwood House, an assessment and respite centre. We'd seen a psychiatrist at the time, and he said he could help Stewart, so they put him in for a week to try to get him into a toilet routine, but it didn't work. I didn't think it would, but the psychiatrist was confident. I think they gave up in the end. He hated it, and he begged me not to let him go back. I think because they were trying to get him in a toilet routine they were waking him up all times of the day and night, he didn't like that, torches shone in his face. It seems to have stayed with him, that, you know, and he just wouldn't go back in.

He will just keep travelling

Stewart likes to be at home, he likes his own things around him, and he's happier. The problems have still been there over the years, you have to watch him like a hawk, or otherwise he tends to take off. If he travels anywhere on his own the chances are you won't get him back. You know, he'll just keep travelling. He talks to somebody, goes away with them and then he'll go on to somebody else. We've lost him many a time, a weekend at a time. We've had the police out. Then there are other things like there's a pub right on the doorstep, we've taken him there. We've left him for an hour and then we've gone back, and chances are that he wasn't still there when we went back. He couldn't cope with it and then, of course, he always ended up in the hospital for some reason. Getting an ambulance and getting himself taken off to hospital. So we've had a lot of problems that way and it's been very hard going. If he goes outside to have a smoke you've got to check every five minutes to make sure he's still there, otherwise he would take off.

The Courts

Going through the court thing is terrible, you think there's no end to the problem and you wonder what's going to happen at the end of it. You're not in control and you think, 'I can't do this any more, I've done everything I could have done and it's up to the judge now.' I wouldn't like to go through it again. After the court thing it was just a question of keeping him in and taking him everywhere.

You take him, you bring him back. I had to learn to drive, I hated it, but I had to learn to drive so I could take him wherever he went. Even now I hate going out in the car, but it's just one of those things. People talk about him because wherever he goes, his mother's in tow. A lot of people with learning difficulties have their own responsible lives, they're up and they're away and they're gone. But because of all the things that have happened in the past we've had to tighten our hold on Stewart.

There have been a few blips since then, but we got them ironed out and now he's on pills and he's a lot quieter. Before he was wanting to go here, there and everywhere and we got no rest; he's a lot quieter, a lot more settled, but I don't know if he's any happier. If he asks to go anywhere he goes, we'd take him. But we've been trying to force him to go somewhere: "Do you want to go tonight, Stewart?" "No, I'm not bothered." It's just the opposite; it's not like Stewart at all. Anyway, it's a relief for us. It's an awful thing to say but it's easier for us now. The only thing Stewart likes is his music, otherwise he just sits there on the chair watching the television.

We realise now that he is never going to manage on his own

We always thought as he got older that he would get more sense, and there would be a time when he would settle down, but he would still have a life where he could go and do things. We realise now that he's never going to manage on his own, and there'll come a time when we're not there to watch him and he's got to have provision where he's got somebody to look after him, really. Not one of these where he's in a house on his own, and copes on his own, because he just wouldn't. He'd end up having parties and inviting all sorts round.

A lot of people take advantage, but there again it's his personality as well. He knows a lot of people and a lot of people look out for him, so it works both ways. He's very popular. Wherever you go there's always somebody shouting over to him and nobody walks past him and ignores him, they always shout over if he hasn't seen them. You could go up town and leave him for five minutes and come out and there's a crowd around him. He seems to know everybody and everybody seems to know him, so it's just his personality.

Contact with social workers

Social workers tend to come in if anything goes wrong but they haven't got the provision to really keep an eye on him. They've been good over the years, though, we can't fault that. If anything's gone wrong and we've needed them, they've been there to get proper things in place, and they've given us a lot of help.

He's actually got to 33 now, and it's only recently that the social worker has actually realised that there was something wrong with Stewart. He has a syndrome that's very, very rare; it's called Williams syndrome. I'd never heard of it, but all the problems over the years, and the trouble with his digestive system, it fits this to a tee. The social worker had been dealing with somebody with Williams syndrome. He thought it fitted Stewart, so him and the nurse that was coming to the house at the time got together and decided to see if it was the syndrome that Stewart had. They wrote to my doctor and the doctor kind of pooh-poohed the idea, saying, "What's the good of labelling the boy at this time of his life?"

But anyway, in the meantime, they'd phoned Newcastle, for the genetic research lab, and they wrote to me. So you can imagine the shock when I got this letter out of the blue to say that they'd made an appointment for Stewart in the February. I didn't know what it was about, this gene clinic. I was absolutely furious, and I got on to them. What they said was they'd realised what it could be, but they didn't want to upset me, they wanted to have a word with the doctor first. With the doctor's response they were going to let it drop, but then the doctor must have rung the clinic or something. So I went to the doctor, to see what was going on, and he said it was actually the social worker and the nurse who had arranged it, and that they should have told me about it first. So anyway, I made an appointment with the social worker and the nurse and gradually we got there. They told us what had happened and what they thought was wrong, and if I wanted to go through with it I could, if I didn't we'd just stop there, and that was that. But once you find out that there could be a possibility of something like that, you want to know.

I spent all those years thinking I was a bad parent

So, I spent all these years, you kind of think you may be a bad parent, that it's maybe your fault, and then all of a sudden you think, "Gosh, there's been a reason for this. It isn't that he's just been a difficult child, he's had a reason for it and nobody's known or picked up on it." So we went ahead with it and they said more or less there and then, we think the social worker's right. And that was before he'd been tested. It's called Williams syndrome and it actually has a lot to do with the nervous system. So your co-ordination is bad, and your memory is bad. One of the things about this syndrome is that they're all people like Stewart, very outgoing, very friendly, they can make people think that they can do such a lot, and yet they can't. But people are taken in and let them do more than they're capable of doing. So all these years he's been getting the wrong treatment. There's special schooling, special things they should do, which Stewart never had. He had the wrong type of schooling to start off with.

All the paediatricians that he'd seen didn't pick up on it. The doctors don't know too much about it. It's a syndrome they don't really come into contact with a lot. They gave me all the information, and it was really everything about Stewart, Stewart to a tee. All the problems we'd had over the years, things that are still cropping up, lack of calcium, different things that just fit Stewart, and I thought, "Well, if I'd known this years ago I could maybe have had more patience." Instead of shouting at him, "What are you doing this for?" and "You'd no need to do it like this, you could do it this way", you could understand that they can't do it that way, they had to be taken through it gradually.

He was 32 before we got a diagnosis

So he got to 32 before he was actually diagnosed with this. But that too had an effect on Stewart because when it started, he thought there was something wrong with him. This was because we took him to see these doctors from Newcastle and because they said he'd got this and they talked about it in front of him. I tried to explain to him that there was no difference. He was who he was and it didn't change him or anything. It's just that now all the things that he's found hard to do over the years, we've found a reason for it. I tried to deal with it quietly, but after that he became a little bit depressed and ill, and I think it was just because of this. So this last year has been hard.

He's on tranquillizers and things to keep him quiet, but he's not the same boy so it's a shame. I think if this had been found out years ago it would have been behind him, but because it's happened now, he seems to have withdrawn lately, from being an outgoing boy to one who's really been holding to the family. He won't go anywhere. He's stopped going to People First meetings, he's stopped going to his Wednesday club, he won't go to the disco.

We were having problems, real problems after he'd been tested, and I had to get the doctor to get me an appointment with a psychiatrist, but they wouldn't look at him because he had learning difficulties. I was told the psychiatrist said that he couldn't help Stewart. But in the meantime I'd actually got word from another doctor who deals with people with learning difficulties from West Cumbria. He came to see Stewart and he actually put him on strong pills, you know, just to quieten him down. He said it's either that, or Stewart being a bit miserable and everything, so he says he could be on them for quite a long time.

Coping mechanisms

I take it a day at a time, I really do, and I keep thinking I'll get through it. There are times when you're really down and you think, there's no way we can get through this, but we have. It does cause a lot of arguments but when it's good it's good and when it's bad you just have to get through it a day at a time. Stewart's the same, he lives for the day. He doesn't think that his actions have repercussions for him and for the family and you can tell him as many times as you want and he'll say, "Yeah, I know, I won't do it again", but give him a couple of months and he's forgotten all about it. Basically we do cope, I just don't want to see the bad times coming back.

Where does support come from?

In times of crisis, support comes from the social workers. We know that if we want a break there are respite houses now, but we haven't used respite a lot because Stewart doesn't really like to go away from home. But apart from that, I don't think there's much support.

We've never really asked the family. I've two elderly parents, but I've never put on people, I've always thought, "Well, Stewart's our responsibility." We've just done it ourselves really. I think the mother gets it all really, from washing sheets to changing beds and sorting everything out. I've always felt as if I've been on my own in that way. I found I could be quite ruthless now to get what I want for him. I'd go ahead and not let things stand in the way and try and fight for what he wants. But at one time I would've wanted to hide. You know, when we first realised about Stewart, you want to hide things that are going on. It wasn't talked about, we thought we were the only parents that were trying to deal with this, and it isn't until you meet other parents that you realise, "Gosh, there's lots of people, it's not just us." Doctors could say, "Well, it's not just in your family. Other people are having the same problems and we'll put you in touch with them." It would be nice if there were groups, when you first find out there's something wrong with your child.

Uncertainty over benefits

We never knew about benefits and things like that. Somebody had to tell me. They said, 'Put in for it, you might get it', so we put in for it and we did get it. I'm sure it was a parent that had said they were getting this benefit for their child. It was pretty frightening – the first question they ask you is, "What's wrong with your child?" What do you say? "Well, I don't know; they've never given him a label"? I had to go to the doctor's first at the hospital, and my own doctor, to say I was going to put in for it and I hope they'd support me.

Other people's reactions

People think you're trying to get things when you don't deserve them, but you know it's 24 hours. You can't go to work because you can't leave him. You don't like to go to these organisations or departments, because you've got to tell them what he's like and you've got to discuss all his private business. You've got to have doctors examine him in front of you. It wasn't very nice at all, really nerve-racking when we first put in for it. Now I'm blasé.

Other relationships

His brother and him get on but they're not close. His brother's got his own family. He works full time, so he just comes over now and then. He's not one of these that says, "Come on Stewart, let's go out." He doesn't go out a lot himself anyway because he's busy looking after the kids.

Stewart's had girlfriends. At the training centre he had one special girl that he really liked, and they were always together at the centre. When the centre closed down they went to different workshops so he lost contact with her. Then he got somebody else who was a little bit possessive, so I think now he doesn't really want much to do with her. But he hasn't a permanent girlfriend now.

The future

I'm very worried about the future. I don't think about it too much. I should, I mean at the moment we haven't made a will, but keep talking about doing it. I haven't made plans but I've talked to the social worker and said Stewart would have to have a place in sheltered accommodation, maybe with three or four people but with somebody there constantly. The social worker said, "We're really going to have to make provision for him now", so I was kind of leaving it to the social worker, but the social worker's left his job now, and we've never really been contacted by anybody else. There's such a big caseload that, really, if everything's going right for a while you're taken off the books until things go wrong again. So where the social worker was keeping in touch with him every so many months, because of the trouble that Stewart got in, it's all stopped.

We would think about Stewart moving on but he just wants his own house. He thinks that if anything happens to us he's going to have this house. I don't want to disabuse him but he couldn't cope with it on his own. There may be a way of getting people in with him. Apart from that I haven't done anything, we keep saying we're going to have to sort it out, but we haven't got round to it. You don't want to think that far ahead.

I wouldn't have missed it

Sometimes you wonder what life would have been like. Maybe you would have gone on holiday, had a good job and plenty of money coming in. And then I think about it and I can really honestly say that we've been right down in the depths and we've had some really good highs. When Stewart is good, he's a smashing lad, he's really great, outgoing, bubbly, friendly and I keep thinking, "Well, I wouldn't have missed it." I really would have missed out on a lot I think. I wouldn't have got to know people that I have done, people with disabilities and things, because you don't think of mixing with them really. You don't come into contact with them. It's enriched my life because I've met people whom I wouldn't have thought of meeting and realised that there's something to fight for out there.

I had a relative that was in Dovenby Hall and I didn't know till I was quite grown up that they were there. If I'd mixed with people with disabilities and realised that they were individual people, I could maybe have visited him or got to know him. You think you've missed out on a lot, but I haven't because I've had Stewart. I might have been a shallower person, I'd have been frightened of my own shadow, maybe just going to work and having a holiday and having a good time or having a nicer house. I wouldn't give it up at all.

I think my husband would have liked a nice quiet life. I don't think he can cope as well as me. But when you've had a child it doesn't matter what they're like, they're there and you're dealing with them every day. You can despair at times, you could feel like getting hold of them and shaking them and saying, "Behave!" or "What did you do this for?" But you know at the bottom of it they're there, they're just there to be loved and you do as well as you can for them, that's all.

Chapter 12
Knocking the system

Kathleen Croucher

Kathleen has a daughter, Marilyn, with Down's syndrome, and a son, Martin, who was seriously injured and disabled in a motorbike accident. Kathleen believes that Marilyn was wrongly diagnosed with epilepsy and damaged through the drugs she took for it. Written here are some of Kathleen's experiences, recorded at her and Marilyn's home in Carbis Bay, Cornwall, during the summer of 2001. At that time she had been a widow for three years, and Marilyn was 49 years old.

Rohhss Chapman

The beginning

I didn't have a good pregnancy with either of my children. I went into hospital with toxaemia the night before Marilyn was born. I had a natural birth; it was a good birth. No one ever told me there was anything wrong with her. As she was born I did ask what was the matter with her eyes, and she said, "We don't know." Then after that they said would I take her back after a fortnight of being at home. When I went back there were an awful lot of young doctors all lined up looking at her, but not one of them told me. They all looked at her hands. I still never found out.

My mother didn't believe in clinics. She had eight children and I was the last one. I took Marilyn to the clinic doctor and my sister came with me. The doctor looked at Marilyn and said to me, "You've got a cabbage. Go home and have another child." It was such a shock, you know. I came up the road and as I did – I was crying by this time – my local doctor was passing in a car. He stopped the car and come over and said, "What's the matter?" So I told him and he said, "Oh, well, I'll give you a letter to go to Great Ormond Street." So we went, and there they were much kinder, you know, and they explained she was a Down's Syndrome because she had a chromosome too many, but that in some ways I might have been fortunate because they were usually gentle children. I came to terms with it pretty quick, because she was a lovely baby.

I was living with my mother and father. But adversity made me wake up. I said to my husband, "What we will do is save hard and get a deposit for our own property." He thought we'd never do it but I went and got a little part-time job. I never took money home; I put it straight in the post office so that way we did get a deposit.

I agreed to let Marilyn go

At that time they said all the Down's syndrome were uneducable. So there was no education that was available. I even tried to get her in the nursery because she was ever so clean, but they wouldn't accept her because she was a Down's. Now they would let her in but they wouldn't then. It made me feel terrible. All of it made me feel terrible. If you relive it you still relive the agony. It doesn't matter how many years go by, it never goes. From there I just determined to keep her at home.

Then a council lady came by and she said they were starting up a group in a little church hall for children like Marilyn; I think there were about another seven at the time. So I said I'd go down and look. I was a bit shocked. It was a run-down church hall and there were very big tall fellows and tiny little Down's syndrome all mixed in together. I did say to the teacher in charge, "Why are they all sat on the floor tearing up paper?" She said, "It's good for their frustrations." But I said, "My daughter loves books, she doesn't tear them. If I had to come back and you sit her on the floor does that mean she's going to start tearing her books?" "Oh," she said, "It's good for them. We know what's good for them." Then she showed me all the tapestry work that she said was taught to them. That was very nice; I thought it was marvellous. I agreed to let Marilyn go. It was the worst decision of my life. I let her go.

One day she had a throat mark from ear to ear. I asked how it happened and they said she ran into a rope when they were playing. So I had to accept what they said was true. Then she had a bad laceration on the eye and the nose and they said that was an accident. I took her to the doctor's and he said, "How did she come by these serious injuries?" I said "Well, the little church hall she goes to, they said it happened by accident." So I said, "Have you ever been in the place, doctor?" He said, "No." So I said, "Well you ought to go and have a look, there's big grown-up adults as well as little children."

Then she was again attacked and had four lumps out of her arm, where there was no flesh. Again they told me lies. I seem to have lived my life with lies. What happened then Marilyn started every night waking up and coming down and sitting in the big armchair. And I knew something was worrying her but I consoled her and put her back to bed. But then when she did it another night, it was a frosty morning, and she let herself out the house and she only had a little tunic on and little snow boots. She must have walked about four miles and she ended up at a friend's house. They took her in and then he came on his bicycle, because we didn't have phones in those days, to tell me that Marilyn had turned up on the doorstep. We then agreed that something was wrong. We wouldn't let her go back. So the council came knocking at the door and they threatened me that if I did not return her then she would be erased from the church-hall register. I said, "There's nothing you can threaten me with, I'm not even breaking the law. Until the law states that these children have got a right to education you can't do anything to me or to my daughter." So off they went.

After that Marilyn was happier. She had been there about six months and it had done a lot of damage. And I'll tell you what was the worst damage of the lot: my mother used to go and pick her up, and my mother always used to say she was the cleanest child in our family. And every time this lady in charge, she would hand my mother, wrapped up in newspaper, Marilyn's dirty underclothes. My mother said to her, "I brought this child up as my daughter and she never ever was dirty, only since she's been here." I've got that problem with her now mind, only now she's 49.

I do know that she will read

One day we saw an advert for a teacher who came to the home and privately taught them. It was £1 an hour, which was a lot of money in those days. Especially when your husband was only earning £14 a week! I got in touch – I'm still in touch with her now, she's marvellous – she said to me, "Before I come in, I must be perfectly honest with you, if your daughter cannot be taught I will have to tell you." So I said, "That's fair enough." So anyway – Miss Kell said to me, "I've only been with Marilyn five minutes and I do not know if she will spell but I do know that she will read." Of course I was over the moon, wasn't I? From then on Marilyn started having Miss Kell at £1 an hour for two hours a week. Marilyn loved it.

There was still no centre for her but we weren't worried because we had Miss Kell. Then there was a new centre opened at New Malden. But by that time we were on the move because our house was going to be knocked down. There was no new centre where we moved at the time. Miss Kell had got Marilyn through the assessment just before we moved and they (the council) would pay for Miss Kell's education. The council paid for it. But after that it turned out she couldn't manage the journey from Thames Ditton to Mitcham, and so Marilyn was quite isolated again. First of all she missed her friends because they don't like change at all. And also there was nobody at Mitcham that she knew. Whereas where she was born she could ride round and go to anybody's house; they knew her, you see.

I don't want to go, Mum

I've never had a lot of dealings with social workers, only when something like this occurred and I wanted to find out if there was a centre or anything. She was 16 then. So I thought, "Well something's got to be done." So the social worker said there was a place at Manor Hospital, Epsom. And there they taught them and did things … Well I'll skip that because that was another place I should *never* have let her go to. She did actually say, "I don't want to go, Mum." She was nearly scalped, with her hair nearly being pulled out and all that sort of thing. Whether it was the others I don't know because you never get the truth. One of the teachers said to me in private, "Mrs Croucher, take your daughter away." Now you see, I wasn't to blame for that. I knew something was wrong but it wasn't me, it was two dinner ladies – after Marilyn had left – who take the mobile dinners in, and these ladies reported the one in charge for caning the little children on the legs.

So when she was 16 and because she was so lonely I let her go to Manor Hospital, and then she was very, very bad. She had a nervous breakdown. I nursed her through that for 18 months. I associated that with what she had witnessed … I did know when Marilyn had a nervous breakdown. I knew the signs because I had one myself. I had that just after Martin was born, and I do know what it's like to suddenly be full of one feeling and that feeling is fear, when your hair stands up, when it takes you all the courage in the world to go from your room up the stairs to another room. And that took courage. And it took a long time. But my doctor was very good. He used to come in the week, and I was able to fight it myself. So I recognised it in Marilyn. You see it's a good job I suffered in one way, because if I hadn't have done I wouldn't have recognised it. It's all part of life.

Marilyn would not tell you everything but it seems as though she was losing the ability, and she's lost it now, if you ask her a question, should she tell you or not. She lost that ability. It's left her scarred quite a lot now.

The new centre
I took her away and to the new centre at Mitcham. It was a lovely place and she seemed very happy so I let her go … Just down the road – they used to drive her in the car and bring her home. Then one day she said, "I'm going to bed now Mum, I feel tired." She used to do everything herself in those days; she can't now … I went in her bedroom, not to check on anything really, and I was horrified that her petticoat had big black finger marks all over it. So I said, "How did you get those marks on your petticoat, Marilyn?" She named this boy. Now this boy was at the centre but he wasn't a Down's syndrome. So I said to her, "Who stopped him?" And she named the teacher in charge. So I went down there the next morning and I said to them that something had occurred with Marilyn yesterday. He said there was no need to be concerned because they had come across it in time. And that was all I ever got.

Another breakdown
Marilyn had another nervous breakdown and so I kept her at home again. She was about 19 by then. She had one at 16 and one at 19. Again, she was

getting very lonely and I told Ted it wasn't right. He, as a director of his firm, had collected so many thousands of pounds for the New Malden Centre where we originated. All right, so we had moved outside the area. But I said, "You worked for that, your money, and I don't see why Marilyn can't go there." So that would mean her coming back from Mitcham to go to New Malden. But I was breaking all the rules. Was it my fault? So one day we were out and I said, "I'm going to get a solicitor for advice." We went into one at random down at New Malden. I told him what had happened to Marilyn and her experiences. It turned out that his best friend was head of mental health. He said, "Well you've come to the right person." So from then on Marilyn was allowed, with me taking her, to go to the New Malden Centre. Lovely.

I knocked the system again

Well apparently I'd got the backs up of an awful lot of people because I'd knocked the system – in fighting for Marilyn's rights I'd knocked it every time. So I thought Marilyn was quite happy at New Malden. The councillors were trying to segregate those that lived on one side of the road to the others on the other side, like they do for school. So the pressure was on – I didn't know – behind the scenes to get Marilyn out of New Malden. So I was up against it, but unfortunately so was Marilyn. There are so many things, it's hard to remember them all. One day their car park was empty, so I put my car there and I was told off – "This is not for the likes of you." Then the Secretary of the Association said, "Your daughter shouldn't be here at all." So then I saw her true colours.

Unfortunately my Martin had this terrible accident. He broke his back. He was 16½ years old. He's 40 now … So we were then going to Stoke Mandeville daily, and we used to drop Marilyn off … One day they phoned me from the New Malden Centre and they said that my daughter was missing. They had all the staff searching for her but they didn't know why, she had just walked out. Oh dear, what with Martin in Stoke and Marilyn lost, I didn't know what to do. Then the phone went. When I picked it up Marilyn was trying to phone, but didn't have the pennies to drop down. So I thought, "Well she is trying to make contact with me." She eventually did turn up. She had walked, I don't know whether it was 14 miles or what, even across a level crossing. Her legs at the top were rubbed raw. I said, "Why did you walk home, Marilyn?" She said, "I want to see Martin." So she had got worried over Martin.

I was told by a man who was leaving (New Malden Centre): "Take your daughter away." He was a teacher there. He said he had seen two tall Down's syndrome men – in love with each other – hold hands together and then swing their hands until they knocked Marilyn flying. He said he could tell me more. Marilyn was really at the worst end of this situation. I said to Ted, "I've had enough." We moved to Cornwall. I went into the centre to say goodbye, and I said to the one in charge that I was sorry to be leaving because it seems a shame a mother living that side of the road has got to take her daughter six miles in the wrong direction. It was so silly. He said, "We don't want your help and we don't need your support. We agree with what the council are doing." I could see his true colours. I was just fighting for her rights but I was just knocking the system all the time.

Moving to Cornwall

The funniest part was when we moved to Cornwall she went to Redruth and she loved it! She blossomed! Again, what happened? They brought in this new rule as they built the John Daniels Centre at Penzance and Marilyn had to be taken away, and she had to go there. For the years that she was at Redruth she was happy as a sandboy. They never had no trouble, never. She goes to John Daniels and she was unhappy. She was back in the same situation.

I think all the silly rules should be ironed out. People should be able to go to the places that suit them. At Redruth, Marilyn had friends, but at John Daniels she didn't have any. I don't know what made the difference. If the environment is a happy one for them I don't think you should move them. This is where the councils come in and say, "Oh – we've got to cut back. You live too far away. You've got to go somewhere else …" This is wrong. Because people who've got children like this, they can never say, "Oh it's only till they're 14 or 16, they're on their own then …" We have got it for our lives.

Marilyn went through hell and back

When she was 16 she became epileptic – well the team at the hospital said this – so she was on phenobarbs. Then 14 years ago (aged 35) Marilyn started acting strangely. It was at the Redruth Centre that Mr and Mrs Davies said they couldn't understand that suddenly Marilyn was doing all her work wrong, which was totally out of character for her. My sister Eileen said to me, "What's happened to Marilyn?" I said I didn't know but she had got ever so slow. I went to the doctor and told him. He said he would do a blood test. He phoned me up to say, "Stop all medication." I said, "What? Even the phenobarbs?" She was on lots of things. So I said, "Do I do it just like that?" He told me it was only a sedative and to do it. So I stopped. Well if you hear people talk about coming off drugs then you know that they go through hell and back. Marilyn went through hell and back. I even put a bed by her to sleep, the panics, the madness, she would fight to get out of the house in the middle of the night. She would go out there and I would bring her in. What I'd done wrong was I should have insisted on her being on sedation to help her come off the phenotol and phenobarbs. Instead of that I believed him. Anyway, now they say she's got Alzheimer's. I think it was damage through the years.

When Marilyn came off the drugs and she was in a very bad state, I went to the tribunal to try and get some money. They had to pay me £3,000 or more ... I had to go through all that ordeal ... Because Marilyn was so bad at this time, she really was bad; I mean we'd be really lucky if one day we could get her off the sofa to go out of that front door. So I put a postcard in a local shop up the lane, and I asked for some help. I was willing to pay someone to come and talk to Marilyn, and take her out. Jane turned up, and thank God she's been with me ever since. She comes every Tuesday; she's done it now for 15 or 16 years and takes Marilyn out. She's marvellous. I don't know what I would do without her. Marilyn would do anything for her.

She used to do everything for herself but now I have to do it all
Last November the doctor came in, a lady doctor – since Marilyn came off the other drugs she had a phobia of water, a phobia of strange people, a phobia of doctors; I've only just in 14 years got her to go back to a doctor. They can confirm that – anyway, the doctor came in and Marilyn kept looking at her, and then she had a panic turn come over her. At that instant Marilyn's eye and arm went and she started to twitch. I told the lady doctor she had never done that in her life. I think they must have wrongly diagnosed her all those years. I only took her there (the hospital) because she had one or two falls and they said she was epileptic. How could I go against a doctor's report? They follow her up with blood tests now, but for the 20 years she was on the other drugs they never did any tests. If they had have done they might have averted the situation which I'm now in. But she was never checked in all those years as to what the drugs were doing to her. Anyway, in November last year she had a very bad epileptic fit. She's now on Epelin Thyroxine and has them in the night sometimes. I've now got her bed next to mine. She will sometimes get severe jerks.

I have to do much more for her. I have to clean her teeth. You name it, she used to do everything for herself, now I have to do it all. She's got this bowel trouble that is persistent no matter where she goes. I take a chance, though. I've taken three holidays. Now I book up a coach holiday in a guesthouse; we've been twice to Wales and once to Blackpool. Never ever on the three holidays has she had bowel trouble. I can't collate it. I just can't. It's a puzzle.

If you put Marilyn in a car you couldn't get her out again. Now I've broken that. That's taken me years to break down. I would say, "Come on. Let's go to the shop in Penzance." I would get her in a car and get her to Penzance. Would she get out of the car? No! No one would make her get out of that car! It was very complex situations of what had happened to her through, I presume, being on the drugs she shouldn't have been on. So I used to say to her in the end, "Come on Marilyn, we're going home." I've got every sympathy for people who have been affected by drugs because they become a different personality. I do sympathise with them. I wouldn't have done, if I hadn't seen how bad it was for her.

But from having someone who was highly … you could have a lovely conversation with her, you really could; you can't now. If you see a picture of her today, she's not got the animation, she's nothing compared to what she used to be. Now she's a Down's syndrome and they age quicker than other children. But I don't think their mentality should have been destroyed so quickly as hers. They also say they get Alzheimer's, but the only thing is her short-term memory. She's wiping up and then she forgets where the knives and forks go. Her long-term memory is pretty good. It's just one of those things.

At the moment …

She now goes to a lady three times a week. The voluntary drivers pick her up and she has her from half-past nine till half-past four. It's a private lady. She looks after one during the day like Marilyn, takes them shopping, that sort of thing. It's just an ordinary house and they get paid for it by the social services. Social services have been pretty good. The one I've got now is very good, the social worker. We were without one before; but Maureen who takes Marilyn said we should have a social worker. I got onto the head man via a friend.

I have never been told things – you never get told

I think I can count on one hand the one or two who have been very good – the surgeon who did Marilyn's hysterectomy was good, and my own GP. He said, "You must take Marilyn off those pills." He said she was not an epileptic. But I told him it was the top specialist who said she was epileptic. He said, "Kathy, I don't believe she is." I wish I'd listened to him, instead of listening to a top consultant. That man knew more.

But I have never been told things. You never get told. I've had to find out things through the back door, through teachers who were leaving, a dinner lady, they've always told me afterwards. Oh no, there's no honesty there. They guard their own backs all the time, all of them … When they are in a situation of working for a firm or social services, they are governed not by the truth but by their set of rules. That is where the trouble comes and I think they all stick together … That's what you're always fighting; it's the system, you see. I'm the sort of person who shouldn't have been in any system or connected to it because I'm too outspoken. You can't help doing it when they are yours, and you are trying to protect them, especially from unjustness …. Life's not been a bundle; it's been difficult. I think I've inadvertently knocked the system. I haven't done it on purpose. As far as people of today are concerned, I think they're lucky, because they've got the wisdom and they know they've got the rights on their side. I mean we didn't have rights, not years ago. I like to think I'm older and wiser now. I try not to knock the system because I think it affects you for the rest of your life.

If I had my time over I would have kept Marilyn free of any system. I would have kept her outside of even the best centres. Because I know the times she was never at any centre she was the happiest, most intelligent person going. I mean Marilyn learned to read in six weeks and yet by education standards she was uneducable. And what's happened is – why did she suddenly start falling over? Why did she suddenly start collapsing? There are so many things that have happened I've never been able to get to the bottom of, I never will. And Marilyn will never tell you, not now. She will tell you less now than she would ever tell you before. She very seldom talks now.

I've regretted that all my life

For someone who is like Marilyn who is so high grade it breaks your heart. Literally it does. Before I committed her to Manor Hospital, Epsom I read about Camphill Trusts, and it said they went away for five days, and brought out the best in them. But to get a grant to send them there you had to be able to excel. Well Marilyn excelled in swimming. She had a survivor award at 14 and she could read. They said she would get the grant. But Ted said, "No kid of mine is going to be away for five days a week." I said it would be better for her because when she comes out they put her in a job to earn a living. And they are all like-minded intelligence; they are graded. But he wouldn't let me do it. I've regretted that all my life. I think that's where things went wrong. That's my feeling anyway. I did all the research but my husband, like all men, he was narrow-minded in a lot of things. He had a brother who had divorced his wife and she had carried on … Ted was a good man but he didn't trust anyone. You were always trying to prove that he could trust you. I think he thought that five days might mean I had a bit of freedom – I'm sure of it. I don't think it was about Marilyn at all. But there you go. My sister said to him, "Ted, you are a fool, she's got a chance to have a grant, have a good, fair education." But he wouldn't listen. He wouldn't listen at all. So there you go. So she ended up in the worst scenarios that she could possibly end up in.

I do worry about her future

I don't send her to respite because I have to be sure she's happy instead of making a rod for my own back. There are always carers and carers. Most are good but if you're unlucky, well you've got to be a martyr to clear stuff up. Everyone will find Marilyn very difficult now because she cannot always control her bowels. I don't think I can even condemn people if they have been short-tempered clearing things up because, quite frankly, it is hard. While I've got the strength, I will.

If I die I want Marilyn to go to the Home Farm Trust. In a way I hope she dies before me because I don't think she would last long. I think she would die of heartbreak. Unless where she went she was extremely happy. Last year she had silent tears. She said, "Dad's been in heaven a long time, when is he coming home?" She still has to come to terms with that. I do worry about her future.

The thing is, they never cut the cord. That's the only way I can put it really.

Chapter 13
Caring from afar

Stella Garcia[6]

6 The names of people and places in the story have been changed to protect the anonymity of the contributor

I interviewed Stella in Spain in 2001 and this is her story, transformed from the interview transcript into a narrative form. Stella is the Spanish mother of Theresa, a child with Down's syndrome, born in London in the late 1950s. Theresa's father was from East Africa and had come to London to study Law. Theresa's parents had met and married in London in the 1950s when both were living, working and studying in London. At the time of Theresa's birth in 1958 the couple already had a young son aged one. Stella's story runs parallel through the text. She eventually separated from her husband, and now she and her son live in Spain. Despite living overseas, Stella has maintained close contact with her daughter's carers and services throughout the years through visits, telephone calls and letters.

Sue Ledger

Where to start?

Well, where to start? There were both of us and we didn't have any free time. We had another child very, very young and then I had to pay the nursery of the other child because I had to keep on working. Earl's Court was a very expensive place. I had to work in a place where I could go on the underground for about four, five stations – no more – because otherwise you have to get up too early and travel too much, so at the end it comes to the same thing. You spend more money travelling and more time and then anyway we didn't save any money, we didn't have any money to save. I've had many jobs. The first job I had was as a waitress because it gave more time to look after the children. José (older brother to Theresa) was about 18 months. I had to leave him in a nursery and that cost me – I don't remember now, but about £3–£5 a week. I had to leave him at ten o'clock and collect him at five. So I have to rush, rush, rush. That gave me every day approximately £10 profit and so we got money and could dedicate the many extra hours to the children.

Theresa was born in January 1958. She came home with me after she was born and lived at home with us. To start with she was fine. Very happy. But there came a moment where Theresa was a very bad eater. It's hard to remember exactly how old she was then. She spat it out and everything. I didn't have time or patience. I suppose she couldn't swallow properly because of the effects it had on her throat. I didn't know what to do. I was worried she was not eating and this is why it was suggested she went away. She was the tiniest child you can imagine. Absolutely small. I had to use handkerchiefs instead of nappies. She weighed about 5lb, very small. She had astounding hair – I remember that!

But anyway, I tried my best to cope with both children when the money was tight and my husband wasn't working. So sometimes he looked after the children, but when he looked after them he couldn't work, so then we only had the money I was earning as a waitress, which was OK but was a very tiring job. Then I would work at another place at weekends to get some more money. I was never used to manual work.

Help at last

We looked after her at home as best we could and, as I said, it was a bit of a struggle – and the eating problems Theresa had. Then, a lady called Mrs Andrews came, an older lady, she was talking to me and she said, "I think that you are doing something you can't cope with – for a while, you should leave her in a home for children." I was feeling awful. I thought well, this child, maybe I am not doing enough for her. Anyway, she came with me to show me one of these places, I don't even remember where it was, not too far from London. I was very reluctant to leave her there. I left her there for a while and then I used to go to visit every weekend. It was very hard. Very, very hard. Very discouraging and very heartbreaking.

Only that lady visited. I think she was some type of social worker or welfare worker. No one else gave me any kind of help, and I asked her, couldn't she be in London? Or couldn't someone help us at home with the child care or something? It was so far from me. I wasted the whole day travelling only to be there for half an hour or so. But what could I do? I could do nothing. Anyway, later on this lady, she disappeared – I never saw her again and then of course somebody else came. I asked her if she could be in a nearer place. She said no, they are difficult to find, these places, and then they took her to Devon. They said it was a lovely place, she will be very well there.

I said, "But I can't go to Devon, you know it's impossible for me. I haven't got the money or the time." So they said, they will very happily send you pictures. So they sent me pictures and she looked very well. She looked quite happy. I went twice but then I couldn't go on. It was not only in Devon, it was right out of the way. I remember both times I went it rained and rained cats and dogs. I didn't have an umbrella and was soaked. I couldn't find the bloody place and I was desperate! It was lucky that I found a taxi and they took me there. I saw the child, saw she was well, and then I thought no, I can't do this. It's too far.

It was a nice house, a kind of country house, better than the first one. There were about 25 children. But Theresa seemed to settle there. In those days she was very well. They were nice people and she had party clothes. They liked her because she was always very cheerful and always on the swing. She made friends with some of the other girls. Anyway, after that they brought her to another place in London – well, nearer London than Devon, of course, and I didn't like it at all and then they took her to that horrible hospital where Deborah (former social foster aunt) met her.

Contrasts

A terrible, terrible, terrible place. When I went to see her I couldn't stop crying. I couldn't bear it, I just couldn't bear it. But then with Mr and Mrs Andrews [the social aunt and uncle recruited by the funding social services department] and everything, we eventually arranged for a new home for her at Amelie Lodge. This was a care home for about 30 boys and girls or young men and women. This took many years to arrange, of course, but in the end, just to see her there – such a relief. Just to see her in there after the other place. I couldn't believe it. It was a nightmare at the hospital – just to see it. There were about 2,000 people there. In my personal opinion, they were like animals, living like animals, treated like animals. Theresa was in a terribly big ward. With so many people of so many different ages. There were adults there too. They kept on going to the toilet, vomiting – really awful. I couldn't bear it. I just said, "I can't go back to that place. I can't go back." And so when, in the end, they changed her to Amelie Lodge I was so relieved, because Mrs Best was very nice and I told her about what had happened and she said, "Don't worry about it; she will be much better here." And then of course she did not have a bedroom of her own, she was sharing with another girl, but they got on so well – she was so happy. Oh, I was so pleased, it was wonderful.

An African experience

When Theresa was in the hospital outside London, I went to Africa with my husband and son. My husband's father – he was the only son in the family – wanted him to inherit whatever they had. We went out to Africa with José (Theresa's brother) just to try. When we arrived there and I saw it, I thought: what have I done – another disaster!

My husband was terribly sick with malaria, so was my son. I wasn't, I don't know why or how I wasn't sick with malaria. When I saw them so sick, I thought I must get out of here. I saved money as fast as could. I didn't spend a penny. As soon as I had money I bought a ticket for my son and myself. I said to my husband, "Just take us to the airport; you can pay your ticket, I'm not going to pay it. I want to go there now." I found an Englishman who was very nice. I said, "Please get us tickets to Europe", and he got the tickets for me – the cheapest possible. So we went to Nairobi. My husband took us in a car and then on the way we were attacked by 20 or 30 hungry 14- and 15-year-olds. We had sandwiches with us and what I did, I cut the sandwiches up so I could give then all a bit of bread and I gave them water and then I said, "Well, I haven't got anything else", so they let us pass.

We arrived in Nairobi just in time to catch the plane and then I travelled with my son from Nairobi to Khartoum, from Khartoum to Cairo, from Cairo to Greece and then we arrived in Rome. In Rome we had to change to go to London and I said to myself, "I'm not going to bloody London again: we have no house, no money, no job. I'm going to Spain." I asked the airline if I could change the ticket instead of going to London. I said, "This is an emergency", and they said, "You can go", and so we went to Madrid. It was the best flight I ever had in my life. It took two hours from Rome to home. We went from Madrid to my mother's house and that was the end of the tragedy, you could say. Two days later, I found a job because I am very good at finding jobs. I found a job teaching English in an academy. Very little money, but it was enough to begin with. And that was the beginning of coming back to normal.

A foster family and Amelie Lodge

Theresa was in England then, living in the hospital, but with Mr and Mrs Andrews looking after her at weekends and such. They were very fond of her. I don't know what I would have done without them. And of course I had all the time kept writing and in touch with Mrs Andrews. She was so nice. She used to go to fetch her at weekends and bring her to her place

I first met Mrs Andrews through her daughter, Daisy. Daisy was working there as a teacher or teacher's helper and she selected Theresa because she was the best at gymnastics, and of course she wanted to talk to her mother. So she got in touch with me and we got on absolutely marvellously. I thought, "Oh, you are wonderful, I thank you so for doing so much", and she took a lot of interest in the child. Then when they changed her to the other place, I could never be grateful enough. I thought she was very happy there in Amelie House and she was happy for many years. The only thing was, when this happened, I just couldn't believe such a thing was happening. But many children there in that house were well kept, well fed and clean, and they go out one day a week to the discothèque and the village and to the swimming pool. It was all right.

The care home wasn't very near the hospital. But Mrs Andrews was living not far from Amelie. She was very caring, a very good woman. She brought up her children in a very caring way. I went to see Theresa at the Andrews' when she lived at Amelie Lodge. Whenever Mrs Andrews arranged a trip I would go to see her at her house because the care home was in such an isolated awkward place to see a child. There was nowhere to go or to buy clothes. There were no trains or buses near there – right out in the country. Nothing around.

The lady in charge was also very good indeed and several times brought Theresa to London. We met in Victoria Station and we had a nice lunch there in a good place and went shopping in Victoria Street and brought Theresa some clothes and things. So whenever she did that, that was perfect, but then of course she said she couldn't do it. Then of course when this later thing (the abuse allegation and subsequent investigation) happened it was the absolute limit.

But you see one day I met them – Mrs Best and her husband who worked in the home sometimes – in the house of a friend of mine, in a very hurried way. I don't remember now. I was staying with a friend near one of the airports and I was to be there for about three days, so I called the home and they brought Theresa. She seemed to like him a lot and he liked her a lot. I was quite happy. I thought, well, they seem to like her so much. But of course Mrs Best was there also.The husband too seemed quite nice. When they told me what was alleged to have happened I said impossible, the man was a nice guy.

There was no indication of anything not quite right. Not to me. And besides these children are not very informed, I must say, about sex. There were allegations that Theresa and several of the others had been sexually assaulted by this man. He died before it came to court or before anyone could find out the detail or the truth about what had happened directly from him. Terrible. And it was a nice place lovely – clean and nice

Now Theresa is living with Dave and Linda [current adult placement carers] and she is quite happy. She is very happy there. She is happy in a family atmosphere, you see. That's what she needs. They include her in everything. She talks a lot more now and she's learning more in that place too – cooking. She loves music. When she came here, they had music in the street and she started dancing like mad.

Reflections

When she was a baby she should have had somewhere to stay nearer us or someone to help us. Devon was ridiculous. I think if she had been in a home like Dave and Linda's or Amelie all the time and not in that horrid hospital, she would have improved a lot. After she was in Amelie Lodge she was quite happy because she had friends her own age. You can't put a child of 14 with a woman of 40. Oh, it was a terrible thing – how could they have allowed that?

At Amelie Lodge, Theresa had good friends and they used to go to the discothèque. She loved that and loved swimming. When Theresa came to Spain she went to the swimming pool. There is a private pool near here but I know the owner and there were some Irish people for Theresa to talk to – otherwise when she is here she cannot talk to people or understand. She doesn't speak Spanish.

I knew she was well; I relaxed a little. But after going to that hospital I must have vomited about seven times – I just couldn't stand the smell. It was a horrible smell, of I don't know what – horrible – and then when I saw all those sad people there I said to myself, "Oh my God." The hospital was the worst place.

She went to school in the hospital and she was one of the best pupils, I must say. That's where she met Daisy – she loved her and her family, the Andrews.

Daisy was a wonderful girl. If she was near and in the area she would go to see Theresa and take her out. Without the foster family I don't how I or Theresa would have survived.

Theresa's father never went to see her. I never understood why. We kept in touch for a while because of the children and he came to Spain once when my son was about 16.

I think now things have worked out for Theresa. If it hadn't been for Mrs Andrews and her family, I don't know what would have happened at the hospital. It has been hard that I have been in Spain and Theresa in England, and at one stage I thought about bringing her here but she cannot speak the language. I think she is happy now and doing very well. I am hoping she can come to Spain to visit this year and I will try to see her in England this year or next year.

Chapter 14
Fostering and adopting

Jean Batchelor

I met Jean in 2000 when she agreed to contribute to a Heritage Lottery Fund project I was working on which explored the history of local Mencap societies in East Anglia. I interviewed her at her home, and her memories of both the Norwich and South Norfolk local societies are included in the book Reclaiming the Past. *For this present book, however, Jean chose to write about her life with her fostered and adopted children herself, and the following chapter tells their story.*

Sheena Rolph

I have had a good life, but it became something special on 31 March 1969. Life was so different in the swinging sixties. There were large subnormality hospitals, many doctors advised new parents to put their handicapped babies in homes. Foster-parents were hard to come by – and single women were not high on the list as prospective foster-parents. We – my friend Joan and I – were turned down by Barnardo's on our first letter of enquiry. However, the London Borough of Barnet were more forward-looking. We answered an advert in Mencap's magazine, *Parents Voice*. We had to give three referees each and then, by the end of March 1969, we were driving down from Kirkham, Lancashire to pick up 'our boys' who were by then 12 months and 20 months old. Barnet had been searching all round the country for foster-parents since they were born. I suspect today they may have been put up for adoption.

Joan had been a cook at a school for deaf children which had closed, so she looked after the boys. I was a qualified nursery nurse and sick children's nurse, but had spent most of the sixties caring for the mentally handicapped as a nurse, but also at a Junior Training Centre (before the education department took over schooling) and at Blackpool Adult Training Centre. I continued to work there until we had our third boy.

When we got back to Lancashire, the phone never stopped ringing. I should think we could have had 50 children within months – we were inundated with requests. Within weeks the local social services were asking us to take short-term foster-children. A two-year-old girl joined the family and then our third boy. He was three days old when they asked us to take him. With four children under five, I gave in my notice and Allan joined us, aged five weeks. The house was too small, so we moved back south, and we arrived in Norfolk – as far south as we could afford.

Three months later Norfolk Social Services placed a 13-month-old little girl with us. She was three months older than Allan, and they became almost inseparable. They were both bright, and whereas Henry and Rolly, the older boys, went to Chapel Road Special School in Attleborough, Lucy and Allan were able to go to Bunwell Primary School from four to eight years of age. It was absolutely excellent for them: both Lucy and Allan can read – and Allan is a great reader still. He would go off to the library and he has read all the James Herriot books, and he tends to read gardening books. You had to fight in those days if you wanted to get your child into a normal school. But even when they transferred to Chapel Road, they were able to go to Attleborough First School two afternoons a week, this time in separate classes, staying with the class. Then they went up to the middle school. This is where Allan had his first girlfriend, Susan.

Children came and went, and that hurt. In 1975, we were joined by my now adopted daughter, Linda, when she was eight weeks old. Our home in Carleton Rode grew and so did our quarter-acre garden. As we acquired land around us it became a ten-acre smallholding. The children had a great life. We had chickens, ducks, rabbits, goats, pigs, sheep and calves – many were given to us. All the children helped, even with milking the goats.

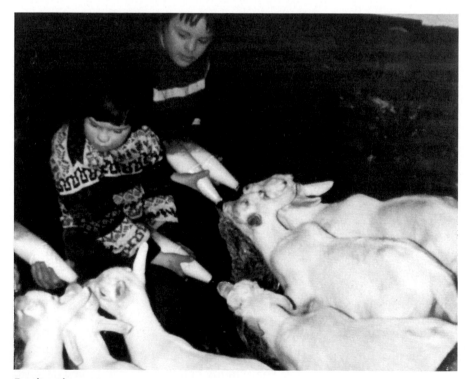

Feeding the goats

They bottlefed their kids, fed, watered and mucked out. They plucked chickens and ducks. Rolly even had a go at sheepshearing. We also ran two pigs during the summer months – they were always called Tig and Tag – and we ended up with two cows! Allan was given a goat and a calf for his birthday, and so we decided that we would have another calf to keep it company. We thought he would like a Jersey, and a family nearby offered us a newborn calf. Because it was a pedigree we expected to pay the earth for it – but they gave it to us. Then Allan was given a lamb and we ended up with 13 sheep and two calves – and the goats multiplied. We would sit around feeding baby goats with bottles, and Lucy would get up every morning at six o'clock with me and we would feed the lambs and let the chickens out. So, all the way through, they did everything for them and became quite adept at handling animals. What better way to learn about life and death, where our food comes from, to care for creatures of all sizes and be gentle, to count eggs, chicks, ducklings, to pick and preserve fruit and vegetables and make bread and jam.

We did do other things. In our minibus we went off to the sea, visiting friends, to Banham Zoo and Bressingham Gardens, where many years later Allan would be working.

We were active members of Mencap. In about 1974 I was a founder member of the South Norfolk and District local Mencap society and I helped to set up and run holiday clubs for children with learning difficulties. We started a group for young mums, for those with pre-school children, and we had a huge group as they brought their other youngsters along as well. We provided a midday meal and everybody mucked in. Social services always sent somebody along, a social worker – they would pop in. We all supported one another. I was really in the background, pushing for things like playgroups, clubs and support. At the time we didn't know any other foster-parents, and we did feel quite isolated.

At first, we decided that if we couldn't adopt all the children - and we couldn't for financial reasons, because you didn't get anything in those days if you adopted a handicapped child – then we wouldn't adopt any of them. But then when Linda was five years old, her home county suddenly had this policy of withdrawing all of their out-of-county children back into the home county. By this time adoption was becoming more usual, and, as she had her own family now with us, we decided that we must adopt her, or she would be taken away.

Life is not always smooth. In 1984 Joan developed gallstones and went into hospital to have them removed. Three weeks later she was dead – cancer. We were all devastated. We had just moved to Great Moulton and knew no one. My family live in East Sussex and Lancashire, too far to give real support. Chapel Road School staff were very helpful, as were the folk from Great Moulton Chapel, a policewoman friend and Linda's godmother Louise.

I felt very vulnerable, and worried about what would happen to the family if something happened to me as suddenly as Joan. She was only 54. I was younger. I made enquiries to Mencap and Home Farm Trust. Basically they were willing to take them but not able to guarantee to keep them together. It was in the days of larger homes, and understandably, finding five vacant places in a home would be unthinkable. It was awful when Joan died but they still had me. If I died without making provision, they would be taken back to their original authorities; to lose their mother and their brothers and sisters would be traumatic. Eventually, in 1987, we moved down to Sussex to be near my brother so that we had family support nearby.

I moved back to Norfolk in 1996. Now the children are all adults and living their own lives. Today, ten years on, my three eldest are living in different homes in East Sussex, and they see each other when I go down to visit my brother. They settled in their new way of life and I am very happy for them. Although the family have gone their different ways, I am still in touch with them – they come up to Norfolk to visit and I always see them when I go south. And the other two live near me in Norfolk. Allan was for a while at an excellent Mencap college in Northumberland, and Linda joined him and they came back to me for the holidays.

Allan and Linda

Allan had the choice of returning to Sussex or Norfolk. He chose Norfolk and began working at Bressingham Gardens, where he still works for one day a week. When Linda left college she lived with me for a few months until we were able to set up a home for her and Allan in the same village as I live. This is run by a Christian charity called 'Prospects'. Linda attends an Adult Training Centre five days a week, but Allan goes to college, works at Bressingham Gardens and Tesco and on a smallholding, and one day a week does gardening and woodwork with me. They both visit me at least one weekend a month – and often more frequently – Allan has just rung up as I write this to ask if he can come and stay from Thursday to Tuesday! And they both always come at Christmas time. We also go visiting our relatives in Sussex and Blackpool. We are members of the same church where they are much loved and active members of the congregation.

Allan and Linda, on Allan's 30th birthday

Reflections – changes and continuities

Life changed dramatically over the time Joan and I fostered, from those times in the 1960s when you had a problem to get hold of foster-parents for children with learning difficulties, to the 1970s when people were beginning to adopt – and right up to the present, when adoption is the norm. The other main change I have seen is that suddenly there was care in the community … and there are Allan and Linda, living in a small group home. The family was my life's work, and the best thing is that the family and I are still in close touch, even though they are in different places, and all grown up. I chose to do it and it was my life, it wasn't a job. Looking back, I shall always appreciate the Norfolk Inspection Unit and social workers who thought of us and treated us as a family, which indeed we were.

Chapter 15
Fight for your child

Mr and Mrs York

Mr and Mrs York are a Jewish couple, now in their eighties, who have lived in Hackney all their lives. Their only child Ben has learning disabilities and has always lived at home with them. I interviewed them in December 2001 and this account has been derived from that interview.

Sue Ledger

Ben was born on 5 December 1963 in Dalston. He will be 38 next week. When he was three years old he was talking, but all of a sudden he didn't talk at all. For years on end we took him to the doctor at the Queen Elizabeth's Hospital in the Hackney Road. He said, "He'll never talk. You'll be banging your head against a brick wall trying to get him to talk." I said to him, "It's not true. I bet I make him talk" – and he's talking now, isn't he? So they were wrong, weren't they?

Ben was born in hospital, Bearstead, and when he was born his breathing was bad so we knew straight away something was wrong. But up to three years old he was talking. Then it stopped. He didn't talk for years on end. We couldn't get a word out of him. At three years old he was a lovely child, then all of a sudden he stopped talking. I said, "Is he deaf; can't he hear?" They examined his ears and his voice – nothing. He was walking fine – physically he was fit but just stopped talking. He is talking a lot more now, though.

The doctor sent him to a school in Albion Road when Ben was about four. They didn't teach him there. They were schools for handicapped children – special schools. I had a struggle to bring him up – it was a struggle. Some people came, nurses I think, and tried to help us a little bit, but other than that we have had a hard time with Ben, a real hard time. When Ben was small there weren't many services for children like him. It's different now.

We were pretty much on our own. Mencap and things didn't really get involved with us. We lived next door to a factory so we didn't have much contact from neighbours.

Just us two brought him up. Hard work. My family [Mr York] were all wiped out, all dead. My wife has a sister but she didn't help. We got him to talk again just by talking to him all the time. The doctor had given him up completely. They tried him out for writing when he was three or four. Did some tests –

he scribbled a bit. He was only small and they said they couldn't find anything wrong. He went to Bancroft Road Hospital for a tear-duct operation when he was about nine months old . Even now Ben can't give you a full sentence but he uses words. He is conducting himself. Words are coming through.

At school they were all handicapped. Ben couldn't really conduct himself with these people – he kept himself to himself, really. He didn't really have friends as such – more companions. The teachers were nice; they cared very well for those children. The school is pulled down there. He left Albion Road when he was 16 years – we took him up to the careers office but they said they couldn't do anything, so he had to go to Albion Road Centre. We never had help at weekends. He had some short stays. They took him out on day trips to Southend and then to Margate for a week with his Centre. When Ben was little no one else looked after him, just the two of us.

We would like more respite, now we are older, but it is hard to get it as there are cutbacks. Ben goes to Ramsgate for respite. He likes it there. He has always gone there. Ben loves swimming. They used to take him out more in the evenings and at weekends but it has stopped. Now he just goes out during the day. More cuts. Ben has never had friends. Never gone to other people's houses. We would like him to branch out. Ben knows how to cross a road, he knows the area well, but he can't use the buses as he doesn't recognise the bus numbers.

When I was working I had to leave off work at four o'clock to get Ben, and my wife had to leave her job at three – my wife worked in a school – to make sure we were both here to look after him. He was a bit violent at times when he was younger – used to throw things about because he couldn't express himself. You imagine if you can't get your words out, you can't talk. He would wonder what something was and start pulling and breaking it because he couldn't talk about it or ask us. One time he banged his hand through the glass. He had to go to Homerton Hospital and he was there for a couple of weeks, stitched up, and then they sent him away for a holiday.

We've got some good memories, too. Lots of times when he did things, you know. We took him to the seaside, Hayling Island, when he was about two years old. We went into a dining room but he wouldn't sit and eat with the people – he ran out, took his food back in the cabin. We always had to plan around Ben – he always liked the buses, the swings. I tried my hardest with Ben and he's talking now. It's an achievement. We get on with Ben now, we do.

We have always lived in Hackney. We lived in Amhurst Road when Ben was born and then we moved and we've been 26 years in this house. We lived in Amhurst Road for 25 years before that. We've been in Hackney for many years – always been here. I remember the war and the air raids.

I think services have got better now. They have improved a lot. My advice to parents now would be to fight for your child. That's all you can do.

Chapter 16
She is part of our family now

Angela and Neil Harris

Yvette describes herself as a young, mixed-race woman with learning disabilities. She grew up in an inner-London children's home before moving to a registered care home in West Sussex at the age of 20. Yvette still lives in Crawley where she now has her own flat, circle of friends and a job she enjoys.

Yvette has not had contact with her natural family since she was a child and she regards Neil and Angela Harris as her next of kin. They regard Yvette as a very close family friend and a firm part of their own extended family network.

Neil and Angela Harris first met Yvette when they both worked as residential social workers in the 1970s and 1980s. Yvette grew up in the home where they worked and since she left they have remained in contact over many years. This is their story of knowing Yvette and how their relationship has changed and developed over the years.

Sue Ledger

Memories of the children's home
Angela:
I first got to know Yvette in 1979 when I went to work at the children's home in Chelsea where Yvette was living. At that time there were 16 children there, can you believe? I was never her keyworker or link worker – we had a link or keyworker scheme at the time – so I never had that sort of relationship with her. But I was always consistent because I was there until the point where she left and moved on to Crawley. During that time there were some staff changes, but there were some staff who looked after her for the whole period, and I was one of a group of people who consistently looked after her through her adolescence. They were important years – we met when Yvette was 11 and she left when she was 20.

Yvette was the only young person with a learning disability in the home. There was another young person who may have overlapped slightly with Yvette. She didn't have a learning disability but she was visually impaired. Yvette tended to socialise with the people from her school or the Gateway Club.

Yvette went to a special school for young people with severe learning disabilities. It was the Jack Tizard School. She wasn't in the mainstream education system.

Some of the older children had their own rooms but on the whole the children had to share. I can remember Yvette shared with another young girl for a long time, probably four or five years. There were two of them in a bedroom. This girl did not have a learning disability and they were really good friends. This person came in after Yvette – they must have been about 13 years old when they started sharing. This young girl had two brothers who were also in the home and because she and Yvette were so close, her brothers became very protective of Yvette too. Yvette saw these three very much as her close friends.

Neil:
Within the home there was a flat where people could practise skills to be more independent in preparation for when they left and maybe moved to their own place, but Yvette never used it. Before she left she had her own room and then was able to do more for herself. Back then it was like most children's homes in the 1970s; it was a very different client group that you looked after than the kids who come into care today. Genuinely I would say that the 16 young people there could have been fostered, including Yvette. There were few issues with people's behaviour or any destruction of property and because of this you could create a much more homely environment, much more group living. On the whole the young people seemed to get on quite well together and Yvette was fully accepted by the other children.

Angela:
She was quite protected by some of them, especially some of the older children who would really go out of their way to look out for Yvette. We can honestly say that, all the time we were there, there were no issues that we were aware of in terms of Yvette having a learning disability, going to a different school, special transport. She was never bullied. She was always accepted. She was accepted for who she was, too. People would row with her but they would treat her as an equal. They would fall out with her and have their say, and Yvette would have her say back but, if it ever got so that someone seemed to be getting the better of Yvette, my memory is that someone else, one of the other children, would always step in to protect her saying, "You leave her alone", or something similar, which Yvette liked.

Neil and Angela:
We didn't have any problems with accessing ordinary services such as the GP. Yvette has always been very able and keen to do things for herself. She has always had a really strong character and was very much someone that people knew locally. She would go out to the shops and, as she got older, she might be in the local pub on a Friday night. We always had really good relationships with neighbours.

Apart from the special school Yvette attended, we don't remember any other specialist help such as speech therapy or specialist social work or psychology.

The school was very good and many of the initiatives around increasing Yvette's independence skills were led by them – so through the school we would have had some contact with specialist learning disability services. They would come to see us and Yvette at the children's home if necessary – making plans about getting used to the local environment, and using money and shops. We supported Yvette to learn about budgeting. She had an allowance and used to go and buy a certain amount that she could cook herself, and that linked in with Hammersmith College when she went there later on. The only other person was a dietician, as Yvette has always struggled with her weight. We were trying to work out the best way forward of trying to support Yvette to eat a healthy balanced diet. They came to see Yvette at home – I think this was better for Yvette because, as a teenager, it was harder to take advice from staff who over the years she had come to regard as her family.

As Yvette had no family contact and no contact with anybody else outside the staff team and school, no independent bit at all, the local authority advertised specifically for a social aunt and uncle. But the idea of recruiting also came very much from Yvette because she felt that she didn't have anybody. The role of social aunt and uncle was almost like that of an independent visitor today and perhaps a bit more, as she used to go and stay overnight with these people. They were formally assessed and approved as social aunt and uncle before being introduced to her. The people selected were a white Irish family. The fostering team organised this. She would see them about once a month. They would come and visit her at the home and go out with her and if there was any special event going on in the family she would often join in. I can remember that she was invited to their daughter's wedding – she may even have been a bridesmaid – and she talked about them as her aunt and uncle, her cousins and her niece and nephew. That was the language that she used and if there was any special event for her like a birthday party or celebration they would come along.

Neil:
When I first started working in the children's home around 1985 this friend of Yvette's was in an adjoining flat preparing to leave care. At the same time there was another young girl also preparing to leave and I am sure Yvette thought of these young people as her family. So there were all these people whom Yvette was very close to and who moved on and for a long time Yvette would still talk about them as though they were still there. And I think that must have been quite hard for her seeing them move on. She was very close to the officer-in-charge and his partner who also worked at the home – she was in fact Yvette's link worker. In fact at that time she was much closer to them than to either of us. In fact when Yvette moved to Crawley they were the two people with whom we expected her to have a lot more contact.

Neil:

I was employed as an RSW (residential social worker) just before I came to work at the home. I remember Yvette was learning to use the buses at the time.

Angela:

I started off as an RSW there and I worked my way up to deputy and then when the manager went off to complete his social work training I managed the unit. That was after Yvette left, so I had worked my way up to deputy while she was there.

It was funny because there was this consistent core of people who had cared for her throughout her adolescence and there was also, very importantly, the support staff. The cleaners – there were three of them, and they all knew Yvette very well and were very fond of her.

Neil:

Because she had been at the home so long Yvette really was part and parcel of the nuts and bolts of the place and I can remember that it was myself who drove her to Crawley with her link worker at the time. The day she left it was awful, everyone was in tears. The cleaners were in tears, and the staff. There was this whole line-up of people saying goodbye and crying. And I was trying to make it something positive about Yvette starting her new life …

Leaving London and moving to Crawley

Angela:

Yvette stayed on at school and had links to the local college. Through that she was always interested in cookery, which she did there. She was always interested in Keep Fit and would go down to Chelsea swimming pool to do aerobics. I remember going with her when I was on shift and she was keen and kept it up when I wasn't working. I remember her with the Jane Fonda workout video and her leotard on! Yvette is still interested in exercise and keep fit now. She also loved dancing as a teenager; she loves anything social.

Yvette, our close friend, loves any social gatherings, loves to be part of it, absolutely thrives on it. As she got older, she would sometimes go to the pub. Some of the children who had left but still lived locally would come back to the home and visit her and take her out to the pub. This was often on a Friday night, though obviously only when she was old enough. She had a little social circle of people with whom she has a shared history and interests. But Yvette's main interests have always been people, socialising. She knew the children from the home, obviously, but she also had contacts with other friends from school. As she went to a special school this was a different set of contacts. Some of them lived locally on the estate where the home was and they would come and visit her at her home.

Sometimes in the evenings there would only be two or three staff on a shift with up to 16 children. The pattern would be to cook dinner and then eat and then we could concentrate on getting the younger children to bed and sorting out anything they needed. After nine o'clock they would be asleep, and then the home would have more of a 'teenage home' feel. On Friday and Saturday nights we would get a video in and get some sweets. At 11 o'clock at night we would all settle down and watch the video with the teenagers. Then there were a few staff flats above the home and staff would sometimes pop in or, on occasions, invite residents to a party, etc., if there was a birthday celebration. There was more social interaction between staff and residents in those days, almost like a family feel. I don't think it would be the same today.

Yvette was quite caught up in the home, her social life was quite a lot around the home. And of course we did have holidays. I can remember taking her to Devon. It was hilarious actually, she and I still laugh about this now, because there was this sign up saying there was a barn dance. We'd rented a house down there and there was a sign up in the village saying barn dance at such and such a farm and we spoke to the locals and they said, "Oh yes, come, come along", so we went along and it was literally a barn dance, in a barn with bales of straw all the way round. It was incredible, a brilliant occasion, but of course we turned up, London kids, disco gear, all dressed up. Yvette was dressed up to the nines and all the locals were literally in their jeans and T-shirts – really dressed down. We were all glitz and glamour and high heels and Yvette, as we said earlier, loves dancing. We got there, the music started and the first person up in the middle of this huge barn in all their disco finery was Yvette and she just danced the whole night, she absolutely loved it. Yvette has always had a lot of confidence – she has always had a strong character. If we think about it, the potential for not-so-good outcomes for Yvette is immense. She's been rejected by some very important key people in her life who have left her. And she moved out of what had been her environment, her networks and locality to Crawley. She could have been very unhappy and isolated but she's not and that's down to her force of character.

I wasn't involved in the decision-making at the time but I know there was a big debate about risk. And risk management. This was particularly in the context of living in inner London as it was seen. But Yvette had all her links there and, although things have all turned out very well in Crawley now and Yvette is very happy, and has been very successful, I think in retrospect it probably was the wrong decision. I know there was a debate. On the one hand, Yvette has the children's home, where she had lived for many years, as a base to come back to, and she had all her connections with the Gateway Club and other organisations in the area, mainly for people with learning disabilities, where she was very involved. On the other hand, there was concern about her travelling alone, 'London being a dangerous place'. Sadly I think in many ways the fact that Yvette had some independence worked against her. I think it was very much the practice of the time, and for all the best reasons, people somehow thought people like Yvette would be 'better in the country'. At that point she didn't have anyone who was clearly her advocate, someone who was there solely for her. I think that all the people around her for all the right reasons perhaps made the wrong decision. Yes, if she had been consulted properly and her views taken seriously into account she wouldn't have gone.

The move was extremely traumatic for Yvette and it took her a long, long time and many, many years to settle into Crawley and every time we saw her in the early days she would say how she didn't like it. And then she would come up to us for the weekend and she'd want to phone the children's home. She'd want to find out all the news from the manager.

A friend of the family
Angela:
I was quite friendly with Yvette's link worker at the time of her move to Crawley so when she would be going down to visit Yvette in her new home I'd go along. This was only occasionally; it might be only every six months, say. But then the turning point of it was when she became very ill and her Crohn's disease was diagnosed. She was in hospital for a lot of weeks, perhaps about six weeks. She was really ill and lost a tremendous amount of weight. She was in an isolation ward for a while. She really was extremely ill. So during that time I went down to see her more often. At that time she really didn't have anybody of her own and that was the first point really when I said to her, "Why don't you come up for a weekend?" And that was where it started really. Yvette began visiting us at our home for the day and then for overnight stays. I think that during the first few years she came up maybe twice a year, it wasn't very often. I went down to see her occasionally but she'd come up to us twice a year. To start off with, she usually went and visited the children's home in Chelsea and then came up here to us in Uxbridge. So it was quite slow to take off really. Nowadays she travels to us independently but to start with she didn't. The staff in Crawley would take Yvette to the coach and put her on the coach and phone us a few times to make sure we were meeting her and that we had found each other OK. Really early on they drove her up and I picked her up and dropped her off, then gradually the staff in Crawley did an independence travel programme with Yvette so that she could get the coach from Gatwick herself. She does all that herself now, orders her taxis and gets the bus. She usually gets a bus to Gatwick and then catches the coach from Gatwick to Heathrow and then I pick her up. We've got our little point where we always meet. On the way back she does the reverse and gets a taxi back to her own flat. At Christmas time we give her a lift to the foster-aunt and uncle from when Yvette was in the children's home.

Neil and Angela:

At the children's home, there would be a meeting about twice a year. When I think of the records that were kept then, it was so different. There wasn't a care plan. It was well before the Children Act. I think her social worker was very happy for Yvette to stay at the children's home as she was happy there. Although she was happy, no one seemed to be thinking about what's it going to be like in ten or 15 years' time. The planning seemed to go instead from meeting to meeting. Long-term fostering seemed to take a long time to arrange then and was not pursued across the board as actively as it is now. Whereas if long-term fostering had been pushed for many of the children, including Yvette, it may have given them wider social networks later on. Or even if she had stayed in Chelsea, moving to local accommodation, I think she would have developed a wider network of people more quickly, as she had existing contacts to build on, whereas in Crawley she had to start from scratch. Although saying that now, after all these years, Yvette is beginning to catch up in this respect and she has a wider circle of people.

Yvette has always liked her own company and she has always liked to do things in the order she likes to do them and she has a set routine. I mean I can remember her routine at the home, as Yvette was a big *Dallas* fan and there would be '*Dallas* evenings'. She would do her washing on a certain day of the week, her ironing another day, even at a certain time, and that really never altered at all. You could run your watch by it! In terms of her independence, school did an awful lot to encourage and support Yvette.

When I first met Yvette there was some letter contact with her family but then that stopped and there was none at all. In all the time we worked alongside Yvette we don't remember any discussion of her cultural heritage. Her natural mother is white and her father Caribbean. I can't remember any specific piece of work or focus on that. Unfortunately I think this was quite common then. The focus was more on the issue of disability.

I think now Yvette's life is transformed. She has a job and hopefully she will soon get paid for it. She has her own flat, which is something that she has always wanted. This was her ambition even as a teenager. I think the flat was a real turning point for Yvette settling in Crawley – after she got her own flat it became her real home. She's got her friends now, a widening circle. It's taken time, but she has got there. There are people like us, and her social aunt and uncle whom she still keeps in touch with, sees regularly and regards as family. We see Yvette as a very close friend of our family; we will always stay in touch. It's difficult, as I think there was a period in her life, from the age of 20 for about ten years or so, when I don't think she was happy.

As I say, I don't feel that the decision for Yvette to leave London was right for her at that time. I think it's all worked out now and that's great, but as a young adult Yvette was starting again in a completely new place with strangers and that must have been very hard. It's nothing to do with the care she was receiving as I think the care she was receiving was very good, very good. I certainly [*Angela*] went down there often and met with the people and they were very concerned for Yvette and concerned to do the very best for her. But I think fundamentally she was unhappy. She had lived 20 years of her life with people who did not have severe learning disabilities and, whether that was right or wrong, that was the environment in which she had grown up and that had afforded her a lot of attention from a lot of people. And then she moved to Crawley, away from everything and everybody that she knew, to live with three other people with learning disabilities. Yvette wasn't used to that. Although she was used to the school environment and people with learning disabilities there, that is quite different from your home living environment. Also when she first went to Crawley, Yvette was living with people who needed a lot of care and she may have felt it detracted attention from her. I don't know, but I can see it could have felt like that. Most people move from a specialist to more integrated services whereas in Yvette's case it was almost the reverse.

Neil:
And her status changed too, as she was a well-established figure in her local community. She was considered an adult, ready to leave a children's home, and she had that status within the children's home as a 'near-adult'. The younger children certainly looked up to her. The age range in the home at the time when Yvette left would have been between five and 18.

However, the support Yvette received in Crawley, even from the outset, was always very good. Tony and Ann were excellent, really. They could understand that it was a hard time for Yvette and they did all they could to support her to maintain all contact with ourselves and her foster-aunt and uncle. Now it seems as though things have almost come full circle. Yvette has quite a full and integrated lifestyle. She is linked to college, has a job, and has friends with and without learning disabilities.

If I could have changed things in terms of how things were arranged for Yvette, and from our ongoing friendship with her throughout the years, I would have liked her to be given more credit. I think an independent advocate would have been really helpful for Yvette when she was younger and having to make decisions about where she would move to after the children's home. Nowadays I don't feel Yvette would need an advocate, just someone to sit down and listen carefully to what she thinks and says, and take that very seriously.

I think that the care given to Yvette was consistent and protective but it was almost an attitude of 'we know what's best, what's good for you'. I think that if more work had been done with Yvette on her cultural background then it might have helped her develop more of a sense of 'who I am, where I'm from and where I might be going'. Issues of people's ethnic and cultural backgrounds were not really spoken about then – at least not very much with the young people themselves. God knows why, but people didn't think to do things like life-story books with kids then. Yvette would have been a wonderful person to do something like that with. As carers in a children's home we had very little information about Yvette's background.

When we were worried about Yvette some time ago we used to talk to the staff in Crawley a lot. Tony and Anne were both very good. They were obviously very fond of Yvette and really took to her. Now there is Jamie and he is also very good and Yvette seems to get on well with him too. To start with, there was no support to us from social services, although we were regarded as Yvette's closest friends. We worked directly with the home – there was no link with social services as there is now. We would deal with the link worker in Crawley; talk to them before Yvette came to stay. Now we just deal directly with Yvette to make arrangements to see her and that works. We would really hope that Yvette would come to us if she had a problem. She talked to us an awful lot in the past when she had some worries about a relationship with her partner. She's also talked about her hopes, and she asks us for advice as you would a family member, but might not always choose to follow it! Just like anyone else.

Part of the family
We feel very, very proud of Yvette. When she comes to stay we will generally always meet up with our extended family. We will meet up for a dinner or maybe go out, and she is so relaxed, respectful and nice to people. By the way she behaves and acts it shows she has been really well brought up.

Neil:
But it's a weird situation in some ways because I'm not that much older than Yvette really, so it's almost like I'm not at all a father figure but an older adult who was a carer but is in fact a very similar age.

Angela:
I think she sees me more as a mother figure and I do feel very protective and caring of Yvette. She knows all our family extremely well and when she comes up she always wants to make a point of seeing everybody. She always comes up for Christmas and usually around the time of her birthday. At Christmas we always have a large family gathering, there's always about 20 of us and Yvette is always there. Every year she gives a speech and she is hilarious because all the men cry. She will say how much we all mean to her, thank us all with special

thanks to Angela and Neil, and she will say how good it is to be part of this lovely family. It's always a lovely speech and it's become part of our Christmas now. After lunch people will be looking around, as if to say, come on, it's time for Yvette's speech now.

When Yvette comes up for the weekend, it's really nice for me as the only female in a household of males, Neil and my two sons. It's like having a friend up for the weekend; we do things together. She loves to go shopping, so we always shop. She loves to eat, so we always go out to dinner. We have to go to see the family, so if we are not going out to eat with them then we have to pop round for a cup of tea and say hello and she'll ring them from here to make arrangements. She really is accepted by everyone; in fact there was one occasion where she stayed with my mum and dad. If she comes up and I'm at work, or Neil is at work, my mum comes to meet her and they go off shopping. It has developed over time and Yvette is like one of the family.

The most difficult time was when she wanted us to adopt her and then she wanted to change her name to Harris. That's when I found it really hard and my protective instincts came out and I thought, "Right, we'll have to adopt her." But then we talked about it, and talked with Yvette and explained that we couldn't adopt her as she was an adult but that we would always be there for her and things have really moved on. Yvette contacts us much less now that she has her own place but we easily pick up where we left off and the visiting contact is just as frequent. She regards us as her next of kin and we see her as part of the family. Just the other evening I [*Angela*] was on the phone to Yvette and we were ending the call. She said, "Bye. Love you lots!" and I said, "Love you too!" and I really meant it.

Neil and Angela:
We see ourselves as always being in touch and here for Yvette. It doesn't feel like a big commitment or responsibility but a close friend. She has achieved such a lot and now has a firm base in Crawley. At the same time, she has maintained her links from childhood with people like ourselves. In the end it's all worked out very well.

Chapter 17
Triumph

Nellie Corcoran

Nellie Corcoran is of Irish origin. She separated from her husband when her daughter Ann was very young and Nellie brought up Ann and her sister Sue alone as a single parent. The family have always lived in the borough of Kensington and Chelsea. I interviewed her in London. This chapter is the resulting narrative.

Sue Ledger

Ann was born on 27 October 1965. From day one I knew something was wrong. The sister in the hospital took her away to wash her. On the fourth morning I asked why I wasn't allowed to do so. She said, "I will send a doctor down to talk to you", and he explained everything to me and said that Ann would be very backward. I was very shocked at the time and looked at this tiny little person in the cot. But, the strangest thing of all, I wasn't worried.

I took her home and I got quite a bit of help from the hospital regarding feeding her. I was told she would be quite placid.

From day one Ann was anything but placid, which helped. When she was coming up to three years old she had an enormous amount of energy and nowhere to put it. I rang around to see what was on offer and I was lucky to get her into a nursery in Cheyne Walk, Chelsea, with children who had no problems. That got rid of all the energy and we had a much better life. She was there for two years and then she was very lucky to get into a school for handicapped children. It was called Dame Evelyn Fox School and was run by a very austere lady. She was very nice to us all. Unfortunately, that was closed down and she went to a school called the Jack Tizard School. She wouldn't get on the bus in the morning and wouldn't get off in the evening (help!). The bus driver used to have to glamorise everything to get her going. She was always full of mischief and very happy.

But as time went on, I realised she wasn't talking, and no matter how hard I tried I couldn't get her to say any words. We went in search of a speech therapist but they were like gold dust in them days. Eventually we found one, but still no words were coming. Then out of the blue came the Makaton sign language. First Ann was taught it, and then I was taught it as well, and at last we could communicate a bit better. She learned it very quickly and we would have great fun making signs to each other. As time progressed, she was doing very well and we got together a mothers' group and we could discuss various things with each other.

Then one morning I woke up with pneumonia and there was no one to help with Ann, so the lady who used to help on the bus told me about a home in Swiss Cottage called Hobbits House and she asked if they would look after Ann until I got better. It was a lovely place and eventually she went in to stay part time, as I had to get full-time employment. She loved it there and was very happy. Then after a few years it changed hands and I took her home for a while.

We used to go out a lot at weekends on coach trips organised by the church. We also went to Lourdes in France. Although Ann had no speech, it was amazing how she got what she wanted across to people. On the last night we were offered a bottle of wine. Not everyone wanted it but Ann held up her glass for some, so she was always on the ball. Everybody loved her and the women took turns to look after her at night so I could go out.

Ann is a great character and we've had lots of laughs and fun. She loves shopping and would carry it home and put it in the fridge and then would make signs to me that she wanted a cup of tea. She is very affectionate. Gives me lots of hugs and kisses. Eventually she went back to Erich Markus House – the name had changed as well. She didn't settle down very well so I used to take her home at the weekends. Ann is very outgoing and is full of mischief, a big smile, but can have her little tantrums like us.

Ann is a great character

However, there came a day when she had to leave school and progress to a day centre. It was very well discussed with the headteacher and she advised which one would suit Ann. We went for Lisson Grove, and Ann started straight from school. Poor Ann had to go with not a familiar face in sight. She took to it very badly and I was up every week to see how things were going. It took a long time for her to settle in but again she came through. She's been through a lot. She's very sensitive and gets quite upset when she's not sure of her ground.

Through the years she has got on very well. She has been on holiday to many places: to her home town in Ireland, then France twice, to Wales, to Cornwall and to the Isle of Wight. She is a very good traveller and used to enjoy it very much.

Ann has an older sister, Susan, and they are very close. She would take Ann shopping up Kensington High Street and take her to get her hair cut and shampooed. She loved all the beauty treatment and used to show me what she had done. We all used to go to the Holland Park to play tennis and go for long walks in the summer. Sue keeps in close contact with Ann and visits her at her home and brings her presents. She is very supportive in all areas.

Nellie, Ann and Sue on Ann's 18th birthday, 1983

Now I must give the placement manager from social services a mention here. Since getting to know us she has done so much in trying to find Ann a nice place to live. A big thank-you to her.

Ann is now living in her new home. It's a beautiful place run by lovely people and at last she is very, very happy. It's been a long journey but I never gave up hope. Ann contributed a lot to it herself.

She's a dear little daughter and I am very proud of her. I wouldn't have been able to cope the way she has. She is a *star*.

Chapter 18
We didn't depend on anybody

Irene Winder

This is Mrs Irene Winder's story about bringing up her son Raymond, born in 1960 on the Marsh Housing Estate in Lancaster. Irene herself grew up here in the 1930s, having a difficult home life, including times in the workhouse; her parents separating; and then, aged seven or eight, being sent away to the institution of King's Heath Residential School, which she recalls as being in Birmingham 14. This followed negative primary schooling experiences in Lancaster. Irene remembered: "They shoved me to one side … There was too many in a class. If you couldn't do what they wanted to do that was it, your face didn't fit. So I used to get bad-tempered and that's where I went wrong, you see. They didn't give me a chance." Irene is currently trying to establish why she was sent away to Birmingham, and the exact location of the institution. Returning to the Marsh Estate, Lancaster, at the age of 16, and having to live with her father rather than her mother, she was under local authority supervision until she was 21, at which point she married and started to raise her own family.

Nigel Ingham

I didn't know what was going on then, did I?
Early years

I have five boys and a girl. Pauline were born in 1957, Thomas was born in 1954, and Phillip was two years after, after Pauline. And then there was Raymond. Born 1960. He were born on Marsh. Mark was born in 1968. Edward 1964. I would never have another lad at home. Raymond was a big lad. But you know he were the only one that were born on the Marsh … I did have a midwife, I had him at home … It was quite an experience for anybody, considering I didn't know nowt. I didn't know how to put a nappy on or feed a bottle or what. It was an experience that, you know, some women wouldn't have took on! They would have left and walked out. You know what I mean. Yeah, it was an experience. It made me grow up more. Summat I never learned at school, put it that way. So I was backward myself, I always was – but I never liked school anyway.

Raymond was a lovely little lad. 'Cause I didn't know what was going on then, did I? I mean I wouldn't know whether there was summat wrong with him or not, but he always had bronchitis and pneumonia in that house. Always. Then they had wooden floors, and underneath when the tide used to come out, you know, high, you could fish in it. That's how deep they were in them days. And you always had a funny smell, a fungus smell. And I used to say, "Don't pull them floorboards up, Raymond! Don't pull them up!" "Well, I want to see what's inside." I said, "Dead bloody fish." Oh, he was a funny lad.

He was a lovely baby, was Raymond. It was a shame he weren't like the other lads. I mean all the other lads and Pauline was perfect in every way, they had nowt wrong wi' them, but Raymond was just the opposite. He's the only one I had at home. Whether it was just one of them things I don't know. He probably took after me, but I wasn't deaf and dumb, you see, but Raymond was. I couldn't let him go out. No way. Because he hadn't the sense. He didn't have the sense of right or wrong, you just had to be careful what he did, you know. If he went out to play, me lads would have to look after him. And they all understood what Raymond's like. So they looked after him. Pauline looked after him a lot. Actually I think she spoilt him a lot. 'Cause she used to take him when he was a little lad.

They arranged for me to see a specialist
Medical assessments
He had to go through all these operations when he was little. I didn't know he was deaf and dumb at the time – I only thought 'cause he was slow on talking, like you do. He used to have bronchitis a lot, you see. And they thought that was 'cause of him being deaf, and dumb. Because he had that bronchitis and pneumonia he went into that Beaumont Hospital at the time. He was in an oxygen tent for, they thought, you know, that'd help him. When he was at infant school, they said there was summat wrong with Raymond but they couldn't pinpoint what it was, why he couldn't speak. So they arranged for me to see a specialist at clinic. They took a test on his ears and found he was completely deaf at the time. That's why he couldn't speak, because he's deaf. He said he could learn to speak but it took someone else to learn him to talk and he'd need the operations. So I went to see an ear specialist at the hospital, Lancaster Infirmary. And they said, "We'll have to take him in and give him an operation or two." So he kept going in for ear syringes and then they decide to operate on him and put pins in. And they put them in their ear so they can hear better, yeah.

You don't talk to my lad like that
First school
When Raymond went to the infants at the Marsh … they (teachers) never hit 'im or owt, wi' knowing what he was like. He couldn't speak at the time. The teachers, because of his disability and that, they couldn't touch him. He was only there until they got him to that special school. He'd be about five when Raymond went. He used to get a lot of abuse, like kids do at that age at Marsh

Infants. If they were deaf and dumb they used to call all sorts of names. That's what Raymond got bad-tempered with. He may not be able to hear but he understands reading and lips. All my lads told me everything. They never kept anything a secret. I said, "Wait 'til I bloody get 'em. I'll show 'em. I'll call them a few names, never mind owt else."

You see they didn't know how to take me on Marsh because wi' being in a residential school they thought I was there because I was a bad girl, but I wasn't a bad girl really. But I could stand up for meself, put it that way. No one could get the best of me, so when I come home, and they used to say, "Watch out, Irene's about. You can't touch her … You know she's been in that residential, you know they can look after themselves. She went away because she was a bad 'un." So they never knew how to take me. So they wouldn't tackle me, you see, because I'd been to that school! But if they only knew. But I could fight if I wanted to fight.

Oh that's good, Raymond, you're talking
Special school
He went to Sunnyfield School when he was about seven from the Marsh Infant School. They didn't want him to go out of town because I was always ill so they decided to wait until Sunnyfield School was built And that's when Raymond went. He was one of the first, you see, in that school. Education office decided that. He needed a lot of attention. They do speech therapy and learning different things. When Raymond went there when he was a young, very young boy, I had to take him to school on the bus because we had no transport, no bus pass. For the first few weeks, I had to take him into school meself and bring him back. And then eventually they got a bus at the bus station. So, as he was about eight, I took him to the bus station and left him there with all of the rest of the boys and girls. And then he used to come home on his own, on the same bus. He know which bus to catch when the other lads used to say, "Come on Raymond, on the bus." So he knew that. But we didn't have a lot of help in that way with Raymond.

But when he was at school there, they found out that he didn't have an age of a seven-year-old boy, he was more like a five-year-old, like a child, like a baby's mind. But he was always a happy lad. He got on very well with the teachers. He did have his tempers, like any child does have tempers, but he was special, needed attention. Anyway when he started to learn to talk they had this machine or something, and they put them on the ears, and they start to learn them like that, whispering and showing what to say. Well, I used to do that anyway, when he was a little lad because he didn't know what he was doing you see, and I used to tell him to "stop this" by mouth-reading not by hands, because I wouldn't know nowt about that. And so when he knew what was wrong, he would stop, and he wouldn't be bad-tempered. But if you just ignore him, he would get very bad-tempered and he wouldn't know when to stop 'cause he's a highly-strung lad.

Anyway, so he learnt to speak. At first he used to shout. And he had a big voice when he started shouting. So when he started saying his words, "Oh, that's good, Raymond, you're talking." I didn't mind him shouting, 'cause it was learning him to *talk* even though he was deaf at the time, because he wouldn't hear himsel' talking anyway. Anyway the doctor decided to operate on his ears, and as far as I know they put pins in his ears to make him hear better. And every time he had his operations on his ears, he was hearing a little bit more every time. I thought it was great because it should have never happened to Raymond. Well I don't think so, anyway. When he was six months he could hear everything. The doctor said he was a healthy lad. It could have been the injections that lost his hearing and he couldn't speak when he had pneumonia. Or it could have been the atmosphere in the house – the dampness and the sewage. And George said, "Oh he's damn shouting again." I said, "Well, at least he's talking, George. He's talking and that's what. He'll ease off as he gets older."

But he wouldn't admit he was deaf, because he liked to be with the lads and do what other lads liked to do, you see. But he couldn't read – he'd never been able to read. He could always focus on black-and-white pictures, not colours. He was good at drawing. But when lads used to go out playing football in the grounds at Sunnyfield, he had to join in, because they made him join in, to make him feel like a lad of the age they were. But sometimes he'd just walk off and smile, 'cause he always had a smiling face. He never showed his temper or owt like that. He always smiled, so they knew there was summat wrong when he smiled anyway 'cause it wasn't natural, it wasn't natural for a lad to keep smiling like he did. But he was a happy-go-lucky lad.

This headteacher, he used to take him to his house. He got well in touch with Raymond. He had a nice personality, Raymond, until someone started him off and then he'd flare up. And he couldn't control his own temper. And he wouldn't trust anybody. Anyway the teacher learnt him a lot until he left there. He used to like going to his house 'cause he had a right big house. We never had nought a patch on what they had. They always had money, you see, but we hadn't. He used to pay a lot of attention to him at school, tell him what's right and what's wrong.

I always went to see his pantomimes and things like that because it was a good school really. I think they did marvellous for Raymond. And that teacher, he was really good with him. He helped him a lot, from the time he went to that school till the time he left, and went to college. Then he still went with him. They had nights out together, even then – Raymond and this teacher.

His wife thought Raymond was a well-mannered lad. He knew how to act in front of people. He still does.

Raymond was a big softie at first. He didn't like hitting anybody, you know, but he was more or less pushed into it. He had to. I said, "Now, Raymond, you're old enough now to fight back. You don't let them get the best of you, 'cause if you do they'll only come back to you, and you'll have more to put up wi'." "All right, mum. I will do. Now you've told me I will do." And he did. He used to fight at school. He'd be about nine or ten when he started talking and hearing, that's when I told him to fight his own battles. I said, "And if the teacher has owt to say, you tell 'em to come to me." One day he had a fight at school. The headteacher told me "Well, these lads were bullying him … And he got that bad-tempered with hisself … he just let go, sort of thing." I said, "Well that's only natural for a lad to do that. You don't think he's going to stand there and let them do it to him, or call him names." I said, "Well I'm not disciplining him for that, 'cause if the other lads are doing it to him, why shouldn't he do it back? Because I learnt them not to fight, but now they're getting older, they've got to show that if the other lad's provoking him all the time, he's got to put up with that or fight back and it'll stop." And it stopped, just like that when Raymond started fighting back. But the teacher didn't like him fighting because Raymond gets out of control, you see. I'd rather him at Sunnyfield (than Marsh Infants) because he was with the lads of his own type. I was quite happy when he went there. The teachers did wonders for him really, because I mean I don't think he would have got it at Marsh Infants! No way! No way.

We didn't depend on anybody
Family and neighbours
What a life I had with that lad! Oh, I used to say, "Raymond don't do this. Raymond. Now your sister will look after you. Now do what Pauline tells you to do." And Pauline always looked after him. She was like a mother to him. Like she had to do. She had to grow up quick with me having five lads. And I tried to go out to work an odd time but it never lasted because I couldn't leave the lads because they were running here, running there – firebugs! I called them 'firebugs' because we had a coal fire then, you see. And we used to go picking coke, picking coal and logs, stuff like that, we had to do because we hadn't the money to buy them. Down quay, on the railway, you know, dropping coal and they used to tip coke. So people could pick the best coke out and take it home. We were never short of a fire, no. No!

Me and me husband and kids used to come as well. It give 'em summat to do as well. Yeah, we used to go blackberry-picking and make me own pies and that! Owt to save, you know. I had to learn to cook even though I didn't cook when I was young. When I got married my sister learned me to do it.

She used to take them off me hands every so often to give me a break, with me being ill a lot. And I've always been ill off and on, never got rid of it, you know.

So we had a hard time of it. We never expected anybody to do things for us; we did it ourselves. We just looked after ourselves, once the kids started getting a bit older. We didn't depend on anybody. We never had social workers. They never come to see how Raymond was or how the family was. We was that sort of a family but they never bothered us. Even though I was ill, they never come. No we looked after ourselves. I wouldn't ask anybody for anything because I was brought up bad myself. And I think Social Services was a right washout them days, put it that way. They never did me no good. They never did me sisters any good. You know, I mean, we just looked after our own.

The brothers liked him but couldn't cope with him really. Raymond was such a heavy lad and quick-tempered. But they were all right with him. They were still close together. Anyway they were quite good with him. And Pauline was extra good 'cause she was, she'd be like a mother. I mean she's been part of me more than the lads really because she was always there, you know, there to help me in any way. And as she got older she were more clever than me, so she was telling me and her dad, you know. I mean she was there for me, not for her dad really. So I mean she knew that she had to grow up quick anyway wi' having the lads.

First time I went to university he was about three or four. Pauline was looking after him and the lads then and I worked at university. I worked there three and a half years, at night. Thomas went in the army and he'd send me a little bit of money. Anyway, Pauline looked after him and I was five to nine at university. And then Pauline decides she wanted to get away from home for a while. So I says, "Well you go, Pauline, you go. I'll still manage. I'll still manage." So she says, "Right."

When Pauline went away … It was only like getting a break from everybody … too much pressure wi' looking after lads, you know. I had a good neighbour, and me husband. He had to keep an eye on them every so often, but Phillip was the next eldest so he had to cope. He were working at slaughterhouse at the time, but he was always in at night when I went to work, you see, so I'd always make sure they were all right before I went to work, never left 'em without anybody, because I knew what they were like – they were firebugs! Well, their dad used to come home about six, or he might be home all day. So there was always somebody there. I had a next-door neighbour used to come and see if everything was all right, so I had good neighbours that way. I only had one good neighbour. We kept ourselves to ourselves; I mean never mixed with everybody.

He can look after himself
Growing up

Before he left school he went out with these lads. It's his first time out with some lads off the Marsh Estate. And they decide to go to Morecambe. And I said, "Well you'd better look after him, because he doesn't know his way about … owt like that. He's never been left out on the street on his own or owt like that." "We'll look after him, Mrs Winder, oh yeah." So I says, "Well I'll give him his bus money to go on the bus, on the train." So he come back with two policemen. And I wondered what was going on; them lads were supposed to look after him. "Has he got lost?" "Oh no, Mrs Winder. It's about a train fare." I said, "They were supposed to look after him. I give them the train fare to go to Morecambe and bring him back." So he could enjoy himself, you know. "Oh no," he says, "he didn't have no bus ticket, train ticket." I says, "Why not?" I says, "I give them money." He says, "Well – all they could say was he spent it." I said, "Raymond wouldn't have spent his train money. I know Raymond. He wouldn't spend his train money. Not when I've told him not to, you know. Not if he wants to get back." You see he didn't know his way back anyway, unless them lads come back with him. They didn't stand up for him. And Raymond was just stunned, you know, because he didn't know what to say to them. So he says, "I'm sorry, Mrs Winder, but you have to go to court with him." I said in court he should have never been fined because he was a lad who depended on other friends. They said in court, "Well I'm sorry, Mrs. Winder, you still have to pay the fine of three pound." But I think that was disgusting, 'cause Raymond was like a child. The police said to me, "Oh, you have to trust your boy to go out on his own to find out right and wrong. … Because it's cruel to keep a young lad in all the time knowing he has a disability." He was a lad who couldn't trust anybody after, you know. He'd think twice about going with anybody actually. He saw his brother get beaten up outside Victoria Pub. He said, "No one will get the best of me like that." It frightened Raymond actually, because he was just starting to grow up. He was only about 15. So that's how he learnt to fight – he could fight, Raymond.

We'll look after you, Raymond
Leaving school: college and work

He was always a smart lad. He wouldn't go to work in a dirty shirt or anything. Always spotless. He must be just right to go to school. When he was ready for leaving school he went to college on Morecambe Road. That's where the teacher said he'd be best at college for a year or two, just give him some idea. He was 16 when he left, went to college until he was 17. Before he went to the college he had to sign up. They signed him up. And they said, "Oh well he'll get a grant." And I will get so much allowed for him. That's the first time he ever had owt off them. And he would get his family allowance just the same. So like I was getting two books, one to look after him, and one whatever he needed, but he always got that hisself for pocket money. 'Cause he always looked after his money, did Raymond, he was never one for spending his money. So that's when he went to college. And he stayed there till he was 17.

And his first job was on the dustbins! He liked it. He used to bring me little glasses off the tip, little things. He was there about nine months. Then they finished him. Raymond didn't like that. He liked his money. Even though he couldn't drive or owt like that. He liked to feel as though he were a man. He's got to look for a job, he's not one for sitting around for long. So he went to the Yates and Jackson's Brewery. He went hisself to get a job. They took him on 'cause he was a strong lad, he was. He was working with two mates and he still has contact with them. They said to Raymond, "We'll look after you, Raymond, we'll tell you if you're in the wrong or right." And Raymond said, "All right, all right, all right." You know, just like a father to him.

Before he got Yates and Jacksons, he worked as a chef. The chef, an oldish fella, he liked Raymond, and he's told him, he said, "Now Raymond, you're going to learn about facts of life. We're going to have a night out. I'm going to take you somewhere where you've never been before and there's a lot of women there." So when he got to this place, it was – what do you call them places? Men dressed as women! But Raymond didn't know at the time. He looked at this woman, and he thought, "There's summat funny about this woman." He says, "Why what's wrong with her?" He says, "Well she looks more like a fella than a woman." And he says, "You're right, Raymond. It's a man dressed as a woman." He says, "Well I'm not bloody going with another fella!" He says, "What do you think I am?!" So that was his first experience of – what do you call it – homosexuals or? So he wasn't so sure about women for a while after that!!

I think he's done marvellous
Leaving home: married life
He's been married twice, so I mean Raymond's done well really. He left home at 19. He got on with this lass. They started going out together. At first when they said they were getting married at 19, I said, "Raymond, don't get married yet. Wait till you're a bit older." "Oh no. I'm getting married, I'm getting married." His first wife took him for everything he got 'cause he had to depend on a woman anyway, you know, to do everything. And he always give her his wages. Then he married this nice lass. She's got the brains you know, not like us. She's an Oxford girl, been to university and all that lot. She met him down Morecambe one day when he was a bouncer. She worked at the power station at Morecambe. She was a woman who did all the orders and give people orders.

Raymond and Irene

They wanted the same things but just Raymond was different from her, you know, in that way. But they were meant for each other, I think. So anyway, when he met this young woman they hit it off right away. They moved to Torrisholme and they got a nice house there, biggish house. And they were living together for 11 years. Then she said, 'cause they had a bargain with each other, she said, "I'll tell you what, Raymond, we won't get married till I've got all me ex–" what do you call them – diplomas or whatever you call them? … "So what we'll do, we'll save my money and live off your money" 'cause it costs a lot of money to – even though she had money – but it cost more money for degrees an' that … And so she passed all that. She even got the cap, you know. So she passed all that and then they decided to get married. 'Cause they both want the same thing, yeah. And they have no interest in having children anyway.

They told me when he left school, and he went to college for a year – and they said he'll never change, he'll always be as he is. They can't learn him anymore than they did. But look at him now. He married a woman who has got brains – always in a book. And she learnt him to drive a car. Because he always ride a bike, but he never drive a car before and she coached him to drive. Anyway I think he's done marvellous to drive. It must have cost him over a thousand pounds before he clicked on. But she kept shoving him into it, you see. And she says, "You'll learn, Raymond," Jill says, "You'll learn." So she used to keep taking him out in the car, showing him what to do. When he did pass, he was quite good at it. Only fault was he didn't know his districts. I didn't really want him to pass a test because I thought, he's one of these lads who could really have an accident, just forget one thing and that's it, you know. He likes to speed, you know. He said, "I'm going to take you for a drive." I said, "Oh my God. I'm going on his first-time drive." I thought, "Oh no." I couldn't say no to him so I says – because he was so pleased that he'd passed. I says, "Right-o Raymond." He said, "I'll be careful, you know. I'll be very careful driving it, so you'll be all right." I says, "All right, Raymond. I'll go in." … And he was very good. He didn't speed or anything.

He's done really well considering he's disabled. I mean driving! I never thought he'd drive a car. Never in my life … I think he's done marvellous really for a lad who's had to put up with a lot of stuff and criticism and all that. He's been there over 12 months now, down in Wiltshire since they sold their house. When he first went I thought, "Well, Raymond, I'm going to miss you. Because I'm used to you coming down with your car and taking me for a ride." I said, "That's goodbye to me rides." He says, "Well I can't help it, mam, but," he says, "you've got to get on with life." I says, "I know you have, Raymond. And I'm glad you are getting on with your life."

He said he'd never come back to Lancaster to live. I am proud of him. I think Raymond has done pretty well. He's got a head on him where money is. I mean everything goes in the bank with Raymond. The bankers pay all his debts. But she's got a lovely job. She works at college, university down there. They work hard. Raymond will be the only one in our family who will have money, 'cause he always liked money. And he's always worked. And down there there's more jobs than there is here. And that's why he likes it. You can go from one job to another if you want to, but he's quite happy where he is. He's passed all his fork truck test. He's done all that. Considering he's disabled, I think he's done wonders. I mean, a lot of people wouldn't have time for him. And he's driving vans as well. They're quite happy with him, because he's a good worker, you see …

I've helped him the best way I can
Reflections
It was a funny life, actually. Put it this way, I wouldn't like to go through what I've gone through now, what I did have to go through. Summat I didn't expect. I mean my dad and mam separated, then my dad said I wouldn't make a marriage because I'd been to a school like that (King's Heath Residential School), and then I proved I could make a marriage, 'cause I'm the longest one out of family who's been married … Well as a child I never mixed with children, you see. When I went to that school, and before I went to that school I never pushed a pram, never had toys or anything to do with kids, child play and that. I never had owt to do with that. So when I went to school, I was wi' more of my own age. So when I come home I was different, it was a life different again, me life

wasn't the same again, so what I learnt at that school, it was no good to me at home, because everything changed. Because I had to go out right away wi' what I had on my back, only had clothes on my back. I had to go out to work. And I didn't know what to do for the best 'cause my dad wasn't always there, my dad was always at work, or out gambling his money away. I love children, definitely do, even though I never mixed with children when I was a child – they never let me touch any children, never babysit or owt like that till I had me own children. I had me own children and that's when I started realising what life's all about!

He's the one I was mostly worried about, than any of the others, because I know they can cope with life. We've stuck together and I've helped him the best way I can. That's all you can do for 'em. When he comes through he'll always pop in, because his mate's down road. He always comes to see how I am. If he doesn't he'll ring me up and ask why I haven't telephoned him, you know. We're that close, you see, whatever goes on for Raymond I feel it you see. I don't know what it is, but it's a – it's just the way we are. When they were kids we were always a close family. We went everywhere together, you know, we went for walks together. All things like that where we couldn't afford to go anywhere, we always walked it to Morecambe, or to Heysham, come back and walked it. I always walked them, because they got tired when they got home! We had a bit of peace then! But as I say, we done everything together. And that is a family way of doing things. I mean they tell me everything. They even now, grown up, they tell me everything.

Conclusion: emerging themes

The stories in this mid-point of the book show continuity with the earlier stories. However, the 'witnesses' also note the changes that have occurred during the lives of their sons and daughters. Mr and Mrs York and Mrs Garcia, for example, say how different it was 'then' compared with 'now'; how little help and support was available when their son and daughter were children. Although the long-stay hospitals continued to grow during this period – and continue to feature in the stories here – nevertheless changes were afoot that were to bring about their eventual running-down and closure. The policy switch to increasing care in the community meant more emphasis on care by the family, as alternative services were still few and far between in the late 1950s and throughout the 1960s. There are four distinctly family-related themes that emerge from the stories:

- family life and relationships within the family
- the family as advocates
- family losses
- family gains

Family life and relationships within the family

This period, as Jean Batchelor wryly points out, was the 'swinging sixties'. Yet it was still a time of expanding long-stay institutions, segregated services and negative attitudes. The passing of the 1959 Mental Health Act brought a change of labels, from mental deficiency to mental subnormality, but also saw, by and large, a continuation of existing services and personnel. The birth of a son or daughter with learning disabilities – or a later realisation or discovery of learning disability – continued to have a major impact on families and family life. In the characteristic manner of the time, Mr and Mrs York were told that Ben would never talk; Nellie Corcoran was told that Ann was 'very backward'; and, worst of all, Kathleen Croucher was told, "You've got a cabbage." The expert opinion of the time was that these children were either completely ineducable, or educable only within special schools. They had no place even in local nurseries, and certainly no place in ordinary schools. The advice to Mrs Croucher was to have another child. The advice to Stella Garcia was to put her daughter into a children's home.

Although forms of care in the community existed prior to this period, this was the era when, with the rising costs of institutional care becoming ever more apparent, this became a major policy initiative. What it meant in practice, as the stories in this section testify, was that families were often left to get on with it (Bayley, 1973); to care for their son or daughter as best they could with little support from elsewhere. Although Nellie Corcoran was a single parent, Stella Garcia's husband was a student and Irene Winder's family lived in poor housing, they had little in the way of support. As Mr and Mrs York commented: "Just the two of us brought him up." This was echoed by Mrs Winder, who recalled: "We had a hard time of it. We never expected anybody to do things for us; we did it for ourselves." This was not uncommon. Other families were left to cope, as McCormack (1978) and Wilkin (1979) showed in their studies of the period.

Families were left to cope and, in practice, this meant that women were left to cope, as the narrators of the stories here testify. The only father's voice is that of Mr York; otherwise these are stories of women as carers. Emma Atkinson's account reflects very much on her struggle as the primary carer of Stewart: "As a mother you fit in with everybody else's needs." What made life particularly difficult in Mrs Atkinson's case was the lack of information about Stewart, and the gradual realisation by the family that something was wrong: "We weren't told anything at all; we never got any information from him [the consultant] to say what was wrong with him." The hit-and-miss nature of services, as reflected in the accounts here, often meant that services were non-existent, poor quality or inappropriate.

The effect on family life of having to struggle in this way was potentially beneficial – but also, in some circumstances, potentially harmful, as the narrators here have indicated. The 'closeness' of their family is a feature much welcomed and celebrated by Irene Winder: "We're that close. We are a close family." The sense of adversity can bring people together, as she has witnessed. It can, at a later date, leave the family feeling isolated, a point made by Mr and Mrs York. It can also, at the same time, leave individual family members feeling jealous (as witnessed by Michael's sister writing in the Trident Café) or stressed (as acknowledged by Mrs Winder when her daughter Pauline spent several years away from the family home after years of caring for her brother Raymond 'like a mother'). Emma Atkinson comments on how difficult it was for the rest of her family to cope with Stewart's problems at home. In particular she reflects that her other son 'didn't get as much attention as he could have'. Family outings and holidays, even just ordinary family life, proved to be out of reach for many of them. The possible adverse effects on brothers and sisters were raised by Glendinning (1983) in her study of the families of disabled children.

The family as advocates
One of the linking threads through the stories is that there were few services available in this period. Those that did exist were separate from the mainstream,

and children and young people with learning disabilities were segregated from an early age in special nurseries and schools, and in training centres. The provision was in some instances second rate, such as the run-down church hall where Kathleen Croucher's daughter was sent – a separate setting for disabled children. The provision of even segregated services, provided they were in the community, at least made it possible for sons and daughters to stay at home with their families. One exception in the accounts here was Stella Garcia's daughter, Theresa, who was moved from children's home to children's home, and then into a long-stay hospital which was "a terrible place … they were living like animals; they were treated like animals". Other exceptions were the infants and young children who were placed with Jean Batchelor and her friend for fostering. Also placed away from their own families, the children who joined this household joined a caring substitute family and experienced a family atmosphere.

Services in this period were patchy. Some were good, including the nursery and schools that Nellie Corcoran's daughter, Ann, attended. Others were less than good and the first intimations of bullying and abuse were reported from the accounts of this period. It became incumbent on families to fight back: to take a stand, to 'speak up' for their sons and daughters. The families in this period acted as advocates. Mrs Croucher recalls how it was necessary to 'knock the system'. She had to fight for Marilyn's right to go to the schools and adult training centres that suited her daughter, regardless of what she saw as petty bureaucratic rules about catchment areas. Irene Winder stood up for herself and for her children, particularly Raymond. She encouraged him to fight back. Mr and Mrs York's advice to parents is to "fight for your child. That's all you can do." After more than 30 years of speaking up for Stewart, Emma Atkinson reflects: "As things turn up you just get on and do it. I found I could be quite ruthless now to get what I want for him. If I needed to get anything, I'd go ahead and not let things stand in the way and try and fight for what he wants."

Resistance has its price though, as Kathleen Croucher found. She experienced misinformation, lies, cover-ups, denials and actual intimidation (through the barricading of her car) as she fought against the system to support Marilyn's rights. In standing up for her daughter, Mrs Croucher was probably herself labelled as a 'difficult parent'. Families were not expected to resist authority or to fight back. This era predates the switch from parents as supplicants to parents as partners. Relationships with professionals could be fraught with difficulty, as the territory of the 'experts' was vigorously defended. In later years, Mrs Croucher may have encountered a more receptive atmosphere as parent–professional partnerships became acceptable, and were even encouraged (Pugh, 1981; Mittler and McConachie, 1983).

Family losses

The stories bear witness to the multiple losses that the people with learning disabilities, and their families, experienced in this period. The most glaring ones are described by Kathleen Croucher and Stella Garcia. The former's daughter, Marilyn, suffered the loss of educational opportunities, the loss of local friends, the loss of confidence, the loss of stability (through unwanted and unwarranted change) and the loss of her health (she has had two nervous breakdowns and now has Alzheimer's disease). Mrs Garcia's daughter, Theresa, lost her childhood and her family home. Separated from her family by a social worker operating on the child-care principles of the time, Theresa grew up in children's homes and later 'migrated' to a long-stay hospital (Rolph, 1998). The decision to let her daughter go to a home was, according to Stella Garcia, "very, very hard. Very discouraging and very heartbreaking." In spite of placements at varying distances from London (including one in Devon), situated at places difficult (and expensive) to reach by public transport, Mrs Garcia kept in touch and continued to visit her daughter. Their relationship has survived the losses, separations and distances experienced by them over many years.

The experiences of the families in this period echo the experiences of families in the earlier period. This is not surprising as, although change was in the air, it had yet to deliver anything significantly different from what had gone before. An important landmark in the preceding period was the publication of the report by the Royal Commission on the Law Relating to Mental Illness and Mental Deficiency in May 1957. The report advocated a shift in emphasis from hospitals to community care. The 1959 Mental Health Act went some way towards supporting the switch to care in the community, in that it lay the basis for community care services such as training and occupation centres, social centres and clubs, home visiting services and residential homes and hostels. However, it stopped short of making these community-based services compulsory. No money was allocated to encourage local authorities to use their enabling powers. Consequently many of them failed to do so during this period. The 1960s, and the stories originating in that period, thus showed more continuity with the preceding era than a time of sweeping change as intended by the Royal Commission.

The reality of local authority provision was that it was patchy. The stories in this section illustrate the tremendous variation that existed between places and over time. Jean Batchelor contrasts her experiences in Norfolk with those in Sussex, and Stella Garcia and Kathleen Croucher reflect on the inadequacies of local provision for their daughters in the 1960s, even in London. The different circumstances of families influenced their response to the lack of (or inappropriate) provision in their local areas. Jean Batchelor initially moved from Lancashire to Norfolk, and Mrs Croucher was able, through her husband's work, to press for Marilyn's admission to a training centre outside their catchment area. Other families, however, including the York, Winder and Garcia families, seemed to have little choice. Unable to move home, and with no recourse to pressure or influence on events, they had little alternative other than to accept what was there – or to do without. And what was there? What were the local authority provisions in this period?

Special schools played an important part in the stories told in this section. In some instances, they were preferred to the mainstream schools of that era. Emma Atkinson, for example, fought for Stewart to have a place at York Special School, and Irene Winder kept Raymond at Marsh Primary School only until Sunnyhill (Special School) was built and he could go there. Neil and Angela Harris comment favourably on Yvette's experience of the special school that she attended daily from the children's home. There were also occupation centres provided by local authorities for children with learning disabilities. Although these were initially housed in unsuitable buildings, nevertheless provision for children exceeded the services on offer for adults. In most areas occupational centres for adults, now called adult training centres, developed much more slowly compared with those for children. It was only from the mid-1960s that more adult training centres began to be built. This delay meant that many adults aged 16 and over remained in the special schools which had long waiting lists and were generally overcrowded. The regional variations in services persisted throughout this period. At the end of the 1960s, the Seebohm Report noted that for years to come, many parts of the country would not have the resources to provide adequate community care services. It concluded that 'the widespread belief that we have "community care" of the mentally disordered is, for many parts of the country, still a sad illusion and judging by the published plans will remain so for many years ahead' (DHSS, 1968, 107, para. 339).

The changing nature of services, and the often illusory nature of community care is nicely illustrated in Emma Atkinson's account. She notes the passing of the local special school as educational policies changed; and later the changes to, and the closure of, the adult training centre as policies switched to dispersal to smaller units. Social workers, although often helpful when around, have come and gone from their lives, leaving the family – especially Mrs Atkinson – to develop their own strategies for coping. This has led to their particular family losses, especially the loss of freedom for both Stewart and his mother. As a consequence of their encounter with the criminal justice system, their world has had to become more enclosed and inward-looking in order to ensure his safety. Without the safeguards and protection of his family it seems likely that Stewart would, by now, be in an institutional setting. It is a mixed outcome: "The only thing Stewart likes is his music; otherwise he just sits there on the chair watching the television."

Family gains

There were gains as well as losses for families in this period. Several witnesses recount how they had the good luck to meet the right people at the right time – those individual stars who really made a difference. Services could be patchy, poor or non-existent, but there were people around who cared enough to put themselves out. Jean Batchelor put herself out in giving up her job to become a foster-mother for children with learning disabilities. Mrs Garcia cites Daisy and her parents (Theresa's social aunt and uncle) as people who made a difference to Theresa's life in helping her get out of hospital. Kathleen Croucher was disillusioned with statutory services but full of praise for the home teacher of Marilyn's early years and the voluntary visitor in more recent times. Irene Winder recalls the headteacher who made a difference to Raymond's life by giving him attention at school and inviting him home. It was the social worker, 32 years after Stewart's birth, who recognised that he had Williams syndrome – a revelation to the Atkinson family. This changed everything, especially for his mother, who for years had longed for information as to what was wrong and how best to help.

The real stars of the stories here, however, are the sons and daughters with learning disabilities – for what they had achieved against the odds and for making a difference to the lives of their families. Irene Winder, for example, says of Raymond: "He's done really well. He's done marvellous." And Nellie Corcoran says of her daughter: "Ann's a great character." They have enjoyed 'lots of laughs and fun, lots of hugs and kisses'. She concludes: "She is a *star.*" Emma Atkinson's life has been 'enriched' by Stewart. Although life can be difficult there are immense rewards: "When Stewart is good he's a smashing lad, he's really great … outgoing, bubbly, friendly." In spite of the struggles and the occasional feeling of despair, she 'wouldn't have missed it'. Without her own family to care for her, or act as her advocates, Yvette became part of Neil and Angela Harris's family. They speak of her with love and pride – love for Yvette the person, and pride in what she has achieved: "We feel very, very proud of Yvette."

There is pride in the achievements of sons and daughters in the stories, but tempered with the acknowledgement that life has often been a struggle and – for Kathleen Croucher and Emma Atkinson –still is. The stories are told with some regret for opportunities missed, for separations that might have been avoided and for taking advice that, with hindsight, was best ignored. The stories are partly celebratory, previewing accounts published by parents whose sons and daughters were born later (Boston, 1981). Although grounded in hardship and struggle, the experiences reported here do not fully replicate the reports of other parents of the period that refer to 'the daily grind' (Bayley, 1973) and 'managing day to day as best we can' (Hannam, 1975). Mrs Atkinson, however, comes closest to it when, in later life, she admits that her coping strategy is to 'take it a day at a time'.

In some respects, from the perspective of the 21st century, the period 1959–71 looks like a foreign country. Discussions about services for people with learning disabilities continued to use the language of mental deficiency, mental subnormality and mental handicap. There was only very limited discussion of provision for service users from ethnic minorities, despite the emergence of large migrant communities in many cities. Debates of the time focused very much on administrative matters, and said little about the service users themselves or their families. The effectiveness of services tended to be evaluated in terms of the number of institutions such as training centres, and the numbers of places they offered to children and adults. The quality of care, and the quality of the experiences, were not considered. Only now through oral history, and the testimonies of family witnesses, are the stories behind the services emerging. The stories here show how families overcame challenges – often from the various services in place to 'help' them – and how, in spite of everything, there were many things to look back on with some degree of satisfaction.

Sometimes the experiences were more mixed, and any 'gains' could only be seen when looking back. In a poignant account written after the death of her brother, Michael's sister records her feelings of 'love, pain, jealousy and grief', and in her poem pays tribute to him and to their mother:

> Dear brother
> Special and needy
> Our mother loved you
> More than life itself –
> We loved you too
> But didn't understand
> Circumstances too tragic
> For childhood hearts

Many of the authors of the personal accounts are acutely aware of the changes to labels and language they have witnessed in their lifetimes. We see the ways in which the terms they use to describe the people they live with and care for are not of their choosing, but part of a separate discourse. We see the ways in which they interact with these changing labels and changing attitudes, influencing and influenced by them. These family members, like those of previous eras, have been fierce advocates for their children. A recurring theme is that these narrators have not just nurtured and given support, but have learned and gained themselves from their relationship with their family member with learning disabilities.

References

Bayley, M. (1973) *Mental Handicap and Community Care: A study of mentally handicapped people in Sheffield*. London: Routledge & Kegan Paul

Boston, S. (1981) *Will, My Son*. London: Pluto Press

DHSS (1968) *Report of the Committee on Local Authority and Allied Personal Social Services*. London: HMSO

DHSS (1971) *Better Services for the Mentally Handicapped* (Cmnd. 4683). London: HMSO

Glendinning, C. (1983) *Unshared Care: Parents and their Disabled Children*. London: Routledge & Kegan Paul

Hannam, C. (1975) *Parents and Mentally Handicapped Children*. Harmondsworth: Penguin

McCormack, M. (1978) *A Mentally Handicapped Child in the Family*. London: Constable

Ministry of Health (1963) *Health and Welfare: The Development of Community Care. Plans for the Health and Welfare Services of the Local Authorities in England and Wales* (Cmnd. 1962). London: HMSO

Mittler, P. and McConachie, D. (1983) *Parents, Professionals and Mentally Handicapped People*. London: Croom Helm

Pugh, G. (1981) *Parents as Partners*. London: National Children's Bureau

Rolph, S. (1999) Enforced Migations by People with Learning Difficulties: A Case Study. *Oral History*, 27(1), 47–56

Report of the Royal Commission on the Law Relating to Mental Illness and Mental Deficiency 1954–1957 (Cmnd. 169). London: HMSO

Unsworth, C. (1987) *The Politics of Mental Health Legislation*. Oxford: Clarendon Press

Wilkin, D. (1979) *Caring for the Mentally Handicapped Child*. London: Croom Helm.

Poems by Tom Hulley

fits

you looked distant this morning
jumpy and near the edge

would the increased dosage
be enough to hold the storm?

it's too hard watching you fall
taking all the impact

but worries about the levels
of drugs keep nagging

innocent chemicals which
offer you a better life

lie in the red box
despite their claims

turquoise and grey

sam got a good report
she announced it
before the day began
as she donned
her turquoise top
her multicoloured velvet coat

she wore crescent moons
turquoise and silver
making a subtle match
with god's favourite colour
and the devil's pipes

when she returned
the table setting she had made
that afternoon
was yellow and red and green
like a karma chameleon

she expected praise
for her artistry before she left
to plunge once more
into the pool
dazzle the swimmers

with her grey glinting eyes
the only place in nature
where grey belongs
and looks good —except
on clouds and far horizons

easter – written jointly by sam and tom

holiday time staying in bed
waiting for dee to help me to dress
choosing earrings
visiting my brother visiting friends
sitting with granny for coffee
in her room
painting boiled eggs for the children
eating chocolate eggs with sugar shells
strong white teeth
looking at lenten lilies in the garden with
mum on the arbour I had built
for us last summer
driving to therfield to see the pasque
flowers on the hill the anniversary of
the resurrection
'you get knocked down you get up again'
on the first Sunday after a full moon
in late march

Part 3

Participation ... the promise of change at last?

1971–2001

Edited by Rohhss Chapman, Sue Ledger and Melanie Nind

Introduction

The period of history for this final section of the book begins and ends with a strategy for learning disability: the 1971 *Better Services for the Mentally Handicapped* (DHSS) and the 2001 *Valuing People: A New Strategy for Learning Disability for the 21st Century* (DoH). It is characterised by a policy emphasis on presence and participation in the community, but once again, our witnesses tell us some of the more complex picture of how such policy has translated into people's lived experiences.

The official history of the period is one of a new era of community care with a desire to move away from models of hospital living, reflecting the civil rights concerns of the time. Moves were afoot to develop co-ordinated health and social services, using community facilities as part of the drive for normalisation. There was a shift in welfare ideology in which the role of health services and the public sector was to diminish in favour of enhanced roles for families and the voluntary and private sectors. Care services were being set up and provided by private companies, split off from the social services who became purchasers of those services. With fragmentation then came calls for more 'joined-up' working and concepts of partnership and 'best value' vied with concepts of 'healthy' competition.

This is also a period that begins with the start of a legislative commitment to education for all children and progresses, somewhat falteringly, towards inclusive education. The concern with inclusion reflected the new strength of the Disability Rights Movement and the popularity of the social model of disability (UPIAS, 1976; Oliver, 1983) illustrating how people with impairments are disabled by attitudes, environments and systems. Disabled activists' call for an end to discrimination and for full civil rights legislation culminated in the first Disability Discrimination Act (1995) and the much celebrated and much criticised 2001 SENDA. Also campaigning through the later part of the period were the self-advocacy groups, run by and for people with learning difficulties. In the 2001 White Paper the Department of Health attempted to include, for the first time, the voices of carers and individuals with learning difficulties.

In Part 3, therefore, we might expect to see people with learning difficulties living in the community supported by a range of services, attending their local mainstream schools, and having a say in how they live their lives. Once again, however, the stories add layers of detail missing from the usual history that is told and illuminate both the new and the old attitudes and practices that go unchanged from earlier decades.

Year	Legislation	Reports/policy	Publications	World events
1971		DHSS White Paper *Better Services for the Mentally Handicapped*		Campaign for People with Mental Handicap (CMH) established (later became Values into Action)
1972				'Our Life' (first National conference of mentally handicapped people in Britain, Wallingford) organised by CMH
1973				'Listen' conference organised by CMH
1974			Joseph Deacon's *Tongue Tied*	
1975				'Working Out' conference organised by CMH
1976			National Development Group Pamphlet 1: *Planning Together:* guidelines for service development and multidisciplinary co-operation, e.g., community mental handicap teams	
1977			Normansfield Hospital Enquiry report revealed serious concerns about care within the hospital system NDG Pamphlets 2–5	
1978		Warnock Report (DES) recommended educational need rather than medical categorisation	NDG Helping mentally handicapped people in hospitals	

Year	Legislation	Reports/policy	Publications	World events
1979		*Jay Report* advocated community living with support from the non-medical caring profession		
1980			*Mental Handicap: Progress, Problems and Priorities* evaluated progress since the 1971 White Paper	
1981	1981 Education Act: statementing of SEN, consultation with parents, entitlement to place in mainstream with three caveats	Care in the Community: commitment to community care; end to children in mental handicap hospitals		
1982			Paul Williams and Bonnie Shoultz: *We can Speak for Ourselves*	
1984	Registered Homes Act: new regulatory framework incorporating residential homes for people with learning disabilities			Delegates with learning difficulties attend first international self-advocacy leadership conference in Tacoma, USA. English delegates inspired to set up People First, London
1986	Disabled Persons (Services, Consultation and Representation Act): LEAs to notify SSDs of 14-year-olds with SEN			
1988	Education Reform Act: National Curriculum and local management of schools			Second International People First Conference, Twickenham: 'A Voice of Our Own Now and in the Future'

Year	Legislation	Reports/policy	Publications	World events
1989	1989 Children Act: children's welfare paramount	Griffiths Report and White Paper: *Government Objectives for Community Care*		
1990	NHS and Community Care Act			
1991	Registered Homes Amendment Act			
1993	1993 Education Act endorsed 1981 Act caveats for mainstream education; tribunal for appeal by parents			Third International Self-Advocacy Conference, Toronto, Canada
1994		UNESCO Salamanca Statement. Code of Practice on the Identification and Assessment of SEN (DfE): continuum of provision		
1995	1995 Disability Discrimination Act: first anti-discrimination legislation for disability			
1996	1996 Education Act	Direct payments Act		
1997		DfEE Green Paper *Excellence for All Children*		
1998		DfEE White Paper *Meeting SEN: A Programme for Action*		Fourth International Self-Advocacy Conference, Anchorage, Alaska
2001	Special Educational Needs and Disability Act (SENDA): removed two of three caveats for mainstream education; made educational discrim-ination unlawful	2001 White Paper *Valuing People*. Revised Code of Practice (DfES): emphasis on consultation with parents		

Chapter 19
Enriched lives

Elaine Monk

Rachel Monk was born in November 1982 and has lived with her parents in the community. Elaine Monk, her mother, was interviewed in July 2001, when she explained that she had never wanted Rachel to be treated differently to anyone else and described how the family made strenuous efforts to keep Rachel away from the service system throughout her life. This chapter is drawn from the interview transcripts.

Rohhss Chapman

The birth experience
During the pregnancy everything went perfectly well. I stopped smoking before I had Rachel. It all just happened in the last few minutes of the birth, the last about 25 minutes before Rachel was born, everything went wrong. I felt a bit uneasy because I knew what it was like with Louise and it didn't feel the same. They came in and said they were going to examine me and then all hell broke loose. The midwife said it was a cord prolapse. I had no idea what a cord prolapse was at all. They got me up on all fours, lifted me so I was on the trolley and just flung a sheet over me, and off I went down the corridor. I thought I was going for a caesarean then, I knew there was something wrong. When we got to this other room, they started trying to get this thing to fit onto Rachel's head so when I was pushing they would use a suction thing. But it kept coming off her head and they couldn't get it on and everything seemed to be going wrong. It's really awful when you think back about it. It was about 25 minutes before she was actually born. I just wanted to be asleep and for it to be over with.

When she was born Rachel was like a little waxwork doll, you wouldn't have thought she was alive. The cord prolapse meant that a loop had come down in front of Rachel's head so with every contraction it was cutting off the oxygen to Rachel's brain. We didn't know that at the time; they didn't make it very clear to us.

The next morning one of the doctors came down to see us and he said Rachel was very poorly and she was going to have to be christened because she was going to die. They just waltzed into the ward and all the other mothers were there. They were crying, it upset them, you know. We had to have her christened that day. It was strange really; one minute you were thinking she was going to die and the next minute she was OK. Then soon she was coming home, they packed her off home with us and that was it, we were left to get on with it. We weren't really told what was wrong with her or anything. I knew that there had been faulty equipment but I didn't know what it had meant, no one had ever sat down with us and said what had happened. The only explanation we ever really got was that Rachel would be a little bit slow and that maybe by the time she was five she would be slow walking and talking and everything. I didn't even know children who were handicapped, you know, born like that; I knew nothing about it at all. I just never realised that children could be like that.

Rachel is suing over the birth

Rachel is suing them. If she was going to do it she had to start to do it just before she was 16, which she did. It's up to her what she does. She said she wanted to and there is nothing to lose. I just got a letter from the solicitor to say that whoever is defending the hospital, they want it delayed for another three months. They've had three months to get everything together but they want another three months now so they can do it a bit more. Of course it was a long time ago so all the staff will have gone, and it will be difficult to trace everybody.

We were speaking to a couple of medical experts who came down to London and spoke to the Barrister. It has come as a shock to us really, but they said if somebody had held Rachel's head off the cord while they were preparing for a caesarean then she would have been all right. It took us 18 years to find that out. We were all sitting round a table just like this, talking, and then he just came out with it. He said, "Do you remember anyone holding Rachel's head?" And I said, "No, I'm sure I would have remembered." They said that if they'd held her head off the cord she wouldn't have cerebral palsy.

I'm not sure how Rachel feels about it. She's quite good really, Rachel, she just seems to get on with it. I don't think she thinks too much about things; it's part of the way she is. She's always out campaigning and always busy doing things; that's the way it's been all her life really.

Rachel's early life at home

Rachel cried constantly. I had to carry her about everywhere; I had one of those little baby slings. As soon as she woke up she cried. I used to say, "What's she crying for?", and the only explanation I got was, "Oh, it's just irritation on the brain." I gave her Calpol and hoped she would sleep; it was an absolute nightmare. It wasn't like an ordinary baby crying for food; she just cried constantly. I can still hear the noise of Rachel and the way she used to wind herself up and start crying!

We all got used to it really; everybody knew what Rachel and her cry was like. I could hear it when she wasn't there; it was just in my mind all the time! I didn't get an awful lot of help. My mum was good, she always supported us, but I think other people found it difficult as well, they didn't know how to cope, I think they were embarrassed.

We didn't get enough help

I remember asking for physiotherapy for Rachel, but whether it actually helped her I'm not sure. I obviously didn't think we were getting enough help because when she was about three we started going to a private clinic with her. That turned our world upside down completely because I had to have volunteers coming into the home all day, every day. There were exercises she had to do; at one point I had a big slide in the living room, and a hammock to do exercises! We started going because we felt helpless. We felt something had to be done rather than just sit about seeing this baby cry all the time. We knew there was intelligence there, as she was getting older you could see it, and I had managed to potty-train her. And she could answer 'yes' and 'no'. I knew she understood things I was saying.

It wasn't just physical stuff; she was learning to read and spell and open her fingers. I had to massage her face so her muscles wouldn't tighten up in her mouth and massage her tongue and get her to try and say little words. I thought it was really good. I enjoyed doing it. We did it for 13 years. We used to raise money any way we could.

I don't think the health service was very good

I would have liked it to have been different. If she had been getting ordinary services I think she would probably have gone into the system a bit more and into a special needs school. I was determined that she wasn't going to go.

We had a really excellent educational psychologist, and he started coming to the house. He was the type of person who would come, he would listen to you, and he wouldn't always agree with you; but whatever was said, he would go and do it. If he thought it was for Rachel he would do whatever we asked of him. He stuck by us all these years. He told us he would get Rachel to college before he left, and he did. So I've had his support through the years; any problems in the school I would just pick up the phone and say, "Rachel's missed out on this", or something like that, and he would be right down there and sorting it out for us.

When we were going to the clinic we would go down to Wales every three or four months. They would look at what Rachel had done and ask you what problems you'd had and what sort of help you thought she would need and then they would give you another programme. You had maybe ten programmes a day to do and they would last about half an hour each.

I couldn't have coped if I'd sat at home all day as she was. I think I got my support from people that were coming in. I felt we were really doing something and working hard. A lot of parents are just left to get on with it and they don't know what to do, so you just go out and find out things for yourself. You just get on with it. It's the best way I think.

We met quite a lot of families through going there and they all say the same, they just wanted to do something for their children, so obviously they felt as if they weren't getting enough help. It was stressful. I could see we weren't going to get the help that we wanted. It was made clear really right from the start. One of the doctors phoned me up and said, "I don't think you should go to this clinic; do you realise they are only vets?" Well, I said to her, "I think vets have more qualifications than doctors, don't they?" If I hadn't liked it I wouldn't have carried on with it. I wouldn't have done something to Rachel that I didn't think was right for her. They weren't offering any alternatives!

The Peto Institute
We did take a break from the clinic and went to the Peto Institute in Hungary for a while. You were in a big group of children but there weren't enough helpers. Rachel needed two people to work with her on the plinth so David and I sometimes used to go in together. After the Peto we went for an assessment and then stayed for a month. Then we went and stayed for six weeks and Rachel was in the Peto every day, Monday to Friday. I didn't find it was actually that good going over there. I found out they were going to set up a clinic at Longtown (nearby) in a big house and there was going to be a couple of what they call conductors like the girls that work in the Peto. I found out about that and decided to give that a try and go there.

We paid for the Peto and the psychologist arranged for us to go and meet the Director of Education. He came down and watched her on her programme and realised how good it was so they paid for the next visit to Hungary and then, when we didn't go back there they funded it for us to go to Longtown. I got travel expenses as well to take her. The Director of Education was good because he listened; he became quite friendly with Rachel. It all depends on the person really. I found that a lot over the years. I like to do things personally, it's the best way.

We never had a social worker
We never had a social worker for Rachel until recently; I don't know why that was. I don't suppose I ever had time to think about it, we were just too busy getting on with things. There used to be a nurse came round when Rachel got out of hospital; I suppose she was there for me, to see if I was all right. The social worker now takes so long to reply to letters. Since the psychologist

has gone, there's nobody like him now ... if there were any problems I would have asked him ... and he would have gone and spoken to everybody about it and he would have come back to us and said what's happened. Now he's gone, that's a real loss for us. We do cope all right, we tend just to get on with things ourselves really. We don't ask for much, but it's so much hassle when you ask for anything you just end up thinking, "What's the point?" If you want some equipment for Rachel you find it's easier just to go on and raise the money for her and get it.

The local community

Rachel's very involved in the village because I wouldn't send her away to school. I thought it was better if she stayed here where people knew us and could help us. The mothers would pop in and bring their children. A lot of Louise's friends were about as well, so Rachel's had a really good childhood as far as being involved in the local community, and then she went to local school. She didn't start with everyone else, that was the difficult part because they had to have a lot of staff in place for her to start at school and she could see people going down to school and she wasn't. That used to upset us a wee bit. But she eventually got there and they put the support in for her. It was OK; I wouldn't have had it any other way.

Rachel goes to college

She went to college and she got settled in and had a really brilliant support worker. This was at Carlisle College; she was still at school then ... So we just thought Rachel would carry on and Cath would go with her ... but there was this problem of transport, because she lives over the border they wouldn't fund her. They weren't going to back down and let Rachel go to college. The MP stepped in and there was so much support for Rachel. There are so many people that know her now and how she's struggled through her life and they understand. I think people quite admire Rachel and will support her so maybe all those people got together behind the scenes and said, "This lass should be going to college." Eventually they gave in and funded it. But she didn't get her support worker with her. She'd been with Rachel for seven years; they're really nice together and she really understood her. So Rachel has had all this hassle of getting to know everybody again. They didn't know how to communicate with her and she hated it when she first started going, she'd come home in tears, which is most unlike Rachel.

The college seems OK; I mean she seems quite happy. I don't think they do an awful lot with her. She's good on the computer. She works at People First; she's quite capable of doing stuff and that. But I don't think she gets the opportunities to do much at college. When she first started there she pressed something with her head attachment by mistake, and a rude message came up to a member of staff and they were offended by it. So the next day they didn't put her on the toilet and they said that if she could press a message like that then surely she can ask to go to the toilet. It was horrible. And then they would knock off the touch talker the minute she came through the door. So we had to go in and tell them eventually.

Usually me and David have to sort things out. You know, when something's wrong with Rachel. I know it seems like it's always us complaining about things for Rachel; it's difficult for her because people take advantage of her. They think she can't talk and so they do what they want to do. Its not like we control her or anything because she's really got a strong mind, but I always feel we've got to be there to make sure everything's done the way she wants it done.

Things could happen differently

Someone should have come and got to know Rachel and tried to communicate with her, spent a little bit of time with her before she went in to the college.

Usually I find I don't get on with professional people working with Rachel; it's just a job to them, that's how they see you. I don't suppose they have the time to get to know people. I've found the best support that I can get is from volunteers. They're there because they want to be there; they're not getting paid to be doing it. They're not walking away at five o'clock. They're there because they like Rachel and they want to be involved with her. I just never felt we got the help for Rachel that we wanted. We've had that many fights with people over the years. Just to get something for her, even.

Celebrating Rachel

It's wonderful the way Rachel has turned out and I think she just never lets anything get in her way. She's quite determined and she'll try anything. I think her character is really starting to come out, the person that she's turning into, and she's great! She really is. I hope it's something to do with the way that we've brought her up. She knows she will overcome everything and I've said I'll always support her in whatever she wants to do.

Rachel's future

Rachel says she wants to work, she wants to get a job, I wouldn't put anything past her. If she says she wants to do something she'll probably do it. I hope she wins this court case and I hope she has enough money to keep her going for the rest of her life. If I'm not around, I really worry about if anything happened to me, and she was left to fend for herself. If she wants a bit of equipment that she needs she'll be able to have it. It's nice to see her working. She's had boyfriends. She's done everything really that you would never have expected. She's experienced just about everything, I think.

She's in the campaign group at People First. She's involved in anything that really affects her life and her friends' lives. She'll get mad about things. Recently she's been left without a vehicle, Motability were going to leave us for weeks without any vehicle, so she's gone and campaigned about that. I think she likes to go round training people about disability and disability awareness. She likes to get out there and change people's attitudes. It's been great for her coming to People First. It's a good social thing for her as well. She's always been brought up in the family and in the village; she's always just been Rachel on her own in a group of people without learning difficulties. She goes out to clubs and she's probably the only one there in a wheelchair that goes into the clubs. I think coming here has maybe changed her outlook on life as well. She's speaking to other people and about their experiences, maybe realising she's not the only one.

She used to think about relationships and having a family. If Rachel put her mind to it she would. But, she's kind of gone off men at the moment; she finished with the last one. She said she would like children. She probably could have them you know, it's the getting them part that worries me with Rachel! There again if she met somebody and they wanted babies … another chapter …

Other people's attitudes

When Rachel was born I didn't know that children were born like that, I didn't know that there was such a thing. I think attitudes have changed. I see a lot more parents wanting their children to go to ordinary schools and buildings are getting changed and transport is getting changed, more so recently this past few years. I think more people, maybe more parents, are starting to realise they have got choices. More and more people aren't keeping their children at home and hiding them away. You've got to get out there and mix in with everybody and that's it. I'm very strong for integration. It is going to change.

I don't know where the idea came from for me, but it must have been there when Rachel was born, because right from the start I was not going to have her made different from anybody else. I just knew I had to do it and that was it. I didn't want her to be treated different from anybody else. I find even the doctors are more open-minded about things now. Our doctor, he's seen Rachel growing up over the years and seen what she has done. It's probably changed his attitude.

How my life changed through having Rachel

Having Rachel has changed my life completely. I don't realise because I do it every day. We do the same thing every day and it's not until she's away then I realise how different it is. I really don't know where we would be without

Rachel. I don't have a night out or anything; I do everything with her and her social life is my social life. It's strange.

I'm not very keen on leaving her. I mean she goes to college and things like that. I always like to know what she's been doing.

You have to be positive, I think. I've had my moments when I haven't been! You just have to get on with it and that's it. It's made me stronger; Rachel has just totally changed our lives but she's really enriched them. And I suppose it's changed our attitudes and everything to life. I wouldn't swap her for anybody else; I like her the way she is and the person that she is.

Chapter 20
A family's story

Sue Wilson, Jennie Harris and Norah and Jim Broadway

Volunteers willing to be interviewed for the Witnesses to Change project were sought from parents and carers of students at the adult college James Harris attends. Sue Wilson (James's mother) came forward and James's sister and grandparents were also interviewed. The following accounts are drawn from their own words and provide very different perspectives on what these family members have in common – the experience of living with James.

John Welshman

Sue Wilson (James's mother)
Early years

Before James was born, I had shingles. I had a really difficult pregnancy and I knew that there was something wrong with this baby. It was instinctive. I knew with my other children that they were OK before they were born. I knew that James wasn't. He didn't move much. After he was born, he had lots of different medical conditions. I couldn't get any answers out of the doctors, about what

Sue and James, 2002

217

damage he'd suffered, so I read it all up. I took it upon myself to go to the library and go through all the medical textbooks until I discovered what was wrong with him. I worked out that he had cerebral palsy. James had a physio that came to the house but she wouldn't tell me what was wrong. Eventually I had an appointment with the consultant when James was about nine months old and he confirmed that it was cerebral palsy. But after that, it always left me with an anxiety that it might be something else that they hadn't told me.

When there was a delay in James's diagnosis, I got very angry. I felt that it was important to be told straight away, at birth if possible. I felt I would have coped better if I had known, I wouldn't have all the anxiety of not knowing, all the anxiety of wondering what it might be. It was a relief to know exactly what was the matter with him and to start having some treatment for him. I was told when he was nine months. That doesn't seem very long now but at the time it did seem like an eternity.

Family life
After he was born, I knew that my marriage was very unhappy, but I knew that I could not face life as a single parent with one disabled child, so I made a conscious decision to have another child. I felt it was important for James to have at least one brother or sister, to have some sort of normal life. When I was a single parent with them, I think it was easier having two children than one.

When James and Jennie were small, it was very difficult to cope. I had a twin buggy that I used to have given to me regularly by social services. It would only last a few months and James would break it and they'd send me another one. He must have been in a pushchair until he was well over five or six. So Jennie was walking and running long before he was, and she's two years younger. She was out of nappies before him and talking. But she still had to get strapped in the twin buggy next to James because I couldn't cope with them.

I think it's been quite hard for Jennie. I think she's suffered quite a bit of neglect; her needs have had to come second to James's a lot of the time. It's been hard for my younger son as well, particularly when Joel has had to look after James, helping me to bring him up. He has been able to do that for him for a long time. I think James finds that hard.

We had no help from social services. I tried to get help but he was so violent, he really used to punch Jennie hard for no reason, his aggression was directed at Jennie. He grew from five foot two to six foot two in twelve months, so he had all that testosterone flowing round his bloodstream, he didn't know what to do with his anger. At that point, that was when I felt I couldn't cope any longer. Jennie was subjected to tremendous amounts of violence, and I tried to get respite care. We tried to get some sort of placement for him; we tried everything, and we got nothing.

As for my parents, I think they think James is a small boy, about nine years old. I know they know he's 24 but how much of that they accept, I really don't know. They won't let him drink any alcohol in their house.

I think James was a factor in the break-up of my first marriage. I don't think there was any chance that marriage would ever have succeeded anyway, but their father couldn't hack it, he just couldn't accept the situation really. James doesn't want any contact with his father at all. I think that was really good that he could choose to do that for himself, because I'd tried never to say anything negative about their dad and let them make their own decision.

My second husband has been absolutely fantastic really, because James was nine or ten when we met. Looking back, he just took on these two children as his own; he had no children of his own. He would only have been about 28 himself. He took the children on and he became their father and not only that, I went to university then and we had another child. He gave up his job to care for all three children for about five or six years till we swapped round again, and he's been great with James really.

Having a child with learning difficulties can be an isolating experience in lots of ways. I think we would turn to the family, whether it was the immediate family or the wider family, for support if we needed it, rather than friends.

Reward or burden?

James has been a really rewarding person to live with but then he has been, in lots of ways, quite hard work as well. People do enjoy his company; he is a joy to be with. He's a very happy person. The one thing that we find most rewarding about James is he doesn't question his mood, he is just happy. He doesn't get depressed; he does get angry but he doesn't have highs and lows. He's happy with his life and he doesn't have all the angst that all the rest of us have.

The harder things were in the early days – all the sheer physical hard work. When James was born there were no disposable nappies. James was in nappies until he was about five so I had two children in nappies at the same time. I must have spent my whole life washing nappies. Then there was all the bedding which he used to drench as well, even with nappies on, so it was physically hard. James's behaviour was often very difficult, absolutely hyper. He was very violent when he was a teenager, but when he was a small child his behaviour was very difficult. When Jennie was a baby I used to have to lock her bedroom door with a bolt because otherwise James could get out of his bed in the night and get her out of her cot because he couldn't sleep. Even with the bolts on the door, he'd break them down, so it was hard.

School/service provision

When James was little, we had a physio who used to come to the house and James was placed in a therapeutic nursery before he was one. The therapeutic playgroup had a physio and an OT and a speech therapist. James could go three mornings a week, and I went with him so it was very much a thing for the whole family. Both the mother and the child could work together on a whole treatment programme but most of it was physio for James.

By the time he was three, he was allocated a place in a special school, run by the Spastics Society in Cheltenham. We lived 20 miles from Cheltenham so it was quite difficult. I wasn't keen on him going to this school at all because of the taxi journey. I didn't let him stay. I took him out of the school and kept him at home again until his sister went to school. She was four and he was six. I took him back to the same school but we moved then after a year or so.

As for the social services department, their help is worse than useless. They want to impose their own ideas; they are very judgemental. The Children Act came out when James was about 14 or 15 and that made things so much worse for us. When we were trying to get respite care, to get a break for Jennie's sake because I was frightened he would do something serious to her, the social services were informed by the Children Act which said that the needs of the child must be taken into consideration. James was 'the child' and Jennie obviously wasn't, and because he didn't want to go to respite or any other place, his needs, his wishes were taken into account. That was one of the reasons why they weren't very forthcoming, even though my other child was at risk. I pointed that out to them at case conferences. I had to be restrained from hitting a social worker at one point – I've never hit anyone in my life – because she could do nothing to help find a placement, to give Jennie a break.

I think there have been a lot of changes in provision in the last 25 years. The one thing that is always important to me is the fact that there is nowhere, nowhere that James could now move on to that I would feel would be a safe, secure and loving home that he could live in. That's got to do with care in the community and the fact that there is such a drain on resources for that sort of provision. I think that for people who have homes to live in and families who care about them, those families are faced with very difficult choices. We're faced with the choice of allowing him to go and live somewhere else where he can have an independent lifestyle and perhaps make more of his own choices, but knowing that that care would possibly not be adequate for him. It's about the minimum ratio of staff to clients, the staff could be unqualified, they could be on low pay, they might be perfectly good-quality individuals, but making a short-term commitment to the person. The one thing people with learning disabilities need is continuity, they don't like change, certainly in terms of carers and daily needs.

Over the years, we've had a lot of contact with families who share our experience. We did belong to Contact a Family when we lived in Worcester, and for a while, when James was quite small, I worked as a play leader on a special adventure playground for children with all sorts of different problems. As he's got older I haven't really been involved with family organisations because it's just different with an older person. When he was small, I avoided any contact with those family organisations and I realise why. Because I was 24, and most of the other mothers, certainly mothers of Down's syndrome children, were in those days in their 40s. I had a fairly alternative lifestyle and I didn't fit in with any of those groups when he was small and I don't now he's older.

People's attitudes

I think people's attitudes have changed as James has got older. When he was small, other children were not tolerant and knew that there was something different about him and made fun of him. As he's grown older, he is a very personable person, he's friendly, he's happy, people like him, so that's good. Some people who don't know him still make fun of him, that happens, but he seems oblivious to that. He's well liked and accepted in society.

Terminology has changed in my lifetime. When James was a baby it was the Spastics Society, then mental handicap, and all of that changed after he grew up. I don't think the new terminology has been helpful, really, because James knows – or he did know when he was small – that he had a mental handicap, and he understood what that meant. Now he's had to adjust to having to understanding that he's got a learning difficulty and I don't think he's sure what that means really. I don't think anybody else is, because it covers a lot of things; it stretches the whole gamut from quite severe problems to people with dyslexia and all sorts of things, it's a bit too much of an umbrella term.

I think there is still a very paternalistic and patronising attitude. We've had experience of different organisations over the years. For instance, Rotary in Worcester raised loads of money for what they called 'handicapped children'. They wanted to send them to see Father Christmas in Lapland, which was a lovely idea. But this trip would have been wasted on James because he wouldn't have enjoyed the travelling, he wouldn't have understood much about it. Jennie would have loved it and it would have been great for her but she wasn't allowed to go. It was for handicapped children. A lot of them have those sorts of attitudes, that people with a disability are people who are in need, and that's not true either. I hope more is being done for siblings now but somehow I doubt it.

Work

It's been really difficult for James making friends with other people with learning difficulties. I think part of that's been his own choice; part of it's been that it's just been difficult for him. He's happy to go to the adult college and Piccadilly Gardens in the daytime and make friends there. He likes his life in little boxes and he likes to keep those boxes quite separate.

I think work and college enable him to be himself, to have a role in life, to value himself, to be valued by other people, to know what's expected of him in life. To have a role like everyone else, to get up in the morning and go out. That's I think its primary role and it gives him that opportunity to make those friends in the daytime.

The future

I choose not to think about the future. It's something I've had to think about a lot, since James was about 15. I've had to try and plan futures for him but you plan something and then it goes wrong and it doesn't happen. I've kind of got an idea in the back of my mind that I'd like him to go to a home farm trust, Steiner, or something like that. I'm 50 now, in ten years I'll be 60 and he'll be 35 and I do not want to be caring for a man of 35 when I'm 60. I know people of 60 nowadays are a lot younger than they used to be, but I still don't feel that that's what I want to be doing, I don't think it's right for him and I don't think it's right for me.

So I know that I've got to make some plans, not least because when I am too old or if I were to die, it would be so sad for him to have to go somewhere that he wasn't familiar with or cared for by people who aren't in tune with his needs. One thing I do know is that I don't want my other children to have to care for him if they don't want to. I think maybe when they're older they may want to, but certainly not while they're still young people and have got their own lives to live.

Feelings and fears

I get terribly anxious about him going out on his own. I have to try and just hold that down and know that he's perfectly capable of doing it. In the daytime, he can get the bus to my Mum's and pay for the bus even though he won't know very much about coins. He can get himself a bus ticket quite happily, get on and off the bus at the right place, get the right bus. He's perfectly capable of doing that but I do find that quite difficult.

I am worried about other people taking advantage of him. Somebody like James is terribly vulnerable to predatory men. If I had a daughter with learning disabilities, I hope that I would have given her as much freedom as I give James. It's so difficult, I want James to be safe, I'd want anybody to be safe.

I find it impossible to have any expectations of James, and that's not because I don't think he has any capability, because he has a lot of potential. You just have to learn to cope on a day-to-day basis and not look ahead because the future is always changing. You don't know what's going to be out there;

provision is always changing, the goalposts are always being moved. James surprises us all sometimes, he performs far better than we'd thought and sometimes at a much lower level than I expected, I never know what to expect with him. I never think about tomorrow if I can avoid it with James, there's lots of difficult decisions to make.

But I wouldn't have changed things. I'm glad, I feel privileged to be James's mother, he's a great person. Spending half of my life with James has certainly given me an experience that I wouldn't have wanted to change.

Jennie Harris (James's sister)
Early years
I can't really remember when I first became aware that James was different. I can't remember very much of when I was little, probably when I was about six or seven, maybe. He would have been about nine then. There's only two years between us. He's stayed at the same intellectual age as I was when I was younger.

We lived in Lancaster when I was about seven or eight and he did used to come out a play with us, out in the streets, but then when I got older, I didn't go out with him. I didn't really want to associate with him, because of his difference to everyone else, you know, not normal, name-calling and stuff. When I was a teenager, it was quite difficult, with friends and everything, to speak to them about it. Not many people have got anything like that. Now, it's much easier. I don't know if that's because I've got older or attitudes have changed.

James and Jennie at home in Worcester, 1997

Family life

James is mainly Mum's responsibility, but then if she needs me to come home to look after him, do whatever, I will, just because it's so difficult to find somebody to look after him, because Joel's not old enough. It's different for Joel, because there's such an age gap. Maybe it's because I used to look after Joel and Jim as well. Joel does have something to do with him, but not like I did, like caring. I'm not really sure if the fact that I'm his sister rather than his brother has made any difference. Maybe it has, because I'm a girl, because it's the role that women take, like the caring. I don't know.

I applied to quite a lot of different colleges, but they were all up in the north, so really I think James did have an effect on how far I moved from home. Maybe I didn't realise it. It's not far away so I can come back whenever I need to. Maybe if I was here all the time I would have more responsibility, I'm not sure.

I think my experience has been different to my Mum's and grandparents', because they're older, their attitude to life is different. People's outlook has changed, like Grandma is quite old fashioned in what she thinks. She doesn't treat him like he's 24, she treats him like he's still three, and maybe that's because how he is intellectually, but he's capable of doing much more than he was, if he was three years old. He shouldn't be seen as a three-year-old; he is 24. Mum doesn't treat him like that, because he goes out by himself.

Reward or burden?

People look on the negative side because they see the problems that you associate with discrimination and prejudice against people with disabilities, but they don't see the positive sides. For instance, he loves going out and meeting people. When my friends from university come, he loves speaking to them, he chats to anybody, which is quite good, he's got loads of company, I don't know where he's got that from. He doesn't really care what people think, which is a good thing in a way; there are negative things about people with disabilities in their portrayal.

School/service provision

When he was at the special school he used to go on trips all the time and we always used to wish that I could go, even if it was just to help. I wanted to go. He went to EuroDisney once, and on PGL adventure holidays, and I just used to wish that I could go with him because I thought I was missing out on something. Why is he so special, why has he got to go there when I haven't? I've just got to go to school.

There was no way he could have gone to a mainstream school. I don't think he could. I don't know if I would have wanted him to integrate in the same school that I went to.

People's attitudes

I think it's easier to have a brother with learning difficulties now than in the past because in the seventies they were locked away in asylums, institutions, and now because they've moved out into the community, people are seeing them more and people's attitudes are changing. Because people see them more, you know, they experience it more, their opinions change, they're less likely to be scared. They can see that you can do something, even if you have got a disability, you have got something to offer. I don't know what it was like when Grandma was younger but I know they were locked away. Now I think it is much better, more opportunity, and services are supposed to be better than in the past.

Work

It is good that he goes to the adult college, but then he's still separate from the mainstream, they're still in separate groups. Maybe if they were to mix together a bit more, then that would be even better because he would be mixing with people of a similar age, not intellectually, but you can still speak to them. The garden centre is good because people can see that it is possible to do something, even if it is only gardening, at least he gets something out of it, he enjoys it and it is doing something. He's got independence, he gets away from home instead of being stuck here all the time. He's doing something, he's learning.

The future

I don't know if he's going to carry on going to the college. He obviously can't go there forever. I don't know what happens when you leave. It would be nice for him to get like a job somewhere like Piccadilly Gardens, but I don't think he would be able to, wouldn't be able to cope.

I think about the future quite a lot, because what happens when they are not here any more, when Mum and Ross aren't here any more, what happens to Jim? Is it going to be me in terms of looking after him? Will I be the main person, or what will happen to him? Will he go to live somewhere else, in a home or something? I've no idea what's going to happen. It is quite worrying in a way because if he didn't have a disability, then we wouldn't be faced with that problem. Maybe it's because there's such an age gap between me and Joel and Joel and Jim, maybe I think it's more my responsibility to look after him when Mum and Ross aren't here any more. There's 12 years between him and Joel so it's quite a lot.

Feelings and fears

I don't worry about James; I worry about other people and what they could do, because he's quite vulnerable in a way. You can see that he doesn't understand what you're saying but he pretends that he does, he puts on a sort of front. He makes people think he's more intelligent than he actually is, so that that's a bit worrying when he's out. He's quite vulnerable, that's probably why he doesn't go out by himself.

Having James as a brother has been different to what everyone else has had, like friends and everything, but I don't know any different. It's been good in one way because you get to know what it's like, a different way of life. You get to meet different people. I think it has changed me, it has affected what's happened in my life, like what I want to do when I leave university. I'm doing a degree in disability and community studies and I want to work with people who have disabilities, so it has had an effect. I think that's partly because of James and what I've experienced.

I'm quite glad he is how he is now. Perhaps I wouldn't have said that a few years ago, maybe I would have wanted him to be 'normal', as it were, even though he was normal for him. He is normal. I don't really know what it's like to have anybody older who's 'normal', but now I don't think I would want to, I don't think I would want to change him. He's a good person to have as a brother.

Norah Broadway (James's grandmother)

Early years

When Susan was three months pregnant she had shingles, and she was having injections because she'd had miscarriages before that. Then, when she was having Jennie, she was having injections again and she read on the label that they shouldn't be given people with shingles, so we reckon that that is what caused the damage to James's brain.

James was lovely; he was the most beautiful baby and we always loved him, even when we didn't know there was anything wrong with him. But then he couldn't sit up. The first shock was when that physiotherapist used to come to him and she said he's spastic in every limb. We had a terrible shock then, he was only what, six months old, but we just got on with it. We accepted it right from the beginning.

I kept buying these books for him because I was determined my first grandchild, my first grandson, was going to be able to read. I bought books for reading and arithmetic and I used to lean over him when he was a tiny baby and I used to say to him "A, B, C, D". I wanted him to learn to read the same as his mother; I taught her to read.

James, Norah and Jennie, 1991

Family life

When James was young, he would spend most of the holidays with us, because Susan was working, and to give Susan a break, for James's sake. It's been hard work for Susan to have him all the time. We taught him to swim and everything; this is when we were 60. He's a good swimmer; he loves swimming.

James has learnt how to come over on the bus on his own. He buys his ticket and he gets off and I watch him there and I give him his dinner. When he comes to see us we take him out. He loves walking; we usually go out walking with him. All the residents all know him, he's so polite and he always speaks to them when he comes in.

We love all our grandchildren. We love Jennie in the fact that we can give her money. She understands it but I could give James £200 and he wouldn't have a clue what I was giving him. James and Jennie have got the same father but Joel's is different. We love Joel but we don't really know him. We know James and Jennie because they were there, we were there when they were born, we were there for years and years. The family came and lived with us when the parents got divorced. We knew them like our own children, but we're only just getting to know Joel. He's an independent boy, Joel can cope, he can fight his way in the world.

When they moved away we still kept very close in touch, coming over and seeing them, we were always up, getting the children. When James was at Dilston I was still seeing him all during the holidays. So we've always been in very close contact with James and Jennie. They were never close to their other grandparents; it's a shame.

The real reason we moved here, to Morecambe, was to help Susan look after James. But we also came up here to be near the grandchildren, because we were getting lonely down in Peterborough as we were getting older, there was nothing for us down there.

Reward or burden?

To us James has always been a normal child; we've never treated him as if there was anything wrong with him. He's been our grandson and he's been more than a grandson, he's been like our own child, because we lived in the same street. We looked after him a lot of the time. We've helped him in every way. I think the best thing for him as he got older was for him to go away to Dilston, because we protected him.

He's a credit to us. He's such a wonderful person; he's gentle. He's not a disappointment to me at all because he's not rough. When I see all these rough youths I think, "Oh, thank goodness James is not like one of them." But there again, you see, he'll never be like other boys. He's happy in his way though.

School/service provision

At Dilston they completely changed James. It made him grow up. By this time I think he must have been 17 or 18, but he was still a baby. But he's not a baby any longer. It's made him into a young man. Dilston did wonders for him. They taught him to travel on the train and they had bicycles up at Dilston too.

Susan moved to Lancaster; the services are much better there. She said it was no good, Worcester, it wouldn't have done him any good down there, there wasn't anything for him. I think Lancaster's excellent.

Work

He loves working at Piccadilly Gardens and he can ride his bicycle to get there, he loves riding his bike and he gets on well with them, although he gets very tired. I think it's excellent.

The future

We do worry about the future, but I'm sure Susan will always look after him, Susan will always provide for him. I'm sure Jennie will, and I'm sure Joel will. Joel thinks the world of James and James thinks the world of his brother. It would be nice if James could meet somebody, some companion. People do, don't they?

Feeling and fears

We do worry about him, at least I do. When we take him down to the prom on his bicycle, to see him off and we worry the whole time until he's got home.

Somebody could stop him on the cycle track. I'm going to get him a mobile phone so that if anything did happen to him, he could be in touch with his mother. We do worry about him. He's such a lovely looking boy and he's tall, people don't think he's retarded so they just accept him and he goes off on his way, but if anything happened to him on the cycle track he would be so nervous, he wouldn't know how to cope.

We would have loved it if James had been a perfect baby, but you've just got to accept that's the way he is, and he's our grandson. He doesn't ask for anything; he's always happy, content. He loves coming across here, I don't think we can do any more than we're doing.

Jim Broadway (James's grandfather)
Early years
When James was first born, we didn't realise first of all what was wrong with him. You can always speculate on what caused the problem but the thing is trying to help. What caused it is quite irrelevant now. It's possible when they're born they get starved of oxygen because of something technical, being born they're given oxygen. That makes them cry and get their lungs to open, and if they're short of oxygen at the beginning of birth, some of their brain cells can be affected, so they say. I'm not an authority on it, I don't know.

We were a little bit put out, or concerned, and we did everything we could to try and improve his babyhood. Norah has felt she was over the top in trying to buy books and reading matter, to try and improve his reading ability, because it was obvious right from the very beginning that he had no conception of words. She thought she was dealing with a normal child, you see.

They told us he was spastic in every limb. I'm not sure if I accepted it that quickly. He has got some spasticity in one of hands. His digits aren't working correctly, and that makes him look a bit stupid sometimes, especially when he was a lot younger.

Family life
We lived near Sue and the children until James was about nine years old, I think, when they got divorced. They were living with us for a while in Cheltenham. I had to go and meet Jennie from school. James was brought home, he was at special needs school; it's always been like that. And then Sue decided she wanted to go to Lancaster University, but we've always been in close contact with them. We live near them again now and James comes over regularly. We help all the grandchildren, but we give more to James because he needs it more, although we're helpful, to Jennie and Joel.

Reward or burden?

I don't see how you can say there can be a reward. The only reward you have is if you have perfection. Most mothers, you know what mothers are, they've got the most beautiful babies there are and that's what you want, a perfect baby, now to have an imperfect baby cannot be a reward, can it? I mean imperfect in any way, some are more imperfect than others.

If you're of a religious nature and you think that a child comes from God, then it could be a reward, but I don't think that. I'm not a religious person so I don't think children come from God or anywhere else, come to that. That's the way a reward would come, if you thought it came from God. There can't be a reward to have to look after a child with learning disabilities, I mean James is quite good compared to some of them. Some of them who are really disabled, why should children be born like that and have to suffer like that to enable somebody to be rewarded? That is wrong in its own right. I mean, it depends how you look at it, you can have different views, and I have that view. It's not a strongly held view, it's merely something I would state if I was asked. I don't go around spouting about it.

School/service provision

James went to a school for special needs. He was picked up in the morning from the time he was four years old, to take him to Cheltenham playschool. So he's always been looked after in that respect. There has been a responsibility to try and get him to school and sort of looked after for school, get him ready for school in the morning. A bit of handful when he was very young, you know, couldn't keep still.

People's attitudes

I think people have always accepted James. When he was very young he wasn't accepted by the other children, they hadn't met people like James before, but I think most people accepted him. He's not obviously retarded.

Work

He does apply himself to what he's capable of. He doesn't shirk anything, he goes to college in the evening and although he probably doesn't take a lot of it in, he still goes, he still tries to do something, he doesn't shirk it at all, or he doesn't appear to anyway. His work in Piccadilly Gardens takes a lot out of him mentally. When he does anything he gets tired, the mental effort is shown in tiredness, that's where his energy is exhausted. He's strong enough in his own right, in his limbs.

James in 1997, aged 21

One gets the impression sometimes he stands back and lets things happen to him. I think when he's taken his own responsibility, say, for travelling he can do some things. I don't know how much. A part of his brain that does the reasoning doesn't appear to be all that strong, some of the cells are missing. I think it was obviously when he was born.

The future – feelings and fears

I don't worry about James when he's on his own. Norah worries about things more than I do, but he's got to be able to go somewhere on his own. What I concern myself with is when we're not here, when we're no longer able to do anything for him. I'm 82 now, you see, and Norah's 77, and Susan's 50. We're all getting older and who's going to worry about him, because he needs somebody to be responsible for him? Jennie and Joel have their own lives to live, and when they marry somebody, they make a contract with somebody else, they can't give everything to James, the other people might object. There's always that thing to be taken into account. I don't think James will ever meet somebody, like a companion.

I don't think there's much can be done; all we can do for James is what's being done, and that's it. I would like to be able to help him. As long as there's somebody that can be responsible for him. I mean, where he is at the moment, he's in good condition, people are looking after him and he's able to look after himself in some ways, and while that continues in that vein then I'll be quite happy. It's when it doesn't continue in that vein, when those services are withdrawn from him, that I might worry a bit.

I don't think we can do anything more than we do. He likes coming across here and having a meal and going for a walk on the prom, that sort of thing, he doesn't ask much of life. I'd say that for James, he has tried. But I'd say a lot of that has to do with because Norah helps him to try, encourages him. He's a nice boy. I always feel in my mind I feel sorry for him because he can't live a normal life. I think he's happy in his own way.

Chapter 21
No turning back

Jan Thurlow

I contacted Jan Thurlow, having been put in touch with her through a friend, and asked her to contribute to this book. In response, she wrote this chapter about the early years with her daughter Clare.

Sheena Rolph

It was about 6pm on the evening of Saturday 18 June 1977, after a long labour, that my second child entered the world. I felt both exhausted and exhilarated at knowing that my two-year-old son would have a sister, both grandparents would have their first granddaughter and I would be able to have the pleasure, one day, of sharing in the feminine interests girls like to pursue. I lay back on my bed feeling deeply satisfied.

Clare

My daughter, who we named Clare, was taken away as soon as she was born. The midwife told my husband and me that before we could see her she would need to be cleaned and wrapped in a foil blanket to keep her warm before going into an incubator as she was premature in weight, cold and blue. We accepted her explanation without question; as our two-year-old son was small at birth we thought nothing of it. As I needed stitches, my husband was asked to leave the room while the nurse prepared me for the Doctor, who was on his way. As I lay waiting, I was aware of a flurry of activity and muffled voices deep in conversation in the next room, but I could not hear what they were saying. The Doctor arrived, making light of having to carry out a job that seemed pretty undignified. After he had finished, the doctor left the room, a nurse helped to make me comfortable, and invited my husband to join me. The doctor returned, perched on the edge of my bed leaning towards me, and announced he had some bad news. He was sorry to tell us our baby had Down's syndrome as she had epicanthic folds of skin on the inner parts of her eyes and a transverse palm crease in each hand.

The news was a mixture of both shock and disbelief; all I wanted was to hold my baby and see her for myself. I had no idea what epicanthic folds or transverse palm creases were, and felt a little unsure as to what I was going to see. My fears were groundless. Clare was brought to me, snuggled in a blanket, with her tiny face just visible. She was beautiful, very tiny, but beautiful.

The doctor left my husband and me clinging to each other, crying tears of mixed emotions as we cradled Clare in our arms.

Little did we know that the news we received that day was to change the course of our lives as we entered the world of the service system, a world that in relation to children and adults with a learning impairment is often called 'special' but which has come to me to mean separate. My introduction to the world of the 'separate' began when I was wheeled into and remained in a side ward for the rest of my stay in the maternity hospital instead of being taken into the larger ward with all the other new mums. To this day I have never figured out if this separation was for my benefit or the other mothers. Perhaps hospital staff were unsure as to how I would react to hearing the news about my daughter's impairment and they did not want to risk me upsetting anyone else. Perhaps the staff thought it would be best for me to be away from the other mothers as they had their babies by their bedside, and they wanted to save me any upset in explaining why my baby was still in the baby care unit in an incubator. I never did find out the basis of their decision.

Even though I knew nothing about Down's syndrome, its cause and effects, I did know, through the haze of tiredness and emotions, that my bond with Clare was strong from the moment I held her. I knew Clare would be deeply loved, no matter what. She would be a truly welcome member of our family, and we would assist her with whatever she needed, to help her grow, develop and learn, but most of all to be accepted for who she was, even though I knew that she was lying premature, being tube-fed in an incubator. I willed so hard that she would live, so that my dreams of her running around, laughing, playing with her brother and enjoying family life could be fulfilled, despite her needing extra help. Thankfully, after a few days, the doctors thought Clare was strong enough to leave the incubator in the baby-care unit and stay in a cot by my bedside.

What I was not prepared for were the negative images portrayed to me by some of the medical profession. On day four of Clare's life a doctor walked in and abruptly told me not to bother to try to breastfeed her because 'they' don't suck very well. It was as if 'they' were aliens from another planet. Besides, little did he know, this negative prediction was far from the truth. As tiny as Clare was she had a strong suck and drank her milk as if it was going out of fashion. Over the next few days of my hospital confinement there were more negative comments that hurt my feelings: things like "she probably won't talk because she has a big tongue", or "she probably won't walk because 'they're' usually floppy". On one occasion a doctor swept into my room, looked down at Clare, snug in her cot, and in a rather offhand manner flippantly suggested that I should go home and have more children, then promptly left. I felt quite shocked at this remark, which was so insensitive because it seemed to offer no validation of Clare as a person, or offer any consideration for my feelings. The very thought of having more children within a few days of giving birth was the last thing on my mind or, I would imagine, on any new mother's mind, for that matter.

Perhaps the worst comment of all was the cold, clinical statement: "They don't usually live beyond the age of five", which was blurted out by a nursing sister. This was a comment I knew I would never forget as it cut to the core of me. How could anyone say such a thing? Thinking is one thing, saying is another. Besides, how would the sister know unless she, like the other bringers of gloom, had mystical powers and could see into the future? What seemed strange was that nobody predicted when my son was born what he would or wouldn't do in his future life or how long he might live. I couldn't see any difference. Yes, I wanted to know more about Down's syndrome, as well as the best way of stimulating my baby, who I accepted might possibly be slower at learning new things than some other children, but the negative remarks and ill-informed prognosis were just unhelpful and hurtful. All I longed for was to take Clare home, away from the clinical world of hospital professionals and back to the security of my family, to get on with life in the best way I knew how.

Homecoming
Having experienced the negative, hurtful images portrayed regarding Clare in the hospital, I was keen to avoid a similar sort of thing when I arrived home. I did not want to be faced with the stumbling hesitation or awkwardness some people show when they first meet someone who has just been bereaved and cannot find the right words to say. I did not want to be treated in that way. Clare had not died; on the contrary, she was very much alive. But what I hadn't anticipated, and was quite surprised by, were the different responses from people I knew, or was acquainted with, when they heard our news. Those who did not know me very well brought me flowers and cards with emotional verses. Later, I discovered some I knew well wondered whether to send a birth celebration card or not, but thankfully they decided to. Others felt unsure as to what to say to me, and a couple of people whom I expected to be understanding and accepting just seemed to avoid seeing me for a while. One lady I sometimes chatted to at the local shop was convinced that disabled children were a punishment for some wrongdoing in a previous life. Whose previous life, Clare's or mine, I was not sure, but I never waited around to find out.

All I knew was that my closest friend, who was more like a sister even though she lived in another county, my parents, brother and husband, would be an anchor of love and support as we entered the unknown. Sadly, I was unsure of the reaction from my elderly mother-in-law, who initially found it hard to look at or even hold our baby. I knew the family were initially shocked on hearing Clare had Down's syndrome, but their responses were positive, which reassured me. I also realised everyone had a different way of coping with this unexpected news, and I tried to understand my mother-in-law's response or lack of it. Was she hurt for her son? Was she worried about how he would cope? Did she possibly feel disappointed? Did she blame me? Or was she just overcome with a sort of grief? What I just could not figure out was how she could not look at or want to hold Clare for some weeks after she was born; after all she was just a baby, a lovely, tiny, vulnerable baby.

I tried very hard to understand my mother-in-law, who found it hard to express her feelings. But after some weeks she told me that, in her days of midwifery and nursing training during 1920s, babies with Down's syndrome or other obvious impairments were allowed to die as it was thought to be for the best. I was horrified at such a thought, and while it sounds unkind or disloyal to her to even mention any of this, it made me realise what negative attitudes and values invaded and still invade the medical profession and society at large. While I never knew what my mother-in-law really felt about Clare, thankfully, over time she came to show a great love and kindness to her.

The first year

Like most parents of new infants, we made new discoveries about Clare. From the time she was newborn, we noticed that she had no involuntary reflexes to grip like babies usually did, and she also had the predicted low muscle tone associated with Down's syndrome. These things in themselves were not a great worry because we knew, with regular daily physiotherapy, even in play form, her muscles would grow stronger. My greater concern was for the unusually jerky head movements combined with a cry, that she showed when she was held over my shoulder after a feed, as well as the regular occurrences of upper respiratory infection, accompanied by serious bouts of croup. The dry, hoarse-sounding cough racked her tiny body, leaving her exhausted and her face tinged with purple as she struggled to breathe. Although we kept a croup kettle going in her room during these attacks, it brought little relief, and many times she would end up being admitted as an emergency to the children's ward of the general hospital, where she would spend several days in an oxygen tent. The ward became quite a familiar place to me as I stayed with her, willing her not to die.

Having had the experience of raising my son, I had some idea about the developmental milestones children usually went through. While I tried not to compare Clare with other children of the same age, it was easy to see that her development was very slow. Instead of her smiling at six weeks, it took six months, but it was still a very exciting moment to witness. At a year old, Clare was still unable to sit unaided despite the regular physiotherapy.

To compensate, I used to prop her up with lots of cushions in her pram so she could see what was going on around her.

It was around this time that the local authority began to provide home tutors for pre-school age children with 'special needs'. The tutor visited once a fortnight and set Clare new tasks each time she came. Unfortunately, she was unable to accomplish any of the set tasks, regardless of how much time the tutor and I spent working on them with her. There were times when I sensed the tutor's mild frustration at this lack of progress, but I kept telling myself we were not in a race, and that

Clare at 18 months, just sitting

every child varied. While on one level I tried to develop a philosophical attitude, on another level I began to question myself and wonder if I was doing enough to help her, even though I regularly spent time each day giving her physical and sensory stimulation designed for young children by the Down's Association. Despite Clare's need for lots of attention, I was very keen not to neglect my son who also needed my time and attention, and finding a balance as a mum and just purely enjoying my children was very important to me.

I felt pressure each time the home tutor visited, and because of this it came as no great disappointment when I learned she was leaving the area and a replacement could not be found. I suppose, looking back, I did not want anyone else to say anything derogatory about Clare. Another doctor who visited my home to assess her had already told me that she had a severe mental handicap and would probably need institutional care by the time she was five years old. The idea appalled me and all I wanted was for these bringers of gloom to go away.

As with any new baby, the first year was a challenging one, often dotted with sleepless nights. But, for us, there were added, new concerns. While Clare had a healthy appetite, which was wonderful, mealtimes took a long time, as she could not chew and had a tendency to choke easily unless her food was well puréed. Her jerky head movements were increasing and this was put down to poor digestion and poor muscle tone. Her ability to track objects reassured me that she could see, even though her hearing was in question. Despite these things, I instinctively felt she had another underlying problem, but I didn't know what.

A new diagnosis

It was when Clare was about 15 months old that I bravely accepted the offer of leaving her at a nursery, run by our local Mencap Society, especially designed to give mums a break for a few hours a week. I say bravely, because I had never left either of my children with anyone other than a family member, usually my mother. The nursery was situated in the town centre, convenient if I wanted to shop. While I was reluctant to leave Clare at first, part of me wanted the independence from using my mother to look after her, no matter how willing she was to help. I felt she had done enough, and had difficulties in her own life to deal with, as well as getting older and more tired herself. Leaving Clare at the nursery gave me the valuable opportunity of spending time with my son on our own before he began nursery school. It also turned out to be a blessing as one of the qualified nursery nurses noticed Clare's jerking head movements and asked if she was epileptic. Not knowing, seeing, or having had any experience of epilepsy, and certainly never thinking that the head-jerking movements could be a form of seizure, I felt a strange sort of relief that someone else thought that Clare could possibly have other medical problems, and that this was not my imagination.

With the suggestion of epilepsy in mind, I returned to my GP, who referred Clare to a paediatrician who in turn carried out an EEG. It confirmed that she had a type of epilepsy, which the paediatrician told us would be difficult to control. That was probably one of the more accurate prophecies, because, despite a cocktail of medication, as Clare grew, her seizures changed and became worse. I found them distressing to witness, but what they were like for her to endure I'll never know, particularly when she went from one fit into another, going blue through lack of oxygen and gasping for breath. All I knew was that Clare could not be left unattended. The seizures came viciously and abruptly with no warning, leaving her limp and exhausted.

The 'special' school

While we were coming to terms with coping and dealing with Clare's epilepsy, and making trips backwards and forwards to the hospital fortnightly, I was introduced to another part of the world of the 'special' – a special school. Clare had not attended the local Mencap nursery many times before it was announced it was going to close. The head teacher of the local special school held a meeting and announced he wanted to offer nursery places in his school to the children who used the Mencap nursery. The school could offer more facilities, teaching input and funding, and mums could continue to have a break in the knowledge that their children would receive appropriate stimulus, physiotherapy, speech therapy and hydrotherapy. The idea sounded reasonable enough, so it was arranged for me to visit the school with Clare.

I had no idea of what to expect on my first visit. My only comparison was the Mencap nursery. The special school was in the grounds of a long-stay institution, built originally to serve the children and young adults resident in the institution, and the journey through the large, wrought-iron gates round the grounds of the institution unnerved me. On entering the school my heart sank as I saw the classrooms with the contorted bodies of children lying on beanbags. I was upset seeing so many disabled children in one place, motionless, staring up at the mobiles hanging over them. I reassured myself that probably more activity went on than one snapshot visit could show, and reminded myself that each of the children was some mother's son or daughter who loved and cared about them.

By the time I reached the head teacher's office, I had already decided this was not the place for Clare. Maybe I was in denial, I don't know. Maybe it was because Clare did not have the same physical impairments as the other children I had seen. I could not pinpoint why but I had an overwhelming sense this was not the right place, and if Clare attended the school I had let her down. All I wanted to do was run out of the place with Clare in my arms, go home and shut the so-called world of the 'special' away. Despite the strong urge to leave, I did not give in to my emotions, and instead spent the rest of the afternoon talking with the head and nursery class teacher. Thinking I might have some concerns or feel insecure about leaving Clare at the school, the perceptive headeacher arranged for me to meet some parents whose sons and daughters were attending the school as day pupils. The parents spoke very highly of the quality of the teaching and the care the teachers took. In my heart I knew that early learning was crucial to Clare's development, regardless of how quick or slow her pace of learning would be, so it seemed unfair not to give her this opportunity.

The following week I took Clare for a few hours to school and put her in the capable hands of her teacher, a lovely lady. Feeling overwhelmed and not knowing if I wanted to go or wanted to stay, I retreated to my car, where I sat and wept. Who the tears were for, I do not know, there were too many mixed emotions to decide. It was some time later I learned that many new parents on their first visit to a special school reacted in similar ways to mine, thinking that their children should not be there either. It was some comfort to know that my reaction was not out of the norm.

An 'overprotective' mother?

Despite Clare's growth and her newly diagnosed epilepsy, I instinctively felt that she still had some underlying medical problems, but again I did not know what. All I knew was that the daily routine of physiotherapy and playful stimulus, combined with the extra help from school, was having little effect on her development. She was also at times very lethargic. I felt sure that when I raised these concerns with the paediatrician he thought I was fussing, overprotective or even overreacting, and did not really take me seriously. All he seemed to say was that Clare had one of the severest cases of Down's syndrome he had seen. As the weeks passed, little changed for Clare except she seemed to sleep more and more. I realised the cocktail of medication for her seizures could have some side effects and might be making her more sleepy. In our fortnightly consultations, I asked the paediatrician if he would carry out further blood tests to put my mind at rest, to which he agreed. A week later it was confirmed that the blood test showed Clare was suffering from hypothyroidism, an underachieving thyroid gland, which causes brain damage if not treated in the first year of life. This was another blow as Clare by this time was almost three years old.

No wonder Clare could not do many of the tasks the home tutor had set, no wonder she could not sit unaided at a year old, no wonder she was so lethargic. I just could not understand why the hypothyroidism had not been picked up sooner, particularly as it only took a simple blood test, of which Clare had had many in her short life. The only explanation I was given by the paediatrician was that the physical signs of hypothyroidism were masked by the Down's syndrome. Here was yet another thing Clare had to live with, and my only way of coming to terms with this added impairment was being thankful that the diagnosis was made when it was; left much longer and the consequences would have been dire. It was just Clare's ill luck that screening for hypothyroidism was not routine when she was born, as I believe it is now.

Thankfully, the daily thyroxin treatment meant that Clare had more energy and strength. She learned to crawl in a fashion and generally be more active, giving her opportunities to explore things around her. Her poor co-ordination meant she lacked the pleasure and independence most toddlers enjoy from finger-feeding themselves, and her inability to concentrate to hold a spoon or a feeder cup for more than a second or so meant someone had to hold their hand over hers while she did so. But we would not give up on her. Clare's class teacher was a gem and devised a way of working on each task, developing a programme that could be followed through at home as well. It was during our discussions about the best way of working together that it really hit me just how much we all take so many things for granted. What further challenges were ahead for her, I wondered?

As Clare grew and generally became more alert and active, there was a point where I thought she was having too much thyroxin, because combined with her ever-increasing seizures, she slept very little at night even though she looked and seemed very tired. As soon as she was awake, she was wide awake and ready for action. She couldn't be soothed or coaxed to go back to sleep, despite it being two, three or four in the morning. This pattern of sleepless nights was almost a way of life. To try to offset this, my husband and I did a sort of shift system, taking turns to be with Clare in these twilight hours, so each of us could get some rest. As my husband had a demanding job to do during the day, tiredness took its toll on him. In an attempt not to wake my son and allow my husband to sleep a bit more, I invariably took Clare downstairs to the sitting room so she could play and work off some excess energy. I lay on the sofa watching her, so at least I could rest my body even though I couldn't sleep. I cannot begin to count the amount of new dawns I saw breaking, and the piles of ironing I got through in the wee small hours.

Over the next few months I became more and more exhausted. I was also pregnant with my third child. I do not feel it fair to go into detail about the difficulties we encountered living with and trying to manage what I call the 'fallout' of Clare's impairment, as it was not her fault. All I knew was that I felt burned out, and reached a stage where I was desperate for practical hands-on support coming in to my home regularly day and night to help me with Clare. The head teacher at school arranged a meeting with a social worker in my home so we could find out what services were available to help us.

The world of social services
My husband and I had never encountered the world of social services before, so assumed, rightly or wrongly, that they would be able to help us. Unfortunately, the first meeting with the social worker about Clare, who was seen by them to have 'special needs', was where I learned again that 'special' really did not mean special. At least not in relation to one of the dictionary definitions of the word, which means 'additional to ordinary'. I logically thought that there would be additional help and support services to supplement the ordinary. The ordinary to me was Clare living in our family home.

On the contrary, the newly qualified social worker who met with us was more interested in practising her psychology on me, as she asked if I felt guilty when I had had Clare. I deeply resented this question, partly because I did not feel at all guilty when Clare was born, and partly because the issue of whether I felt guilt or not was absolutely nothing to do with requesting more help at home. In the next breath the social worker then went on to inform us that, because of lack of resources for children's services, the only thing on offer was long-term fostering. This bald suggestion stunned me and I felt hurt and offended. Being exhausted did not make us unsatisfactory parents; not, that is, unless the fosterparents recruited by social services were superhuman. The thought of Clare leaving our family was upsetting enough, let alone passing her over to foster-parents I did not know. I could not even begin to visualise this faceless couple who would be bathing, dressing, or making decisions for and about my child. Besides, what if I bumped into the foster-couple with my daughter in the town and did not like how they treated her or how they had dressed her. I also wondered if their energy levels would flag too? Would they be as patient with her? Would they go the extra mile and stay up all night if necessary? Would they run out of energy too? More importantly, would they love and accept her like we did?

Even though I felt desperate for support, this was not the support I had in mind; the whole idea of long-term foster-care for Clare just seemed to insult me and undermine my role as a mother, and ours as a family. While the policy of foster-care may be centred only around the interests of the child, our child was part of our family, and to me these two interests could not and should not be treated in isolation from one another. All we wanted was a few hours a week of practical assistance in our home to help me help Clare and my other children. It didn't seem a lot to ask.

Chapter 22
A blessing in disguise

Joyce Mays

Joyce Mays lives in London. I was put in touch with her through a friend and asked her if she would contribute to this book. Within a short time, she had sent me this chapter describing family and community life with her daughter Emma.

Sheena Rolph

Where to begin?
It's funny how one puts things off for ages before suddenly making a start on some task. Some months ago we were approached to see whether we would be interested in contributing Emma's story to this book. The question is – why sit down and start today?

Emma and me, 1996

I guess the answer to that is that this weekend we celebrated Emma's twenty-first birthday. A special birthday for a special person, and we celebrated in style! A surprise party with Emma's friends, a meal out with the family, a fuss in our synagogue on Saturday and, after the sabbath, a West End show.

243

What shall we tell you about Emma? Her birth? Early years? Struggles over education? The impact on our family? The impact on our community? Where we are now? Our hopes, and fears, for the future? Or maybe we should just focus on more positive aims – what can we communicate which would help others deal, directly or indirectly, with similar situations? This last option is the most tempting and so probably worth resisting. Tempting because it offers a 'cop-out'. Maybe this way we can avoid answering the first questions, which are more personal and painful.

Our family

To explain a little about us as a family, we are an orthodox Jewish family and have always been closely affiliated to our community. Orthodox Judaism demands quite a high level of self-discipline. There are strict dietary laws affecting what we may or may not eat. We keep Shabbat – which means that Saturdays are a day of rest. We go to synagogue, we do not work, travel in cars, watch TV or operate other electrical equipment. Shabbat therefore provides a sharp distinction from the hustle and bustle of everyday. It is a tranquil day spent with family and friends, taking the time to take stock and do some thinking and resting. Alan has a fine baritone voice and takes an active part in the synagogue service, and Shabbat mealtimes are a noisy affair in our house as I enjoy singing too.

Emma and Mark

Alan and I married young. Like most young couples we were struggling financially. Alan was a law student when we met and I was still at school doing A levels. I gave up thoughts of further education, found a job, and we married when I was 21. Mark was born a couple of years later, and we felt very blessed. He was a bright, contented baby with a huge smile, sunny personality and loving nature. We thought we appreciated how lucky we were. We were wrong. It was only after Emma's birth that we truly appreciated how fortunate is the gift of a healthy, normal baby. Emma was born on 27 January 1981. Mark was then three years old.

Emma's arrival – so many questions, not many answers!
My pregnancy with Emma was entirely unremarkable for the first eight months. I have never suffered morning sickness, and apart from feeling tired in the early months, otherwise felt fine. I don't remember having even a cold; I was careful about diet, even giving up artificial sweeteners on the grounds that they were 'chemical'. There is no family history of any type of abnormality in either of our families. Mark was by then attending a small morning playgroup nearby, Alan had qualified as a solicitor and I was happy as a full-time mother.

When I was 34 weeks pregnant a routine scan picked up an excess of amniotic fluid. We were told in 60 per cent of cases this meant nothing. However, in a minority of women, it could indicate a problem with the pregnancy. I was not unduly anxious, probably partly because I am a born optimist and convinced myself I would form part of the trouble-free majority, and partly because the ultrasound operator had seemed hesitant and uncertain. In the early 1980s ultrasound was far less precise than it is today. However, then, as now, the quality of information depends largely on the skill of the technician. I was asked to return for another scan, which I did two weeks later. The second scan still showed excess fluid. The operator was unsure about the baby's measurements and thought the head was large in proportion to its body. A second scan operator was consulted who decided the reverse – the abdomen was large relative to the head!

Alan is not a born optimist. He had been suffering pangs of anxiety throughout the two-week wait and was now very worried. I was even more convinced that nothing whatever was wrong, and that the scan technicians would not be capable of diagnosing their way out of a paper bag. In any event, so close to the birth there was nothing to be done. As a precaution it was decided that the paediatric team should be alerted when I went into labour in the event that the baby had a bowel blockage.

The labour was long but straightforward. I remember the births of all my children vividly – not the pain, because pain can never be accurately recalled – but the exhaustion of the last pushes and, eventually, the relative speed and 'swoosh' of the baby's body slipping out. I remember my immediate rush of excitement, disbelief and joy at having a daughter. I remember my immediate rush of love. Then I just remember silence. Emma did not cry, and she was a dark blue, dusky colour. The student doctor who delivered her, nurses and paediatrician all fell silent. It took several minutes to register this as strange. I could see her taken to a table on my right, and could see a small foot waving in the air. Her colour worried me, as did the lack of a cry, and the foot, I could see, was definitely an odd shape. No one answered the obvious question – 'What's wrong?'

As it turns out, no one was able to answer that question fully for a long time. I remember, too, how the midwife wrapped her and said, gently and carefully, that there were quite a few problems, and would I just like to hold her? I took that as a code for 'Would you just like us to do nothing for her?' She was still a blue colour and barely breathing. I looked at her briefly, took in her small but pretty face and quickly replied that I would rather they got working on the baby and get her breathing. Before taking her to the special care unit, the midwife said she wanted to point out Emma had some abnormalities, a cleft palate, for example. I remember responding sharply that it was probably fixable, and could they please get her breathing properly. Even in the few minutes before this brief conversation I could almost palpably feel my insides turn numb and icy. My brain, however, seemed to click into a mode of what I can only describe as 'hyper-clarity'. Although I was shocked to the core, I seemed to enter this exceptionally clear mental zone. It is a state I am struggling to describe in words. I think of myself generally as a clear-thinking, logical and rational person but this was far from normal. I noticed Alan's tears with cool detachment, and felt momentary irritation, which I brushed away as unhelpful.

I asked to see a paediatrician as soon as possible, and cursed the epidural top-up administered late in labour, which had now temporarily physically paralysed me. Alan and I were left alone. Alan was very emotional – all I wanted to do was get to the special care baby unit. No porters and wheelchairs were available, so with Alan's help and that of a student midwife, I was dragged upright and tried to force life back into my legs. I don't remember how I got to the special care unit in the end – but I do vividly remember the battle to walk.

I think I remember all of this because it is a metaphor for the beginning of the struggle. I remember feeling amazed at the surge of strength, both physical and mental, that I experienced at that time. I felt no physical pain and immediately felt quite certain that we could face whatever was in store for us. For me, at that moment, there was truth in the belief that at times of crisis one is 'given strength'. Equally, I am sure it is true that for many the complete opposite must seem to be the case, and they apparently crumple and collapse.

Certainly Alan and I seemed as polar opposites in those early weeks, and I am ashamed now in the light of later events to recall my impatience with – and even envy of – his ability to cry openly. I saw tears as a luxury I could not afford; in any case I felt emotionally frozen. With hindsight I think this was actually deep shock. I describe it now because I think it is important to realise that parents and relatives experience a variety of reactions, all equally valid and needing empathy and support. There is no 'normal' reaction to the birth of an abnormal child. I remember people telling me I *should* cry – all well and good if you can.

As it turns out my 'freeze' lasted for about two years. I did cope incredibly well in the immediate crisis, but when things started to stabilise and Emma was out of immediate danger (which took around a year and a half) I completely fell apart emotionally. I guess at some level I could afford to let go at that time, but I shudder to think how we would have managed if Alan had not assumed the 'cool as a cucumber' persona then. For some three months he coped with a demanding job, an active four-year-old, a still very sick baby and a wife who was a misery – just when things should be looking up. He nourished me then with his strength, and was a rock of calm reassurance that all was well and my reaction was overdue and necessary.

Early days for Emma

Back to Emma. The Royal Free Hospital where she was born was obviously baffled. Emma had a range of abnormalities in a cluster that did not fit any obvious syndrome, including a cleft palate, defective heart valve, skin tags on one ear, a missing pair of ribs, bent fingers on her left hand and two club feet. Her major problem, however, was her breathing. She had a very small jaw, half-size tongue and tiny airways. In the early days she could not breathe unless she was prone (on her tummy). Consultants, registrars, doctors and students buzzed around her constantly. Initially we were told she may have a condition called Edwards' syndrome which is a condition incompatible with life. We were asked whether the hospital should adopt a 'do not resuscitate' policy and whether we wanted her fed. As the condition could not be confirmed until chromosome tests were complete we delayed a decision on this one – just as well, because Edwards' syndrome was ruled out. Emma's condition, however, deteriorated quite quickly.

Emma needed help with her breathing, which had become dangerously distressed. She developed bronchiolitis and, try as they might, the hospital could not intubate her, and she was transferred to Great Ormond Street Hospital for Children. She was critically ill when she arrived and was admitted to the intensive care ward. She suffered a cardiac arrest as they tried to intubate her. I was watching and numb with fear. Eventually the tube was in place. She hung on grimly, hovering somewhere between life and death for four months. For intensive care ward 5b Emma was an old-timer. It is a ward usually passed through quickly. Outcomes either improve or children die – lingering for four months is virtually unheard of. Emma earned everyone's respect – not least our own.

On the home front those early weeks and months were relentlessly grim. Mark had taken to his new sister with chirpy delight and a thousand questions. We decided early on that secrets were not a good idea and we were absolutely honest with him from the start. He asked all the right questions – what was wrong with her? What were the doctors and nurses doing? What was each and every piece of equipment for? Was she going to die?

I remember being discharged 48 hours after Emma's birth and coming home. The feeling of emptiness was indescribable. The next day was Friday and I laid the table and prepared a meal for Shabbat. At the evening meal, Alan struggled through the Kiddush (blessing over wine) before bursting into tears. I was appalled, and actually also started weeping mainly in distress for Mark. This most special day of the week had always been filled with fun and singing, and here were his usually happy parents in tears about a baby who could hardly seem real to him. It fell to the infant to come to the rescue. Rushing from one of us to the other, Mark flung his arms around each of us in turn chanting a mantra: "It's all right; Marky's here!" I was furious with myself for allowing this to happen. *We* were the adults, *we* should be reassuring him, how had life turned so cock-eyed so fast?

Emma at 1½ years old, with Mark

I felt guilty about the effects on Mark for a long time, until it dawned on me that although difficult for him, he was very much up for the challenge. Having had Emma for a sister has contributed greatly to the generous, giving adult he has become. Now himself a young married man and father, Mark seems to view all people as having 'special needs' in some way, and treats everyone with kindness and respect.

Bracha – our blessing

We had expected our community to be a source of strength and support. In the event people were embarrassed and did not know what to say to us. That first Saturday, Alan remembers going to synagogue and being asked tentatively how he was, and how I was and how Mark was. He responded directly: "Why don't you ask me how the baby is?" His memory of people's response is one of acute embarrassment. It is obligatory to call the father of a newborn baby girl to the reading of the Torah where a blessing is said and the child is given her Hebrew name. That Saturday, Alan waited in vain to be called and finally had to ask for what should have been automatic. The memory still makes him angry.

Earlier in the week Alan had phoned up our rabbi who was most distressed and uncomfortable. If the child's condition is incompatible with life, no name need be given. The rabbi went into a lot of detail about what would or would not be required in the event of her death. Alan got the distinct impression that, with death, the rabbi was on comfortable and familiar ground. He seemed less comfortable with a response geared to the possible survival of a disabled child. When the conversation was reported to me I exploded in rage. Not give her a Hebrew name – how outrageous!

In Jewish tradition it is usual to give a child the name of a deceased close relative. In advance of the birth we had picked out what this would be. In the heat of that moment I declared that of course we would name her, and her name should be 'Bracha'. Bracha was not the name we had picked before the birth. It means 'blessing' and I felt that in giving her this name we were demonstrating our faith in the fact that all life is a gift. I felt that whatever time span she was allotted was something we would accept as a blessing. I hoped she would survive and live up to her name, but simultaneously knew that if she did not we would still have regarded her as a blessing.

The wall of silence

I don't think you need to be Jewish to feel this way, and again feel that there are important lessons here for everyone affected by disability and loss. I think we all share in a struggle and responsibility to give life meaning. Today, we have learned many lessons around bereavement. Stillborn children are often named and given proper funerals, parents are encouraged to spend time with them; maybe take pictures or handprints. Such respect is important because it acknowledges that this life did exist.

Equally, I think as a society we can ease the difficulties for families with a disabled member with simple respect and courtesy, for example, asking how the child is, what the child's name is, whether you can help in some small practical way. Every now and then I get a phone call from people who have just found out about the birth of a child with special needs. Or they have just discovered that a child has been diagnosed with some illness or disability. The question usually boils down to 'What on earth can I say to these people?' or 'I just don't know what to do or say.' My answer is always the same. If you don't know what to say, say just that! A card or phone call to say 'I don't really know what to say but I'm thinking of you so much. How can I help?' is fine. If you would normally have given a small gift – do as you would normally do.

This issue about cards and gifts certainly struck me as part of the wall of silence. The birth of our first child was greeted by a flurry of cards and gifts. Shortly after Emma came home when she was five or six months old, our bell rang one Sunday morning. A bachelor friend of ours was at the door with two small parcels. In one was a babygro and card for Emma, and in the other a brightly coloured china mug for Mark. It was our first and only present. Every now and then and to his embarrassment I comment on how unusual this was to our friend, now a married man with three teenage sons of his own. He always shrugs his shoulders in characteristic bewilderment at my praise. Why is something so simple so unobvious?

Our pigheadedness – Emma's progress

Emma eventually came home at around five months of age. She had not even regained her birthweight and weighed around 5lb. She was unable to take any liquids directly, although she had taken to baby food enthusiastically. We gave her milk via a nasogastric tube until she was almost a year. At some point I just abandoned the tube, which she pulled out half a dozen times daily. We diluted her food, avoided all salt and she simply did not drink anything. This continued till her palate was finally repaired at the age of three. Emma continued to give us many medical frights. At her first birthday she weighed slightly over her brother's birthweight, and in her second year the surgeons started to have their turn. The palate repair was delayed because of her breathing difficulties and anaesthesia was – and still is – a complete nightmare.

Developmentally the experts hedged their bets. She was so behind on all her developmental milestones. However, her early hospitalisation and general weakness needed to be taken into account. Nevertheless the early assessments suggested severe retardation. It was unclear whether this was congenital or brought on by early oxygen deprivation. Most unclear was the extent to which we could expect progress.

My pigheadedness seemed to come in useful again. Here was an area where we all had an important role to play. I started to read extensively and we all spent hours playing with and trying to stimulate Emma's development. Mark quickly asserted himself as the guru of thinking up imaginative games and 1,001 ways to achieve a developmental goal. We found the Portage system and principles of 'backward chaining' especially useful. Basically all these have one common idea. Define a developmental goal and break down its constituent parts to simplify the task. Often it is easier to start with the end of a sequence and work backwards to the beginning. For example, if the goal is 'dressing oneself' and the task is putting on pants, you do three-quarters of the job, leaving the child to simply pull the pants up for the last little way. Lots of praise positively reinforces the behaviour, which is eventually learned. Then you simply work backwards, doing less and less, until the child can accomplish the whole task themselves.

Emma soon started to progress and close the gap of her developmental delay. During the first two years I really believed I could 'make' her normal – it was simply a function of how hard we were prepared to work. Certainly her progress began to raise a few eyebrows among the developmental experts who assessed her regularly as she began to catch up. But at some point after her second birthday I reached the realisation that, while we may make continued progress, Emma would never be exactly like other children. This triggered a real crisis in me. People often say the experience of having a special needs child is like bereavement. The child you expected to have is alive in your imagination and dies with the realisation of the difficulties ahead. In their place you must accept the reality of the child you actually have. This was the process I went through then, and I realised that Alan had been well ahead of me. He had worked through the grief and accepted the reality from the start.

Emma turned out to have a fantastic memory and could therefore learn many things. Conceptually, however, it was clear that categorising information, or abstracting principles from one situation and applying them to another, was exceptionally difficult. Music was – and is – a point of contact. Like the rest of the family, Emma loves singing and has a retentive musical memory.

Community education

Once her medical crises were behind us, we could start thinking about schooling. As a toddler she accompanied us regularly to synagogue, where she rapidly became everyone's pet. The community became very used to her and she totally at home with them. Our son attended a local Jewish primary school, and eventually (a couple of years late) we began to dare to hope that she might be successfully integrated there. The school gave very careful consideration to our application and agreed to give it a try.

Emma's progress was incredible to us – although doubtless small by normal standards of developmental progress. Within the school she felt secure and valued. The teachers and other pupils were really wonderful. At the end of each year, her teachers would invariably thank *us* for the experience of having Emma in their class. Equally they always confided how very scared they had felt before having Emma, wondering at their own ability to cope and offer her what she needed.

Emma ice-skating

By the age of ten it was clear, however, that the benefits of integration in a mainstream environment were rapidly tailing off. Emma needed more and more one-to-one help and was therefore spending more of her day withdrawn from the classroom. The social benefits of mainstreaming therefore also began to tail off. We explored local special needs schools and decided on one, which seemed ideal. We could not have been more wrong. Emma was miserably unhappy from day one and the situation deteriorated steadily throughout the first year. The school was not Jewish and that was another major problem. Emma's life revolved around all that was familiar and here she felt like a fish out of water.

Emma had by now become seriously depressed at school. Eventually we decided to transfer her to a small local Jewish school for children with special needs. We had previously rejected this same school on the grounds that the pupils, by and large, had severe difficulties in comparison to Emma. Before we took her to meet her new headmistress Emma kept bombarding us with questions about this new school. I suggested she write them all down so that she could ask them herself. Laboriously she set about this task and I sat next to her to help her formulate and spell her questions. When the list was complete it was mainly really sad. "Will the children kick me?" "Will they call me bad names?" "Will the teachers stop the children being horrible?" We took the list to the interview and the headmistress read them carefully and quietly, folded up the paper, put her arm around Emma and looked her in the eyes. "No, Emma, I promise. If anyone is unkind, I want you to come straight to my office. My door is open; I always want to see you and will always listen to you." She was as good as her word.

Emma at school

Bat mitzvah

Years later when we were meeting with representatives of the local authority to plan a move to college, her headmistress produced this old list of questions and commented how typical it was of Emma to want to be in control of her life, and make her own decisions. Emma really has gone from strength to strength. At the age of 12 she celebrated her bat mitzvah, which is a religious coming-of-age for girls (boys celebrate a bar mitzvah a year later). It was a great event for all of us, and one of the loveliest features was the unembarrassed participation of the community. Emma delivered a speech she had written, which people who found her difficult to understand could follow on an available printed version. The party we held was on the exact scale as the bar mitzvah party we had held for our son two years previously. One of the things that struck me was how our hopes and aims for Emma were identical to those for our son. We wanted her to achieve her full potential, to contribute to her community, to feel needed, wanted and useful.

When Emma was ten years old her baby sister was born. Jenny was immediately the baby of any prospective mother's fantasy. Blonde, blue-eyed, curious, active and intelligent, her birth was magical and, despite the gaps in their ages, Mark adored her immediately. Emma found things more difficult as she struggled to welcome the newcomer. Over the years, however, they have become as close as any pair of sisters and Jenny – like Mark – feels having Emma as a sister has added an extra dimension to her life.

Emma, Alan and Jenny

Emma and Jenny

Reflecting on the blessings

As the years have passed the difficulties have not gone away, but I think we cope with them better. It has been a rollercoaster ride at times, but as we have matured we have found it easier to accept and cope. I can now honestly say I am grateful for Emma exactly as she is. She is a really terrific person, and she contributes amazingly to everyone around her. I feel I have grown personally through the experience of raising her. Because of Emma I went back to college and took the A levels I walked out of at age 18. I went to university and have a career teaching psychology, which I chose to study so that I could learn more about Emma. Her twenty-first birthday was a lot of fun and I hope we enjoy many more celebrations together. Emma still needs support but at her college in Manchester is gaining qualifications and would like to work in child care. We are trying to organise a flat down here in London where she can live near us, but as independently as possible. Emma has grown into a charming, confident young lady, and in case you hadn't guessed, we are *very* proud of her!

Emma's 21st birthday

Postscript

Since I began to write this chapter, Emma has moved into a flat in London near her family. She shares the flat with a friend who also has special needs and they are supported by Kisharon, the Jewish special needs organisation whose school Emma attended between the ages of 11 and 16. Emma currently attends Kisharon College and works in a local nursery one morning a week. She remains actively involved with her local Jewish community who regularly offer her hospitality and support. Her verdict on her new life is 'brilliant and amazing'!

Chapter 23
Through the looking-glass: on difference and disability

Jet Isarin

Jet Isarin currently researches family care and paid labour at the Academic Medical Centre, Division of Public Health, in Amsterdam. I met her when she was giving a paper at a conference in Cambridge in 2001. She was enthusiastic about writing this chapter, which gives not only her reflections about her life with her son, but also a glimpse into attitudes and approaches to learning disability in Holland.

Sheena Rolph

Let's pretend the glass has got all soft like gauze, so that we can get through.[7]

7 *The Complete Illustrated Works of Lewis Carroll, Through the Looking-glass.* London: Chancellor Press, 1982, p.127

Children, they say, are like mirrors. Many a mother will hear herself in her four-year-old rebuking a doll or a smaller child; many a father may meet his equal in his six-year-old explaining how circumstances made him lose this battle. Parents recognise themselves in the image their children reflect. At the same time, however, they recognise how their children, like themselves, interpret and thereby change the things they see and experience. Most children, I think, are not like mirrors, but like interpreters.

Disabled children carry various professional labels describing their defects and deviations. These labels can be very useful for parents who want to understand their puzzling children and who try to obtain the support they need to raise them. These same labels however, can also obscure the image that lies beneath. As parents we live our lives guided by professionals who care, cure and define our worlds. Can we still think and talk about our children and about difference in a non-professional language?

"Of course they answer to their names", the Gnat remarked carelessly.

"I never knew them to do it."

"What's the use of their having names," the Gnat said, "if they won't answer to them?"

"No use to them," said Alice, "but it's useful to the people that name them, I suppose. If not, why do things have names at all?"[8]

8 Ibid, p.150

255

My seven-year-old son is like a mirror. He is different from other children. This difference has been described in terms of professional diagnosis, and has thereby lost qualities that make my son special and loveable – to me. Although every description brings its own limitations, I think it worthwhile to try and find a different vocabulary for those differences professionals tend to call defects.

The fact that my son was different from birth urged me to reflect on my feelings, actions and motives as a mother. What did I feel for this big baby boy who did not like to be touched; how could I enjoy bottle-feeding an infant who could not enjoy being fed; why was it so important for me to feel loved and needed by him?

Being a reflective mother I confronted the painful questions our relationship posed on different levels. *As a loving mother* I wanted to find out *who* he was and tried everything to follow, reach and understand him. *As a thinking mother* I wanted to know *what* was 'wrong' with him in order to acquire means for coping with his strangeness, my perplexity and the incomprehension of our (professional) surroundings. Feeling a bad mother, I started questioning my quest for professional recognition of my beloved son's strangeness: what was wrong with *me*, searching for a professional label for my son, while knowing from literature and by experience how dangerous labels can be.

Recently I finished my PhD thesis on the subject of mothers, professionals and disabled children. Referring to what mothers, professionals and philosophers have to say about love, knowledge and mutuality, I state that acknowledgement of contradiction is a prerequisite for understanding the relationship between mothers and their disabled children. *Who* a child is and *what* it is in terms of professional diagnosis cannot be but interwoven and contradictory at the same time.

My son is a part of every sentence I wrote for my thesis and our relationship was a touchstone for my research. The reverse, I guess, is also true. My reflective exercise affected me as a mother and by this has affected our relationship.

Before long I will be invited to defend my findings before a scientific panel and I hope to do so with fervour. The reflective part of my relationship with my son has found its end for now.

Sadder and wiser, I stand before my son's mirror, wondering how far I have got in my efforts to get *through the looking-glass.*

The little voice sighed deeply. It was very unhappy, evidently,
and Alice would have said something pitying to comfort it,
"if it would only sigh like other people!" she thought.
But this was such a wonderfully small sigh, that she wouldn't
have heard it at all, if it hadn't come quite close to her ear.
The consequence of this was that it tickled her ear very much,
and quite took off her thoughts from the unhappiness of the
poor little creature.[9]

9 Ibid, p.149

Meet my son. Riding his bike, greeted enthusiastically by children and adults I don't even know. Seven years of age, looking more like five, and learning to read and write. Asking his grandmother how she is doing: "Is she still running a temperature?" Telling his 13-year-old sister that she really ought to eat her vegetables, that is, if she wants to be healthy and strong.

My son likes going to school, goes in laughing and comes out laughing, telling me how 'exhausted' he is and how he does not like working so hard, telling me about his 'friends' who do not seem all that eager to come and play with him. He does have a friend of sorts, a neighbourhood girl who is one year his senior and acts accordingly. They play at 'father and mother' and 'teacher and pupil' and they have fun together riding their bikes and walking the neighbourhood dogs. He adores the girl, does everything she tells him to do; from playing at father and mother, to stealing sweets or matches and dropping his trousers. Every now and then she tells him she does not want to play with him anymore, because she does not really like him.

Meet my son. Stroking my hair; telling me after my father's death how all people die eventually, how our dog and my daughter will also die sometime and how I should not be sad. It is, he says, the way things go. Talking to me incessantly about what he is doing, asking innumerable questions without being interested in the answers he gets. He likes helping me and neighbours with cleaning, sweeping, cooking and gardening much better than he likes playing the incomprehensible fantasy games boys his age love to play. His efforts to play at being a pirate, a thief or a policeman go no further than repeating the things he hears other boys say; it is only the knifing, shooting, handcuffing part that really appeals to him.

My son had a cerebral haemorrhage right after birth; he has a cleft lip, jaw and palate; he is small for his age, he wears glasses, he cannot smell at all, he does not hear very well and he does not really understand the rules of the game we call living. He can read, but he cannot tell me what he has been reading. He does not seem to understand the intricacies of the bedtime stories I read to him. He has a large vocabulary, but he does not seem to understand half of what he is saying. He can count, but has problems calculating. He can write – though with difficulty – but he can hardly draw. He goes to an ordinary school, but gets exhausted trying to concentrate, trying not to say everything that comes to his mind, trying to deal with children who make jokes and do not want to be hugged and tickled.

My son does not mirror other people's tastes: he does not like sweets or ice-creams, eats no fruit, no vegetables, no potatoes, no meat. On social visits his own kind of bread and butter, his special drink, his canned baby food for dinner always have to come. He would much rather go thirsty than drink something that is not the right colour, he does not mind going hungry when not exactly the right kind of food is available. Offering him an alternative causes terror and temper tantrums.

We have come a long way. Some three years ago everything was much more complicated; no games, no friends, hardly any social visits and temper tantrums every day, everywhere and about just everything. Shoes and clothes in need of replacement were small-scale disasters. Friends and relatives who unwittingly looked him straight in the eyes were met with aggression. He does not fly off the handle like that anymore. His small stature is a blessing in disguise: he does not behave as seven-year-old boys do, but then again, he does not look like a seven-year-old boy either.

We both have learned a lot. But even now every day knows its moments of misunderstanding. His anger meets mine, my anger meets his: he orders me to make his lunch, I tell him to go and make his own, he tells me he is not my slave and so will not make his own lunch. What is more, he will never ever allow me again to prepare his lunch. My incomprehension confronts his perplexity. He tells me he is afraid in the dark and I ask him why; he does not understand my question and asks me while I am leaving his room, "Mama, what does it mean, 'afraid'?" Still, it is easier now than it was before, there is language and there is my knowledge of his idiosyncrasies which enable me to anticipate and prevent. But it is also more difficult now: *sometimes he seems to be so normal.*

Most of the time now his temper tantrums do not last very long. One moment he is crying, screaming, calling names, slamming doors, retreating to his room, the next he comes back all smiles and goodwill, no hard feelings. And no memory, or so it seems. It is as if nothing has happened.

My son at seven is beginning to realise that to be stared and laughed at is not the way things ought to be. There is the onset of wonder about not being asked for football games and birthday parties. There is deep sorrow when a boy he considers to be his best friend tells him he is a 'weirdo'. Sometimes there is an inkling of the difference between his own accomplishments at games and sports and those of other children. More and more he experiences things as others do. There is, however, no understanding at all about the *what* and *why* of these experiences, no insight in his own part, no notion of ways to prevent things from going wrong. For him the only way to adapt seems to be to copy the behaviour, language and emotions expressed by people he knows. He is very successful at this; reproving his older sister as he has seen and heard his grandmother do, being angry with his schoolmates as he has seen and heard me being angry with him, talking to me as he has heard other children talk to him and each other. He can copy, but he is unable to see or understand the relational differences that exist between peers, siblings and adults, nor those between strangers and intimates.

Meet my son. Being a very sensitive and considerate child, his tenderness towards babies, small children and vulnerable adults knows no bounds. Someone else's pain causes him great distress. When someone expresses just pain he offers consolation – stroking and talking like an adult. When there is combined anger and pain, however, he seems to enjoy the other's mishap. A silent reproach in someone else's pain makes him furious. Desperation makes him turn silent and apologetic. When he is the accidental cause, he is full of reproach and accusation.

> *"Well, now that we* have *seen each other,"* said the Unicorn,
> *"if you'll believe in me, I'll believe in you. Is that a bargain?"* [10]   10 Ibid, p.197

Because my son's mirror is clearer than most people's self-image and catches more than isolated persons, it reflects something most people will not recognise as their own behaviour or emotions. They see something they did not know existed. If they are prepared to look, however, then what they see reflected in a seven-year-old boy is a part of who they are and how they behave.

Because my son's mirror not only reflects the one person that is in front of him, but also the people he recently has been with, his mirror reflects both the here and now and a past not known of. And so the image people see is distorted not only by their own lack of self-knowledge, but also by the bits and pieces of absent people – adults and children – my son brings in. These unrecognised fragments reinforce the estrangement that follows the recognition of unacknowledged personal traits and emotions.

Mirrors not only reverse reality, but they also divide it. There is reality on the one side, appearance on the other, there is the way things are and the way things look, there is being and representation. There seems to be a world behind the looking-glass that resembles ours, but turns out to be completely different – it is our world but in a different way. It is the strange and wonderful world Lewis Carroll's Alice steps into at the moment she succeeds in getting through the looking-glass.

Now, if you'll only attend, Kitty, and not talk so much.
I'll tell you all my ideas about Looking-glass House.
First, there's the room you can see through the glass –
that's just the same as our drawing-room, only the things
go the other way. I can see all of it when I get upon a chair –
all but the bit just behind the fire-place. Oh! I do so wish I could
see that bit! ... You can just see a little peep of the passage in
Looking-glass House, if you leave the door of our drawing-room
wide open: and it's very like our passage as far a you can see,
only you know it may be quite different on beyond. Oh, Kitty,
how nice it would be if we could only get through into Looking-
glass House! I'm sure it's got, oh! such beautiful things in it!" [11]

11 Ibid, p.127

Like Alice's looking-glass, my son reflects just about everything. Could his inner life be like Alice's Looking-glass House: a copy of outer reality at first sight, a different world for whoever takes a closer look? Trying to relate to my son, I had to take a closer look. It has made me see that some things take a turn, while others cannot be seen at all. As Alice, I keep trying to see that bit, the bit just behind his point of view. I can see a peep of the passage that leads to other rooms, if I leave the door of my own inner life wide open. But it is only a peep and, like Alice, I know it may be quite different beyond.

To see beyond the face of things, I have to step through his looking-glass, while at the same time I have to hold my footing in common reality. Losing one side, means losing both. I have to get upon a chair and thus outgrow myself, while at the same time I have to get on my knees so as not to outgrow him. Stepping through the looking-glass for me means entering a literal world without metaphor and without a false bottom. His lack of internalisation and interpretation turns the world absurd. Which it is, in a sense.

For me, as for most people, interpretation is part of my dealings with others. In relating to my son, however, I need more of it and less. I need more because my son's way of being is not self-evident. I need less of it or a different kind because opening my arms, my heart, my being for him is quite enough. My arms I can always open, but my heart and being do not always follow suit. When they fail to do so I need all my interpreting skills to reach my son. The skills I need then are the same skills one needs to understand Alice's adventures in Wonderland and the Looking-glass House. Relating to my son, I feel like Alice walking around in a looking-glass world that is very different from our daily reality, a world that knows its own rules and logic. It is a world that makes no sense and yet is sensible on its own terms; a world that is incomprehensible and at the same time more comprehensive than our own. It is a world one wants to be part of without wanting to belong to it, a world one wants to belong to without being a part of it.

Right now I avail myself of various labels to describe and explain my son's strangeness to other people. I use these labels to postpone judgement, to claim understanding and support, and to create a space in which his ability to reflect loses the reflexivity that frightens people.

Right now I have different ways of relating to my son. I open up, I adapt and I mirror. I try to normalise him without losing his speciality. I try to preserve his speciality without giving up on normality.

As long as I am in front of the mirror, I am part of my son's world but don't belong to it. If I want to belong, I have to try and step through the looking-glass. And so I am in and out of my son's world alternately; losing him as soon as I am lost myself, losing a part of myself as soon as I meet him.

Meeting my son in his looking-glass house is meeting someone in a way I have never met anyone ever before.

Chapter 24
The quilter's journal

Jayne Clapton

Jayne Clapton lives in Queensland, Australia, and is a lecturer in the School of Human Sciences at Griffith University. I met her when she visited the UK for a conference. Her work is concerned with the inclusion and exclusion of people with learning difficulties in society, and this was one of the themes of her PhD thesis. When she heard about our plans for this book, she sent us this chapter about her experiences as a houseparent of young people with learning difficulties in Australia.

Sheena Rolph

Prologue
Narratives woven into a patchwork quilt are autobiography in fabric. They are an expression and interpretation of unique experience, unique positioning and unique relationships. Pieces are brought together not only to declare the artisan's witnessing of the past, but also to make a creative and perhaps inspirational contribution to something new. Hence, it is in this transformative act that the pre-existing social and moral fabrics of our being may be similarly reviewed and redesigned.

> She cries.
> Her blue eyes squint.
> Her skin is pink.
> The warmth of her touch expresses life.
> The miracle of birth has occurred;
> And she is perfect.
>
> Our baby did not cry.
> The blue of her eyes matched her skin.
> Her little cold hand was warmed by tears
> When she touched our memories forever.
> So perfect; yet so lifeless.

Only God knows
Why we lost Karen as a daughter and sister.
But now we have the gift of Sarah;
Whose love and joy
Illuminates thirty-three years of memories.
Thanks be to God.[12]

When I was about seven years old, I went with my parents to the cemetery to visit the grave of my paternal grandmother who had recently died. On the way out, my parents took the time to go to another grave – a small grave. It was the grave of my sister. At that time, and in that place, I learnt that my mother had given birth to a baby girl between my brother and me. She was a big baby – over 5kg; and the birth had been quite traumatic. My mother had needed to recover, so little did she know of the cloud of despair that had descended into the delivery room. Karen was stillborn; and my mother never saw her or held her. However, my father had seen his daughter briefly; and he remembers her beauty; a memory acutely rekindled when, some 33 years later, he saw his second granddaughter shortly after her birth.

My parents were told that, had my sister lived, she would have had significant brain damage, and been quite affected intellectually. Quite probably, she would have had cerebral palsy.

What happened in the cemetery that day was more than my parents passively telling me some family history. This was my first memorable experience of what is now described as 'disability'; and that experience was to lead to an enduring, active and embodied response to people perceived as disabled. From my childhood, this familial event formed my gaze of such others. I did not see people as tragedies, burdens, or, in fact, as potential death. My gaze on such otherness became centred not around the notion of the distressed and suffering stranger, but of the potential sibling; and therefore of imagined relationships.

I recall my mother's willingness to 'mind' people with disability for parents to go out. I remember the respect shown to the Spastic Centre building located a few streets away, and the way the work inside was held in the highest regard. This was work never visited but always reified. And I recollect the disallowing of certain language; for example, to call someone a 'spastic', a 'retard', an 'idiot' or a 'simpleton' received similar rebukes to that reserved for blasphemy. I have since often wondered why these actions, though subtle, were so dominant. Obviously, the stillbirth had had a large impact. But this had not been the totality of my parents' experiences. I am sure, though, that the influence of different experiences initiated particular moral responses.

My father, a war veteran, was a labourer, employed as a council worker, then a gardener. My mother, though employed for a short time, mainly shared her skills in a volunteer context. So their different experiences were ones lived by the embracing of hardship always in tension with determination to seek betterment, 'rightness' and success, often at personal cost. This has been their gift to their children; and to any community in which they have lived. But these actions, performed on the margins, are invisible to popular media portrayal or public award. These actions are primarily acknowledged in the private lives of those in accepting relationships. Therefore, I have gained an embodied inheritance – my body has been inscribed with compassion, sensitivity, respect and empathy; captioning a text about difference formed in my imagination from the seeds of my parents' experience. So it was somewhat inevitable that some of these texts were to become expressed in another medium, namely a vocational choice.

Nursing

After completing secondary school in the mid-1970s, I chose to undertake training to become a registered general nurse at a large metropolitan hospital some 700km from home. This was, in my eyes, an inferior choice. I had always yearned to study medicine, but this proved to be an unachievable goal. Undertaking nurse training, though seemingly gender-appropriate and romantically endorsed as a 'helping' profession, proved to be an achievable nightmare! During the three and a half years of being at that hospital (three years of training plus six months employed as a registered nurse), I could never feel comfortable with the militaristic style of the profession. Compliance to 'authority' through the surrendering of any sense of self was not only commanded, but any form of non-compliance brought reprimand and humiliation. Status was hierarchically determined from senior medical staff down, and this was played out in every arena. The ethos of the hospital was configured on the premises of power, expert knowledge and authority, all of which covertly depended on a dialectical relationship with vulnerability, naivety and submission.

Living the paradox of an environment supposedly designed as an institution of care, but hypocritically flaunting and sustaining oppression, became, for me, untenable. From my background, this seemed nothing short of moral antithesis. Therefore, becoming involved with the Christian Church during this time served, somewhat, as an antidote.

The arrival of normalisation in Australia

After having resigned from the hospital in the late 1970s, I successfully applied for a position as a supervisor in a sheltered workshop. This workshop was run by the Special Caring Services Division, a section of the newly formed Uniting

Church in Australia, of which I was a member. It was a workshop for people with intellectual disability, and was founded on notions of Christian service easily identifiable with the Methodist tradition brought to church union. Like other people there, I became proficient in rubber doormat-making, the main activity of the workshop. In addition, I learnt to spoke bicycle wheels very sloppily.

This was an interesting era in disability work, for the ideas of normalisation principles, espoused by such people as Nirje in Europe and Wolfensberger in North America, had begun to infiltrate practice in Australia. A predominant outcome was a shift to deinstitutionalisation. In Queensland, the director of Special Caring Services, the Reverend Wal Gregory, was approached by the Queensland Government to work collaboratively to move people with intellectual disability from state-controlled institutions to community/church-based agencies to provide community care and employment. Thus, these adults working in the sheltered workshop came from diverse backgrounds – some who had lived with their families since birth, and others who had only recently entered 'community' life, having been incarcerated, in most situations, since birth. This latter group were now being housed in hostels in suburban settings. Diversity included differences of educational and recreational opportunities; but most obviously, differences in familial experiences. Such were the differences in histories that the easiest options for work culture seemed to be to treat everyone in the present tense.

By attending to people's histories, and by ignoring the invisibilities as such, a yearning was created within me to become more actively involved in the deinstitutionalisation process. I was struggling to understand how groups of people could have been locked away from society, when my background had constantly informed me that such people could not only live in communities, but be liked and accepted.

A new life
As this struggle was agitating and desire was stirring, Wal Gregory approached me to ask if my husband, Bob, and I had ever given consideration to becoming houseparents in one of the church family group homes established in a joint project with the government. These homes housed four to six young people with intellectual disability, and both partners were employed full time, 24 hours a day. After much deliberation, we decided to make this move. Interestingly, our friends and families not involved in the church applauded our intentions and read them as sacrificial philanthropy; while friends and relatives involved with the church told us we were fools!

The decision was made. So with a one-year-old marriage, we prepared to move to a suburban, white, Spanish-style house situated approximately one hour west of the metropolitan city. After four months of working in the workshop, and a trail of doormats and damaged bicycle hubs behind me, my husband and I moved in with four young people who had lived in this house for a year – their inaugural houseparents had recently left, but were living in the same town. So began an incredible experience for the next four years.

Who were these people?[13] First there was Angela, aged 17, the eldest and the 'leader'. Having Down's syndrome, she had been institutionalised since birth, living in a hospital children's unit until she was 12, then at another institution until she was 16. She had never known her family. Then there was Simon, 11 years old, institutionalised since a toddler because his autism-like characteristics could not be understood within his family and had resulted in instances of abuse. Desmond was nine years old, and had been removed from his mother as a baby, because the state had deemed her incapable of caring for him. His bilateral hearing loss had not been discovered until he had been sent to school at eight years old to prepare him for transfer from the institution. The youngest and the smallest (size six for clothes) was Wally, aged eight. Having Down's syndrome had been the reason for his 'hospitalisation' since birth, because, it was said, his wealthy parents could not come to terms with the social embarrassment of having such a child. The boys, being under 12, had come from the children's unit where Angela had lived.

It is not unusual that, when writing about such people, their defining deficits are noted. Their incapacities and inadequacies in relation to their intellectual incompetencies traditionally dominate descriptions of their personhood. However, these were not the deficits by which we learnt to focus. Their lives had been determined by the lack of personal histories – stories and photos; the lack of familial relationships; the lack of life's everyday experiences; the lack of educational opportunities; and the lack of choices: these were the deficits inflicted by a stigmatising society which took little responsibility for such actions. The malignancy of these deficits, therefore, flourished in nutritious social media constituted by institutional excesses of routine and depersonalisation; chemical restraint; and physical and emotional abuse – all 'practised' as medicalised care.

Our initial observations supported these conclusions. More than one of the children were still on tranquillising medication. One of our first activities was to ask a medical practitioner to justify this action. No justification could be found other than that it was a remnant of institutional care where it had been used for the purpose of behaviour control to enable better compliance with routines. On this basis, we set about to cease the medication.

Another startling feature of this new household was the way everyone fought to do basic household tasks, such as washing the dishes and vacuuming. Again, another remnant from where there had been no access to such activities.

13 I have purposely chosen to use pseudonyms for the names of any person for whom we cared. This was indeed a hard choice, as I am sure that I could have gained permission to use real names, but I was not so confident that this could have been informed consent, as there are many voids and assumptions in the histories of the people who I wish to write about. It is my hope that *their* own stories can be told one day.

There were other indications of well-ordered lives: beds always well made and personal belongings placed protectively in personal spaces such as bookshelves.

Relational aspects were to take time. There was overt agitation and irritation to flexibility (or our 'induced chaos'). Mistrust and uncertainty constituted the environment as much as the welcoming of a new adventure. Also, we had to understand that they had known each other not just in the constructed context of the previous 12 months, but for many years in the other venues. These had, to a large degree, been the only example of constancy and stability, while other relationships such as those with staff had not only been at the mercy of rosters and rotations, but also resignations and retirements. We were, indeed, the strangers; and it was important for us to know this dynamic. While some found it easy to touch, others were not just shy, but fearful. We were to learn later of their earlier experiences of abuse.

But there was to be another significant episode during the early weeks, which would add complexity for the next four years. After we had been in the house for a week, Wal Gregory informed us that we were to receive another 'child'. Trudy was 16 years old, and in the same institution that Angela had left; they had been close friends for many years. As well as having Down's syndrome, Trudy was an insulin-dependent diabetic. She had a different background to the others in that she had lived with her parents in rural Queensland until she was six years old. Because of the instability of her diabetes, she needed to be closer to medical assistance. This had resulted in her parents undertaking the heart-wrenching decision to have her admitted to institutional care.

I found the announcement of Trudy coming to live with us to be quite challenging. Life with the others had its particularities; but quite clearly, we were able to separate living and any medical concerns. They were not symbiotic. However, Trudy, with life-threatening unstable diabetes commanding control, would call on my experience of medical astuteness and proficiencies not tested since ceasing to nurse. Whether we had the skills and the confidence to meet these challenges was about to be tested. Wal pointedly asked: if I didn't have the skills, who would?

Our visit to the institution in which she was living left a lasting imprint on my sensory memories. Our sight and hearing noted how the environment and activities represented and screamed the characteristics of custodial care. However, my olfactory senses have not been able to erase the particular stench of an atmospheric cocktail of urine, faeces and other body odours mixed with the splashings of bulk-stored disinfectants from state stores.

Trudy came to live with us soon afterwards, bringing her cherished possessions regularly supplied by caring parents. Although she was 16 years old, she was only about 120cm tall. Her skin was dry, her abdomen distended and her hair dull and coarse. She was unhappy, disengaged and irritable. She would sit in a corner with her back to everyone else, and incessantly make an 'urring' noise as she turned each page of a magazine, or did some colouring-in. If we hadn't known otherwise, we could easily have assumed that she had come from a refugee camp in middle Africa. She had the characteristics of malnutrition, but her diabetic diet was large enough to sustain a working, mature male. However, we seemed to be dealing with more than just difficulties of 'settling-in'.

Notions of dispensability

One thing that did come to our attention very quickly was that Trudy had incredibly foul-smelling diarrhoea, for which we sought medical attention. The local doctor thought that it may have been due to intestinal parasites, and prescribed medications, for her and the rest of the household. When these were ineffectual, we sought to find out some of her medical history from the institution. We were informed that they were aware of the diarrhoea and, likewise, had tested her for parasites. However, as nothing had shown up, they could not make any other conclusions other than that she was somebody with Down's syndrome, and people such as this weren't very hygienic, so episodes of diarrhoea could be quite predictable. Basically, this was something we all had to live with.

From our medical backgrounds, coupled with our suspicions of some of the inherent shortfalls of some practices, Bob and I weren't convinced. Although she was interacting more easily, and occasionally would smile, her diabetes was still considerably unstable, subjecting her to other medical opinions. Unfortunately, these were often unpleasant and negative. A memorable example is when she became unconscious through a hypoglycaemic episode at 2am while we were all away at a camp. As she needed an injection of dextrose, we had to seek medical attention from a local doctor in the small town. While reversing her unconscious state, he felt obliged to tell Bob that personally he felt that all children such as these (i.e., with Down's syndrome) should be 'put down' at birth, and not be a burden to society.

This was not to be the only time we were confronted with this sort of opinion. Such notions of dispensability could emerge in very different contexts. A new road-safety policy of the time had declared that all children travelling in cars needed to wear seat belts. However, the taxis which transported children to special schools were often allowed to carry over seven children – so obviously they were not all able to wear seatbelts. When the government department responsible for enforcing the new laws was questioned about this disparity, their response was that children such as these were exempt from the law, and therefore the ambition for safety offered by the law did not apply to such children.

There were other instances where well-being 'didn't matter'. Because of his particular facial features, Desmond had an incredibly small palate. Despite this, orthodontic dental treatment was denied him for some years because junior dental officers declared that having a small and ineffectual bite didn't matter for someone like Desmond. On another occasion, Simon had dental treatment which required a local anaesthetic. We weren't informed that this had been given, therefore neither were we informed that he should not have eaten anything that would have required biting for a few hours. Afterwards, he had lunch, and consequently bit into his numbed lip, leaving a large laceration. We took him to a doctor for treatment only to be told that, because he had an intellectual disability, he would not be caring how he would look in the future; therefore, because it wouldn't matter, it would not be worth suturing his lip. Once again, we were forced to use the response which we had now had to resort to many times. It 'did matter' to this person because of his/her humanity and no other reason would be acceptable. At times it was even necessary to situate this claim by suggesting that if this child was the offspring of one of the opinion-makers, would this opinion still be given? Always, the answer was in the negative.

Our persistent efforts in relation to Trudy's diarrhoea were to endure another 18 months. In that time, she was much more engaged socially, and despite what appeared to be obvious discomfort, we could see that she had an incredible sense of humour waiting to ambush any unsuspecting 'helper'. We taught her how to manage her diet more independently, and then set about teaching her to prepare and inject her own insulin. Progress was noteworthy, but not completely satisfactory. We had suspicions that she may have had a malabsorption problem in her intestine; but all doctors had been reluctant to undertake any invasive diagnostic procedures. By chance at a large hospital one day, Bob met a doctor with whom he had worked at another hospital before becoming a houseparent. They exchanged general conversation about what each other was doing. The doctor explained that he was now working as a gastroenterology registrar, and Bob explained the difficulties we had been having with Trudy. Within a month, the doctor arranged for Trudy to have a small-bowel biopsy.

So after 18 months, with Trudy now nearly 18 years old, we got the diagnosis we had so determinedly been seeking. And, it confirmed our long-term suspicions of what may have been the problem. Trudy was diagnosed with coeliac disease, a condition manifested by an intolerance to gluten in wheat. The disease affects humans by damaging the lining of the small intestine, thus creating serious malabsorption. It can be present from infancy, when wheat products are introduced in a baby's diet. Indeed, we were able to track that Trudy had been showing symptoms of this condition since she was six months old – some 17½ years, ten of which had been spent within medicalised institutional care.

Obviously, the damage was considerable. However, there were some quick responses. Within a week, her diabetic diet could be reduced to be congruent with her size rather than that of a working male. Her hair started to shine; her irritability decreased markedly; and her 'funniness' certainly dominated her life. It would be some time before she had a solid bowel motion; but it was certainly a time of celebration when it happened!

Changes and achievements

However, during this time, life didn't stay still for the rest of the household. Angela moved out of the house after the first 12 months, as her schooling had finished, so she was moved into a women's hostel to be closer to work options. Simon, Desmond and Wally, along with Trudy, got involved with ordinary activities such as learning to ride a pushbike, establishing and maintaining a vegetable garden, building a Wendy House, playing cricket and soccer as well as outings with our friends and families who fulfilled extended familial roles. Holidays and camping activities were regularly undertaken.

We were expected to attend the local Uniting Church, a very traditional 'newly ex-Methodist' church; and that presented some interesting experiences. The first time he attended, Simon apparently stood up on the seat at the end and called out in his not-very-easily-discernible-language, "Shut up, you big fat bastard!" Trudy got through church by 'urring' and counting her way through the hymn book; Wally threw imaginary hand grenades at the senior choir; and I think, week by week, Desmond rendered his hearing aids ineffective. But there was one experience which caused us tremendous concern and that was the church's insistence that these four to five people could not be included with their peers in Sunday School. They had to be in a 'special class' with a 'special teacher'; and this special class just happened to be made up only with these particular four to five people. This caused us a lot of heartache and prolonged discussion. However, it was one battle we would not win; so the only acceptable outcome for us was to go to another Uniting Church where we were not subjected to such restrictions.

Another memorable event was the birth of our first-born son after being with the children for 18 months. I distinctly remember the stares of people when I would go out shopping, and so on. Their looks spoke the words, "The poor thing. Four like that, and she's trying again!" Pregnancy, birth and breastfeeding weren't just new experiences for me as a mother. It was the first time for everyone. Our son, Luke, was born with bright red hair, a considerable talking point among all who saw him. But no comments were as poignant as the questions Desmond asked. Peering in through the nursery window, he turned and asked, "How is his hair going to grow? Do we have to water it every day?" What seemed to be ludicrous questions perhaps encapsulated the particularity of his life. Brought up in a 'hospital ward for handicapped children', there had been no exposure to ordinary family activities such as being with babies; nor had there been any one person who could tell him stories from his own babyhood. There were no anecdotes; there were no photographs; and there was no knowledge of how a baby's hair grows!

Everyone loved Luke. Wally was absolutely enthralled with a baby in the house. Luke became a great playmate. Trudy loved feeding him, cooing in her dulcet tones of "Are you hungry, Baby? Here. You have it!" It was during the pregnancy and afterwards that we could note some distinct differences between Trudy and the others. Having lived with her family for the first six years of her life, she appeared to be much more aware of others; and showed a degree of compassion and care which the boys simply did not have.

As Luke turned two years old, there were some other events which brought their own idiosyncrasies. Roslyn, aged ten, came to live with us from the children's unit. This commenced another 'it doesn't matter' experience as Roslyn had a persistently runny nose. We were battle-hard by this stage, so within six months she had ear, nose and throat surgery to correct the problem.

Friends and relatives were starting to subtly suggest that it was not in the best interests of Luke's developmental well-being for him to be in a house with five others with intellectual disability – views that we would readily dispute if anyone said them openly. By this time, I was pregnant with our second child, and it looked like the purely heavy emotional and physical demands could not be sustained with two small children; so we made the very difficult decision that we would have to resign with Kate's birth. And this is indeed what happened.

The time leading up to the point of separation was made harder with Trudy's health taking more uncertain turns. Her diabetes had been fairly stable since the diagnosis of coeliac disease, with very few hypoglycaemic attacks. However, out of this stability came about four months of life-threatening difficulties. Numerous times we were woken up during the night to hear her thrashing around the bed in a fit, which rendered her unconscious and incontinent. Our local doctor (we at last had a supportive one) had supplied us with an injection that I could administer that would help her regain consciousness by releasing stored sugar in her liver. This would be enough to get her conscious to be able to take sugar orally. While unconscious, most times she bit her tongue, and therefore had a bloodied mouth. What I was to learn most from those episodes, which usually occurred in the early hours of the morning, was the importance of touch. Although I was over six months pregnant, I would sit down on the kitchen floor, supporting her between my legs. As I held her firmly and securely, she would become conscious more quickly than if I didn't hold her. But more noticeably, she would be less frightened, knowing that someone was with her in the darkness between unconsciousness and consciousness.

Reflections

Kate was born, and we not only left the children and the house, but also the community, to move to another town some 300km away. In that time of separation, I wondered what we had all achieved over that four-year period. Physically, and emotionally, everyone seemed to be better off. I must be careful not to romanticise this period. In simple terms, it was very hard work. Twenty-four hours a day for four years (equivalent to 17 years of a regular work pattern), we attended to all needs from domestic tasks to attending to bed-wetting, to enduring severe illness such as hepatitis B. We worked with the other family group homes; and we had the privilege of 'assessing' other children for discharge from institutions into the community.

But what about this so-called 'community'? And what is community? From my experiences and observations, I am left with the following to make sense of. As well as positive encounters, community is the place where one set of neighbours can refuse any conversations between their children and ours – the same neighbours who had vehemently claimed to the local council that a house such as ours would devalue their property; community is a place that can view people with disabilities with gazes of specialness and braveness, but tell them that their needs 'don't matter'; community is a place where options are decided by others who think they have that right, such as teachers who write home to say that Wally needs a haircut; community is a place that appoints professionals to decide if certain people can have access to it; and community is a place where different agents are allowed to flaunt their acts of duty and charity without ever having to enter into a relationship with the stranger among them. The paradoxes of community have, indeed, been enduring mysteries.

Ten years on – any change?

Although some contact was maintained with established relationships, another intimate contact with disability issues was not appropriated until some ten years later. In the intervening years, the disability field was said to have changed significantly. New Commonwealth legislation had been implemented in 1986, and there had been a significant shift of practice from older frameworks of care and dependency to support for independence. Integration, inclusion and community participation, either synonymously or particularly, were ideals being striven for. However, even with this universal legislation in place, along with new policy and program directions, families that I worked with were still experiencing significant hardships in terms of access and opportunity; but most importantly, in terms of understanding of their particular experiences and needs.

Misinterpretation and ignorance manifested themselves in many forms. From my position as a Supplementary Services Worker in childcare services, I saw parents and families continually being subjected to 'professionals' who thrived on discretionary opinions. I found myself in a somewhat liminal position – on the threshold because of the knowledge gained as a pseudo-parent, and of now being employed as a professional worker with newly acquired university knowledge. But in the context of professionalism I found active the same sort of misused power that had underpinned my nursing experience some 15 years earlier. I saw people making decisions about worth, desires and opportunities from the security and distant isolation of nice workplaces, rarely daring to visit families in their own environment. These decisions were made with the power that could determine someone's access to services, to education and to financial entitlements. I also saw first-hand the despair of invisibility felt by families as they struggled to be understood and heard.

But most alarmingly, I was exposed to the crippling effects of guilt constantly imposed on parents by a society that determined that these conditions were self-imposed. I heard stories of how parents were told that their child's condition had been the result of parental sin; for living in particular relationships; and for not choosing certain moral paths. And I found it disturbing that these assessments were propagated by different Christian churches. A paradox was evident. Publicly, churches were involved in service activities; while privately, certain members felt they had a right to police what they perceived as expressions of the immorality of society. Somehow, legislation and professionalism couldn't address these realities.

Epilogue

A couple of years later, we again lived in the large metropolitan city. One evening, we received a telephone call from a friend to tell us that Trudy had been admitted to hospital. She was very unwell, and cancer of the liver was suspected – this diagnosis was confirmed, in fact, a couple of days later. When we visited her that night, we effectively turned the clock back to the late 1970s. She was sitting up in bed when we arrived at about 8pm. Her meal tray, which had been distributed around 5.30pm, was still on her bed-table. With an intravenous drip in her arm, and crying with each small mouthful because of the pain, she was endeavouring to eat her dinner, committed to her lifelong discipline of needing to eat everything provided to meet her dietary requirements. We immediately engaged in conversations of the past, and again, holding her had a small, yet still significant, effect.

When a nurse did come to attend to her, I asked if Trudy could have something for the obvious discomfort she was in. His reply was that she had been offered an injection a couple of hours earlier, but had grizzled when they tried to give it to her. He then declared how they assumed she mustn't like needles; and how they can't waste these drugs, "you know", so it was decided to abandon the attempt. Pulling out my nursing survival tool kit, which I surprisingly discovered I still carried, I made an icy response. It seemed quite unimaginable to me, and now hopefully to him, how this young woman with insulin-dependent diabetes which had required two injections a day since she was six years old, could be scared of needles. I then said that I would be very happy to sit with her while she had the injection that he was now going to go and prepare!

Two days later, after a liver biopsy confirmed the diagnosis of liver cancer, Trudy was moved to a palliative care ward where she was nursed in an individual room. Open access was available to family and friends. During the next ten days that she lived, Bob and I were privileged to sit with her and share that time with her mother, and a couple who had cared for her, as a member of their own family, during the previous few years. We exchanged stories; we laughed together and we cried together. We all made room for each other's need for private space; and we made it easy for friends such as Angela to come and say goodbye. And we celebrated that, even as she was dying, Trudy still managed to ambush some unsuspecting nurses and other professionals. We talked to Trudy about death, preparing her in a way that we hoped would be adequate.

The previous few years that Trudy had spent with Julie and Graham had been as fun-filled, yet as ordinary, as that which anyone could have hoped for. For instance, Trudy went with them for a weekly counter-tea at the local hotel where Graham played pool. She was there as one of the crowd, accepted and always interacting with fun and friendship to the authentic friend. She had regular telephone conversations with her mother who still lived in a rural area; and she dearly missed her father who had died.

This, then, seemed to be what deinstitutionalisation, integration, inclusion, and all the other technical terms were about. This was about goodness and about life, that no piece of legislation or policy or programme could adequately script. It was something that could only be experienced through intimate, yet intentional, relationships; and people willing to engage in them in a profound sense of mutuality. And these were people who were willing to confront evil, to stand up for what they believed was right, and to challenge what they perceived to be unjust. These, then, are issues of morality which have remained unspoken in conversations of deafening silence.

This is a story that begins and ends with death. It is also a story that articulates community exclusion, its plot centring around the defiance and rejection of processes of social death imposed, and continually played out, by different communities towards some members of the human race. It is, and will continue to be, therefore, a counter-story that strives for living.

For it was you who formed my inward parts;
you knit me together in my mother's womb.
I praise you, for I am fearfully and wonderfully made.
Wonderful are your works; that I know very well.
My frame was not hidden from you,
when I was being made in secret,
intricately woven in the depths of the earth.
Your eyes beheld my unformed substance.
In your book were written
all the days that were formed for me,
when none of them as yet existed.
How weighty to me are your thoughts, O God!
How vast is the sum of them!
I try to count them – they are more than the sand;
I come to the end – I am still with you.

Psalms 139, 13–18 [14]

14 Bible verses read at Trudy's funeral, April 1995. Extract from *Holy Bible: The New Revised Standard Version*. Nashville: Thomas Nelson Publishers, 1990.

Chapter 25
A life of campaigning

Ann and Michael Tombs

Ann and Michael Tombs' interviews were recorded as part of an Open University course, 'Care, Welfare and Community', during 2000, and they kindly agreed to our re-editing them for publication in the book. They are very long-standing Mencap committee members who have been keen to see the history of Bedford Mencap recorded. This is now in hand as part of a Heritage Lottery-funded project headed by Sheena Rolph, one of the book's editors.

Jan Walmsley

Ann Tombs – being a Mencap activist

My name is Ann Tombs, and my husband Michael and I got involved with Mencap because our eldest son has severe learning disabilities. At the time, of course, it was called mental handicap.

Sandy's 18th birthday

The importance of Mencap

I think Mencap has been very important right from the very beginning. I feel that it was pressure from parents and from parents' organisations that led to the complete change in the last 50 years from a time when people just went into an institution, to the position now where people have rights and a choice of occupation and of residential provision.

The Education Act (1970), in particular, was the most important, and the Chronically Sick and Disabled Person Act as well, with the change from health to social services. They were all part of the recognition that there should be services in the community, and I think that was largely because parents were saying we want something better for our children who are in the community and we don't want them to go into institutions – we don't think that's the right place for them. I think it has progressed from there.

We have been involved since about 1974, and that was at the start of the change of provision. Mencap worked quite closely all through that period with social services in defining what sort of things parents needed, so, where social services had a hostel which was mainly for the more able, we kept bringing to their attention the needs of people who were more profoundly handicapped and saying that we needed just as much residential provision for them and that they needed day care. Unless you actually make that information known to Mencap and through social services, and in our case through the director of social services, they do not know.

Choices

It all comes back really to the Education Act that people were able to keep their sons and daughters at home, and so you did bring them up as part of your family and as part of the community. We did consider a village community. We thought that would be suitable for our son, but as he grew to be a teenager, it became quite clear to me that that wasn't the sort of life he wanted to lead because he likes, his big passion, is to go to Sainsbury's and he calls the people in Sainsbury's his friends, and he doesn't actually want that sort of cut-off, more protected life; he wants to be out and about with people. And he had that opportunity, even though he went to a special school, not an ordinary school, by growing up in a family, mixing in the community all the time. So he wanted to stay in the community. I think that's how people became more visible.

The welfare visitors' scheme

I was involved in various different organisations, like playgroup, and we started a toy library. So although we actually belonged to Mencap, I was involved in other organisations that brought people together, and the toy library in particular brought young parents together, in a way which Bedford Mencap wasn't doing at that time. And then I got involved with the welfare visiting scheme that started within Bedford Mencap, and so I personally have always seen other parents as being most important for support, and we would see that as a very important aspect of the welfare visitors role – bringing parents together. When Bedford Mencap was started, parents were very isolated, and they did come together; that's always been something that Mencap has done right from the beginning. I don't think that changed except in so far as when there was a school, obviously you had a group of young parents together.

We worked very closely with the Child Development Centre, both as a toy library and with Bedford Mencap, to make sure that parents had access to the information that we had, but we have never been all that successful in getting information to people at birth. On the whole, parents of newly diagnosed babies don't actually want to be involved with Mencap. They reject the stigma and they are too busy with other things. So, although it's good for them to have the information, we found it was more successful to put our information in schools, because by the time they start at special school they are quite clear that their child has a disability and are ready to start looking for help by then.

The Mencap welfare visiting service was started by one of the founder members of the society. The society had previously had a home visitor but he obviously felt that it was not sufficient, and he started off the scheme in co-operation with social services. He co-operated very closely with social services, and health and education used to come to the meetings. We tried to have a team of welfare visitors who would hopefully visit everyone, whether they were members of the society or not, so it was sort of a subtle recruiting system as well as giving them information and support. We were able to take information to people, but we were also able to bring information back on people who were not getting the support that they needed, and what areas we thought we ought to be pressurising social services to move into and develop.

Labels
My son hasn't got a specific diagnosis of his learning disabilities (I'm saying learning disabilities now because that's the current term). He was about two and he still wasn't sitting up and the doctor at the clinic thought I should see somebody else. We went to see the consultant at Bedford Hospital who did a lot of tests and didn't come up with anything, and so I thought that meant that he didn't have anything wrong with him, but in fact it just meant that they couldn't come up with a reason for his slowness. When I complained to them, they sent me to Great Ormond Street for a second opinion, and again Sandy had a lot of tests, and they came up with the same – no explanation for the fact that he obviously had a mental handicap. That was the first time

that somebody had specifically said 'mental handicap'. That is the term that I would have used, and I did use at that time, and I find it quite a helpful term, to explain perhaps why Sandy behaves as he does. Learning disabilities is a less helpful term, and again, it tends to disguise the very real nature of the handicap, in the same way that the doctor originally had said they couldn't find anything wrong. People cling on to the idea of learning disabilities as being, just something that they will get over, that they're going to be slow talking or slow reading and it's not going to be a permanent handicap. It would be quite useful to have an actual label, a diagnosis like autistic, or like we thought he might have Fragile X, because that acts as a protection, because people then understand what the disability is and it's not just somebody being difficult or lazy or naughty.

The first thing that Mencap did was to have a Christmas party. This is the first year that we haven't actually had a Christmas party, and the reason for that is because people have such a lot of other Christmas parties they can go to now. But when the society first began, the Christmas party would probably be the only outing that they would have. Likewise, the Starlight Club was set up as a leisure activity for people to give the parents a little bit of a break, and an outing, one outing, and the same thing with the holiday which was started, and has been going for 40 years now. When that was started, people didn't have holidays, neither the parents nor the people with learning disabilities, so they were both very important in providing support, but also in leading the way, to show that people did want holidays, and did want clubs. The need for the clubs came partly out of the welfare visitor's research findings that there were people who wanted to go to clubs. Jim Nixon, who started the welfare visiting service, was very influential in a lot of these things and he got the other clubs started up. Now there are three Gateway Clubs, and a junior Gateway Club in Bedford, and they are all fully used.

The annual holiday too is very fully used. It's still meeting a need. You would think that perhaps people now would have the opportunity for other holidays, but there are still enough people who wouldn't have a holiday if they didn't go with Bedford Mencap. So the need for the facilities is also leading the way for other holidays.

Other facilities that Mencap has been involved with include the play scheme which, again, we lead the way in, and then social services decided to take it over and then they wanted us to take it back, and we've only done that because they give a grant and the minibus. We have had different parents' support groups and now the Garden Carers, which is quite a big business employing people with learning disabilities to do gardening.

I have realised over a period of time, with my son living in the community, that that was what he wanted. But we have always seen him as needing to be quite protected. He is not able to make decisions for himself, so that is a concern to me, as there isn't any mechanism for making decisions for him. There is quite a danger that he will be pushed into a situation, such as supported living, where he will be expected to make decisions that he is not capable of making. We need to be quite careful about things like supported living. Giving choices, particularly, is quite a dangerous area, and it's going too far with the idea of progressing towards normality, because, after all, people have got a learning disability or a mental handicap, and so they do need a lot of support and help. I do think that it's up to the younger parents now, who have greater expectations, to see if those things can work in the future. I feel that we, with our expectations, have the sort of facilities that we think are right for our sons and daughters based on what has happened in our experiences, and if the next generation want something different then it's up to them to work for it and make that work.

Michael Tombs – What's going to happen to them?
Early days with Mencap
I joined Mencap in Bedford for the reason that most people join Mencap, that I had a child with learning disabilities. We were actually recommended to find Mencap by the staff at Great Ormond Street Hospital. I rapidly became a member of their executive committee (this was something that I think anyone could do if they wanted to) and then not long afterwards I was invited to represent them at the divisional level. And then after a while there I was asked if I would be interested in becoming the National Council representative for the Northern Home Counties, because the existing incumbent wanted to retire. So I was never actually elected, there was never any opposition to any of these things. I also became chairman of the local society and a governor of the local special school, St John's. This was slightly before my son Sandy was admitted to the school. Again that happened because I asked somebody I knew if they could organise it for me and they did.

I served as member of the National Council for about ten years. The council works by setting up subcommittees, and I was a member of residential services, which interested me all along. I finished up as a member of the committee that ran Pathway, which was an employment scheme where people were placed in work and supported. And I was involved in an education committee, and as a result of that I actually became involved with the colleges that Mencap runs. They were called training establishments then, and in the fullness of time I became a member of the Lufton Manor governors and the chairman of the governors down there – though Sandy actually went to Dilston, which is up by Newcastle, because it was felt that that would be more suitable for him. And I have to say that, although I had a lot to do with Pengwern in Wales, I never actually visited.

Then we set up a subcommittee to look after Mencap Homes Foundation, and I got myself on to that and eventually became chairman of it. And that was my major interest on the National Council, because that was when the Homes Foundation was being set up and developed very rapidly, and I think in many ways it was Mencap's major achievement over that period. We finished up with something like 500 homes, having started more or less from scratch in a fairly short time, by far the largest provider of residential accommodation in the country. And the pattern of it and the basic policies and the finances too were all worked out in that period, and I think the lay committee played a big part, though we were very fortunate in the professional director, because he'd got the thing really going and held it together. But of course in terms of the employees and turnover it was far bigger than the rest of Mencap, and so it was to some extent a question of the tail wagging the dog, and there was a very strong move to hive it off as a separate charity, which failed, because the personal interests of the people trying to do it were fairly blatant. I think they saw themselves as being able to run it. And the Gateway too, the leisure activities, was continually threatening to hive off and go and do their own thing, which they did anyway. But the major point, I suppose, is that we were chronically short of money, and we were never able to do some of the things that we'd identified in fact as very desirable things that we should do. Training, particularly, was one big area where we had a blank.

The importance of the 1970 Education Act
To my mind, the key event of the last 50 years has been the opening of schools for the children. I think this had two major effects. One that was obvious at the time, was that people started to keep their children at home with them rather than putting them into institutions. And one that I've realised with a great deal of hindsight was that, with the hospitals not getting any new admissions, the numbers started to go down and their costs per head went up very sharply, which blew one of the arguments for keeping them open out of the water – that they were cheap to run. The schools opened just before we became involved with Mencap. My impression is, that although Mencap in its very early days – when Judy Fryd was starting it up – was saying all the right things, they didn't really have a major impact because they were a relatively small organisation and you couldn't really say then that they spoke for people with mentally handicapped children, or the mentally handicapped. I think you could say that now, but I think then they were really a small minority who were making a case. I suspect that the impetus for the opening of the schools actually came from individual people, probably within the Ministry of Education, and I don't think Mencap can really claim that one, but they certainly supported it, there's no question of that.

The growth of residential care

Looking back, you can see a great schism in Mencap because, as it developed, it did get a lot of people involved whose relatives were in the institutions. I refuse to call them hospitals, because they were not really hospitals at all, they were just institutions. And they took a different view, that they could improve the institutions a lot, but they didn't really envisage the complete shift in the basis of provision that did develop eventually. We strongly promoted residential care, and that was enough to alienate a lot of the people with relatives in the hospital, because they didn't want that.

Nobody mentioned village communities, and they existed of course, but I don't remember them being prominent in people's plans or thoughts. I think one of the aims of perhaps some of the parents and friends at least, was to turn the hospital into something much more like a village community, that was their objective. But many of them quite firmly believed that you couldn't possibly care for people in residential homes of the kind we have now, and that they simply would not be adequate, and that they would lose many of the positive features of the hospital. There was no doubt there was a split on this. And it didn't really extend right up to the National Council because most of the National Council by then, although they may have had their children in hospitals, were mostly very much in favour of what we used to call as wide a provision as possible and giving people a choice. Actually it was a push towards the maximum possible provision for residential accommodation. Though I don't think anybody ever really believed the hospitals would actually close. We never thought that would happen. We thought they'd hang on in some form or other.

I remember Rescare being set up, and it caused a lot of concern. The one angle on that which I think never did get much publicity is it was very strongly supported by the unions, and in particular the health service workers' union. It was COHSE then, it's Unison now. They were giving them substantial financial support, and certainly a lot of background support, which was very sad, I thought. Their local man made some quite outrageous remarks. And we were not happy about that at all. But they had their point of view.

Residential care, other than the hospital institution in this area, has actually been around for quite a long time. Social services ran what they called a hostel, a fairly large one, Brookside in Kempston. This was for relatively able people and some of them used to go out to work, and they did build another one, Orchard House. I remember attending the opening of this, and I remember the Director of Social Services saying we will never build another place like this again, because it was already perceived to be an old-fashioned pattern. It had 20-odd people I think, and it's still there and still in use, in fact. But at the same time, private provision has started to appear, and I think the first attempt in Bedford was by a former nurse from the hospital who decided to set up a private home. He ran into a lot of problems with planning applications and he actually came to see us to see if we could support him and find a way through this, and in the end he gave up that particular one and went to a different place, and got it without any great trouble.

We became aware of the way in which Mencap had been able to use housing associations, which made the whole thing financially possible, on a big scale anyway. Because I knew about it, and was already involved down in London, we put in a bid for one. And got one. That was the first one in Bedford, and it opened about the same time as the one opened by the ex-nurse. We made a big splash of it, organised Brian Rix to come down to the launch, and we got the mayor involved, and even the chief constable. We had all the great and the good, as many as we could attract.

We had a slight crisis almost immediately because one of the residents had to be taken back to the hospital. We agreed to take a couple from the hospital as part of the package, as it were, but the others all came from the local community. And we had all the usual start-up problems. I remember, the day before, suddenly thinking, "What are we doing? This is absolutely terrifying, taking on this responsibility!" I remember feeling, "I hope this is going to work, because we're going to be in an awful mess if it doesn't." But it worked. We did have problems – staff turnover problems initially. Three members of staff suddenly upped and left and, since we haven't got any other homes in the immediate vicinity, we had a problem of getting locums in quickly, and that sort of thing. But then we recruited some more people.

I think it met a need that had never properly been articulated before. The nightmare situation for an awful lot of people who hadn't chosen to use the institution – and their numbers were growing all the time – was: "Suppose we are no longer capable of caring for our offspring, or relative? [because often it's brothers and sisters] What's going to happen to them?" And you face the situation of somebody, perhaps at the age of 50, suddenly being uprooted from a comfortable home and dumped down in Bromham. Because Bromham was the only provision, that was the situation we faced. That's why we did it, that's why we founded Homes Foundation, to cater for people in that situation. And they weren't young people entering the homes, they were largely middle-aged people who were approaching that kind of situation. But then it changed, and I remember talking to the assembled Homes Foundation staff while I was still involved with the one in London, and saying, "One of the things we don't know is whether, in the future, families will choose to have their child go into residential care when the others leave home, in their early twenties probably. And we don't know yet how many people are actually going to choose that route, but if they do choose it, you're probably going to need rather more beds than you think you do." And it may well be that for two-thirds of their lives, they're going to be in Homes Foundation care, and there will be perhaps a bit of a gap between leaving school and going into one of the homes, but it may not be that big a gap. In fact most of them didn't even know how many they'd got in their area. I used to say, "Go to the school and find out how many there are and multiply that by three, and that gives you an idea of what your customers are going to be."

Relationships with the statutory sector

The interest of the Director of Social Services was very important. David Clifton was the first Director of Social Services in Bedfordshire, and he invited both of us round to his house, and I know he gave me his private phone number. I didn't quite realise the significance of that at the time. I always had access to him in County Hall, he made it clear that he supported our general aims and objectives, and we in our turn of course did our best to support him in his situation. I do remember him saying that he'd been to visit Bromham Hospital and he'd formed a very poor impression of it, and I think we were fortunate in having someone who was prepared to take a real interest in the field. I think he made a very big difference to the development of services here. He set up a working party, and invited us to put a representative on to it. And that sat and operated for something like two years I think, producing general policy statements, so we had a very real input there. He came up with this adult fostering scheme, which we did our best to fit in with. It wasn't a great success, unfortunately, but we did try to do that.

We had a member of social services who regularly came to our committee, and if they didn't do anything else at least they listened to us. And we always felt that they were accessible to us, and we could make an input. The contrast between social services and the health service was quite marked. They were indifferent. I mean the hospital itself didn't really want to interact with people out in the community. Perhaps that's slightly unfair, but that's my impression. And although some people went there for short-stay, we got such horror stories back. You know, 'they went in decently dressed and came out in rags' – and this kind of thing. In fact I was assured on one occasion that one of the nurses had been seen wearing the clothes that had disappeared. And there were one or two scandals at Bromham, and one nurse at least was sent to prison eventually. So it was not seen as a place that contributed very much to us folks here in the community.

Of course all sorts of schemes came up. We were told that people were going to be returned to the locality from which they'd come. That never happened. We were told that the whole thing would be handed over to social services, and that didn't happen, largely because of the job implications, actually, when it comes down to it. So they had to find something for a lot of health service staff to do, and one very notable thing is how often, when we interviewed people for jobs in Homes Foundation, the people who'd been working in hospitals came out right at the bottom of the list. They were just not getting the jobs, and in the end we actually offered to retrain some of them here in Bedford. And we took them on, I think. I didn't have a lot to do with it but I know it happened. They came for a short conversion course, and we did have some very good people out of the health service. It wasn't entirely one-way, but they were certainly not ideal from our point of view.

This is an example of the difficulties we had with the health service. One of our members needed a cataract operation, and the local hospital refused to do it, so we were told. And so we quite simply said, "Right. We'll raise the money to have it done privately, we will give this maximum publicity, and we'll march up and down outside the hospital waving banners." The hospital just changed their mind and I believe the operation was carried out fairly quickly. That was the watershed. Before that they wouldn't, or at least they were extremely careful about, admitting people with learning disabilities. After that they were quite prepared to do it. It seemed to me their whole attitude just changed, I think because nobody had ever really put it to them before, you know. In the past you went to an institution like Harperbury where there were provisions for everything, including an operating theatre, and that used to be the situation and they hadn't realised. I don't think they were malicious. They were just ignorant.

Attitudes

When I was at school I had a friend who I knew had a sister who had some kind of problem, I wasn't exactly sure what. And one day he suddenly said would I go and stay the weekend with him because his parents were going away, leaving him on his own. And so I went out there and spent the weekend with him. Looking back, I now realise that this was when his parents were taking his sister off to put her into an institution. I didn't quite realise at the time what was going on, but that was certainly one incident from my youth I remember. But I do remember other people, and I know one family in the vicinity I often used to meet then, had a daughter with Down's Syndrome. Again, it didn't make much impact on me at the time. I didn't really notice, hardly, but there were certainly people about. And if you did go out near Powick, where they all lived, you would occasionally meet a party of 30 or 40 of them, all marching along over the Malvern Hills, or something like that, out for a walk, you know. I remember again being surprised by how upset some of my female relatives were by this. I had a couple of aunts with me and they were quite upset and put out by this happening. It didn't bother me, but again, children, I suspect, are less bothered by this kind of thing.

Chapter 26
Parents in Partnership

Croydon Parents' Group

I came across Parents in Partnership (PIP) when they produced a booklet, called Moving On, in October 2000. The booklet is a collection of stories of young adults with special needs in Croydon, Surrey. PIP developed in the late twentieth century as a mutual support organisation run by and for parents. The booklet suggested that at least some of PIP's members were interested in telling their stories. One of the founders, Daphne Jones, arranged for a group of parents to meet with me one evening in June 2001 in a church hall in Croydon. The transcript from that tape-recorded group conversation formed the basis of the stories now included in the book.

Dorothy Atkinson

Introductions
Marilyn:
My name is Marilyn Pearce. I have 16-year-old twins, Adam and Neil, who were born on 6 January 1985. They both have neurofybroiditosis (NF). The oldest twin, Adam, has physical problems that gave him learning difficulties and has got progressively worse over the years, as well as having asthma and eczema. We thought our other son, Neil was going to be fine and then two years ago he just suddenly lost his memory for no reason. We have had a lot of problems. Because it is such a rare occurrence he doesn't fit into any of the pockets and it's very difficult to get any help for him.

Maureen:
I am Maureen Wright; I have a son, Martin, of 27. He was born on 13 February 1974. He is doing well; he has been through school and college and he is working now for my husband's business two days a week, and he has another job that he travels to. He does one day a week at college. He has Down's syndrome, and has coped really well.

Kay:
I am Kay Vere and I have a daughter, Anna, who was born on 18 June 1979. She was 22 this week.

Colette:
My name is Colette Michael and my son is 29 now. He was born in December 1971; he is my first child.

Daphne:

I'm Daphne Jones. Philip, our son, was born on 26 January 1980, just at the moment the Warnock Report came out. I was aware there were changes in community care. My husband said, "He is all right", because it was a fortnight before we actually knew that he had Down's syndrome. One of the things that kept my husband going at that stage was that perhaps Philip would go into an institution. But as we delved into the national press we realised that things were moving at quite a pace. We have an older daughter and I think another thing that kept him going was the thought that we had another child. We realised that when the pressure was on, we were fortunate to have another child.

Finding out

Kay:

Anna wasn't diagnosed straight away because she's got a rare genetic syndrome. We had to get to Great Ormond Street Hospital to get her diagnosed. That happened when she was about two. We got advice from the physio there so we knew what we had and what it was, but nobody knew very much about it because it was so rare. We went to an opportunity group for about 18 months. When she was three she went to St Giles' School for physically handicapped children.

Colette:

I had one day of thinking Gershwin was OK and then the nurse saw the photo on my locker and said, "Is this a photograph of your husband?" I said, "Yes." We were asked to make a point of being together because they wanted to see us. We were told our son would be slow and it was broken gently like that, and left for us to work this out. When I started quizzing one of the nurses she let it out what the actual thing was. The reason they wanted to see the picture of my husband was that they wanted to know if he was Chinese, because apparently they had made that mistake in the past and told somebody else they had a Down's syndrome child.

Somebody suggested we left Gershwin there at the hospital and went away to have other children. That was one option. But your firstborn, you don't really do that. Then we saw Valerie Cowie who was quite famous. She was very helpful and suggested we had other children. And we did, we had another little girl, and then I suppose this might be the reason why I got a bigger family. I thought it was unfair for one child to have a handicapped sibling so I thought we could have a few more, so we did.

Kay:

Finding out was a battle because it was a rare, unrecognisable thing. Anna had blood tests, but what do they show? Well, it means they can say, they had done their homework, can't find anything wrong, she's fine. But it did take going to the opportunity group to tell us. I think it was my health visitor who had a spot of inspiration, who said there was this nice place. We had tried the local toddler group and there it was very apparent that Anna wasn't the same, she was spastic. She wasn't running around and doing things. So we were taken to the opportunity group and I was saying, "We'll go, because it's got a swimming pool and that'll be nice." We went along and Mary Sinclair saw us. She said, "She's floppy; she's not doing this and that." She said we should get a second opinion. She said, "Go back to your GP and ask for a letter to see a neurologist", and she said, "If your GP won't give you this letter I will come with you." He did, so that was our first battle, and we did that.

The second battle was persuading my husband there was something wrong because Anna and I went into Great Ormond Street for three days or so while they looked at her, and did some tests. There are less than a dozen of these cases in England, so I can't blame them for not knowing what it was. I was told what was wrong and what it was called, and what it meant. They were quite horrendous the things they said, like she will have an IQ of 40. They said she won't marry, this sort of thing. The neurologist was from the old school, and he had an arrogance and attitude which upset my husband. I was told what was wrong, and told: "Go home, talk to your husband and then come back in a fortnight and we will discuss it together." But my husband wasn't convinced, and said, "What's normal?" I said, "I've seen the notes, and they said, 'This family will need support, especially Mr Vere.'" It's taken a good half of her life really for him to accept it. But it is a rare thing.

Anna has Sjögren's syndrome. She is spastic from the waist down and her skin feels very dry and very itchy. She can't sweat very well, so you have to watch her, she could overheat if you aren't careful. She has speech difficulties, quite profound speech difficulties when she was younger. But she has certainly got better and developed. She has a learning difficulty, chronologically she is like a seven-year-old, and she has eye problems, too. It took us two years to find this all out. The hospital were very helpful because they were quite interested, and started doing quite a bit of research when she was six.

Marilyn's husband (Patrick):
The twins were both asthmatic, so we were down the hospital all the time. Adam used to redden on the side of his face, every time he was fed. You could draw a line down his face. We kept asking what it was, all sorts of theories came up. He then developed a bump on his eye which kept growing and the paediatrician at the hospital looked at it and noticed that there were milky coffee marks on his skin, like large birthmarks, and quite a few of them. They said that was a diagnostic feature, they could tell from that that he had NF.

Marilyn:

We had three years of them lifting his vest and saying, "Oh yes, look at that!", but not actually doing anything about it. Then they said, "I'm really sorry about this but he has got NF. I want you to go away for two weeks and I don't want you to look it up in the medical dictionary or anything like that, just come back and then we will talk about it." Then the community nurse who had a lot to do with us because of their asthma, came up and said, "I don't think you should take any notice of what he is saying. I think there is a group for this." She gave me a name and a telephone number. Of course, the next day he flew down to the library. He came back and said, "The Elephant Man had it!" It was just awful.

It went from bad to worse after that because Adam was disfigured on his face. It swelled more, but we couldn't get anybody to do anything. Then my mother went and poured this out to her GP, a big buxom woman who didn't stand for any nonsense. She said, "I will send him to Great Ormond Street, so let me have a look at him." It took us from February to October to get anywhere. When she rang Great Ormond Street they said, "We don't take referrals from GPs." So she said, "We've waited four months of a child's life, and you ring me up and tell me that!" They said, "Oh, all right then, we'll see him", and so we went to Great Ormond Street.

I find you go from one person to another, to another. You go a different day to see each person, and they say, "We don't do that here", so you have to go a different day to see to his skin, a different day to see his neurologist, and a different day to see the facial surgeon. Now Adam has reached transition from Great Ormond Street and has to go to Chelsea and Westminster. I nearly said, "Oh, that's a new one: we haven't been there yet!"

Maureen:

I had my boy. I had two daughters, he was my third child. I was absolutely delighted that I had a son at last and to me there was nothing wrong. They moved me off to the isolation and said, "We have got to move you, your temperature is up", but I thought I felt all right. A nurse came in when my husband was there and said, "The paediatrician would like to have a word with you on Monday." This was Saturday evening. She went off and we thought it was strange, what does he want to see us for? Then the night nurse came in. I said, "The paediatrician wants to see me and my husband on Monday, what is that about?", and she said, "Oh, you have noticed there is something wrong with the baby, haven't you?" I said, "No, there is nothing wrong with him; the baby doctor hasn't even been round." And she said, "Oh yes, they checked him at birth", and then you are really frightened to ask, aren't you? What am I going to do?

Of course, they use that horrible word. I said, "What is it?" and she said, "Well, you have heard of mongolism, haven't you?" and then she said, "Oh no, don't get yourself upset, I wish I hadn't told you." I said, "It's too late, I just want my husband back please." Anyway, they gave me sleeping tablets and said, "We will get him here tomorrow", but they didn't call for him. I had to go to the phone to ring and I was absolutely distraught. I had been taken, wheeled through to outpatients after they told me what was wrong, after the nurse had blurted it out. I had to sit outside and wait to go in, to be told by the head paediatrician, "They think it's Down's, you know and of course you know that he will always be simple. All he will ever do for you is a bit of dusting." I was really devastated. Then they had to take blood tests, and I couldn't see anything wrong with him at all.

It was taking six weeks, and in that time they told me, this was the head man, that they may have made a mistake. When it came to the six weeks to ring up for the results they said, "Oh we have made a technical error, we need you to bring him back, we need to take more blood." We had to start all over again. But by the time they took the next lot of blood, when I went back, I knew in my mind, what they were going to tell me, I just had a feeling. He told me the same story, "We have got places we can put him if you don't want to keep him."

I just thought, "I'll prove you wrong!" I came out and thought of it as a challenge. Let's get on with it. And you know, he's lovely. We've had our moments and it's still worse now he is an adult. But he has done well. I did prove him wrong! But it wasn't handled well.

Colette:
Those weeks, when we were waiting for that test, they last forever. We were in Birmingham when Gershwin was born and we had to go back to London, to Queen Mary's. Everybody said, "Well, I can't see anything wrong with him, he looks perfectly all right to me." And you are just hoping all the time that it was all a mistake.

Maureen:
You want everybody else to know, so you didn't have to tell them. You didn't want the embarrassment of people walking up to you, but people weren't like that, they knew. They'd say he was lovely, but they knew.

Daphne:
It was when our GP was about to retire. He came round one Saturday morning and told us that Philip actually had this Down's syndrome. He couldn't tell me anything about it, so my husband went down to the library. All he could find was the *Encyclopaedia Britannica* in which it said they were cretins, and

that was not helpful. We had a whole weekend and nobody had given us any idea that there was anything like a Down's Syndrome Association. So it was, "Right, well you can go and see the paediatrician on Monday." So we went to see the paediatrician. Our GP had said, "This woman has been struggling with this baby; she deserves to know what is wrong." This is because he didn't feed very well and I didn't know why.

So our GP had never had anybody with Down's syndrome before in his practice although he was about to retire. He had nobody he could tell us to go to and I came in here (church) actually on the Sunday and they said, "Oh how's your baby brother?" to my 2½-year-old daughter, and she said, "Not very well." I couldn't tell anyone because I knew that I would be in tears. I eventually rang one of the ladies I knew very well and then people were very supportive, but also very sad that I hadn't had the guts to say. They said, "Oh, why couldn't you have told us?" We had already told everybody that we had a little boy, you see, and we had a little girl and a little boy, and it was great. And granddad had been down, and he'd said, "Well, you've got cauliflower ears, boy, just like me", all those sorts of things. And suddenly you have to turn around and tell everybody.

When we saw the paediatrician she said, "Your baby has Down's syndrome. I believe you have been told." My husband then decided he wanted another baby. The last thing I wanted was another baby, but I was trying to cope with it because I had been trained as a counsellor and that sort of thing. So I was actually able to step outside to some extent, whereas poor Kingsley, he took it to heart, and his whole life was ruined from that moment, that was his perception.

This paediatrician was not at all helpful because Kingsley wanted another baby, and asked, "Can we have genetic counselling?" "Oh," she said, "'common or garden' trisomy 21, Mongol, whatever you want to call him." Some years later, we took her a little book in which Philip was featured and showed her: "This is our 'common or garden' Mongol!" I was so angry that he wasn't a person to her. Our house was full of books and Kingsley is an academic chap. I had some dealing with kiddies with Down's syndrome when I was teaching at a residential special school for ESN children and I had come across them. I had also come across some older people with Down's syndrome, all trailing around in a group, or just behind their mother, and those were the visions I had.

I sat there and I was like "Aaaghh!" I asked, "Would he be able to read or anything like that?" I was told, "Oh no. Of course there are people who say they can read a bit but of course they don't understand what they are doing, it's just a thing they go through." She said, "Everything will work itself out, go away and enjoy your baby." We said, "Thank you." So we went out, and we had a little Ford Escort then, and I put the baby's cot in the back of the car. Kingsley just flopped over in the front of the car because he had held himself together through the weekend but suddenly was faced with the reality. He had thought "Perhaps she's going to tell us it's a mistake", so it had hit him completely.

So I put the cot in the back and pushed him in the front and I am not sure how we got home, actually. But there was no support, there was nothing. They didn't say "There is a group you can meet", or anything like that.

Marilyn:
You hold their little hands and you think, "Two babies!" and that was before there was anything wrong. I had that experience when Adam had his very first operation, it was done by this plastic surgeon. We went back afterwards and he was a sweaty-palmed, tight-skinned, horrible man and he patted me on the hand, and he said, "You go away and don't worry about it. He will grow, the growth won't, and he will look like everybody else when he is 17." And now when I look back, I think "moron!" That wasn't what happened at all – left to him, Adam could be dead.

Patrick:
Like, the doctor who said, "Don't look in any medical books." Well, I went to the first bookshop I knew – it was near a medical school and they had all the books. I looked up NF and it showed photographs of people with huge tumours on their bodies, as they can come up all over the place. It also referred to the Elephant Man. In fact, that's what he was called at school, after the film was shown on television.

Getting information/finding out more
Colette:
The problem is that Gershwin's additional problem, his hearing loss, was not diagnosed initially. He was about eight before I got someone to say that he was deaf. Prior to that I had taken him to Queen Mary's, just faffing about with speech therapists. I felt like a dotty mummy because I was told he had all the sounds necessary for speech. Another person in Croydon also put him under anaesthetic to test his hearing, which he said was the only way to do it. That was nonsense, of course, because Blethwyn Davies had him for about half an hour and came up with what the actual problem was.

Daphne:
Philip went through mainstream school, but he has a very severe speech and language difficulty. It was put down to having Down's syndrome, but then when he was about five we actually got an appointment and he was diagnosed as having quite severe speech dyspraxia. So it was a different dimension and we were told that the speech problem was the area that was going to cause him difficulties as opposed to having Down's syndrome as such.

Colette:

The thing I found was that you had to find out your own information. You had to go to libraries, you had to read things in magazines and find everything out yourself.

Maureen:

Our children went to an opportunity group, so we all went. We had lots of support; physio, there was a doctor, health visitors. But from the day that you leave the opportunity group, I know you can phone and ask but if you are a mother or a parent you think, "Oh no, it's all right, we will manage, we will get on with it." Nobody ever comes, do they? There's not that support.

Colette:

The opportunity group started after Gershwin was born, and when he was six weeks old we moved out of London. I didn't know a soul. At the bottom of the drive there was this Salvation Army place and I went there to the Young Wives' club to get some kind of contact. Of course, that is where Rebecca was, Elizabeth Blackwell with Rebecca, and so they put me on to Elizabeth. I felt totally inadequate and that stayed with me for a long time. Through that you got the connection with Rex Brinkworth. I thought, "Oh bother, I've come all the way from Birmingham and that's where he is." But we got that connection there with the Down's Syndrome Association. That's what it was called in those days.

Colette:

The people I knew were older parents whose children were older; they hadn't got this sort of thing. I remember the Portage system coming out. What I wanted was someone to come to my house and do something like Portage. It wasn't there then, but it's what I wanted. I did the flash cards and he did learn, but of course we didn't know he was deaf then. Still, he could see words and recognise them, and make the same sound each time. He did learn to talk through reading, so he did learn to recognise print from a very early age.

Daphne:

That is part of the interest that we three have because of Down's syndrome, and because of Down's Babies Association and the work that Rex Brinkworth did. You had the feeling that if you were able to intervene then, although you may not be able to change the world, at least you are actually doing something. Most people are a bit laid-back, other than people like Mary Sinclair at the opportunity group. She said, "Don't you dare let him shuffle-bottom across the floor. He should be crawling." You know, those people were a tremendous inspiration, but it was only due to the setting up of that group by other parents, after your time.

Colette:

What I used to do, Elizabeth had this huge baby-walker and I had a cottage which was terribly small. So I used to take him out every morning to the Salvation Army Hall and put him in this.

Marilyn:

We did try the NF Association but the trouble with NF is that it affects everyone differently, so you could never talk to anybody who had the same symptoms. And then, when Neil got his problems the first thing I did was phone them up and ask had anyone else lost their memory. "Oh no", they said.

Patrick:

But he's done really well. He's very studious. At school his teachers said that he loves school, loves working. School is his life, he loves it. He got knocked down one day on his way to school, but he was back there the next day.

Daphne:

The main purpose of Parents in Partnership is passing on and sharing information. It's why we are together, more so than just having meetings and speakers. We actually manage to find something out. It was in 1992 when we started and two of us had a chat. It was due to when people left the opportunity group and fell into a void in terms of support. It was also the time when they were reviewing the special education needs policy in the borough. I said that parents who had children in mainstream schools had no one, we weren't joined up in terms of being consulted. Although there was this drive for mainstream education we weren't being consulted, and we made the assumption that people who were in special schools had the parents grouping together. I suppose within about six months we realised that wasn't the case, they had no one either. We really started off as a consulting group for the authority, and they have given us a couple of thousand pounds a year since then to do that. But they 'forget' where we are sometimes when it comes to the important consulting.

Getting resources

Marilyn:

It's difficult getting help with Neil, now he has lost his memory, and it seems nobody has come across this before. They don't know why he has lost it and they don't think it will come back. I think if he had lost it through a head injury, everybody would be a little more accommodating. But because nothing happened to him other than the fact that he went out one day, came back and couldn't remember where he had been or what he had done, and complained of headaches, nobody seems to want to know. And he is in this transition period, which makes my heart sink really because at the end of the day nobody is going to help you. You have to just battle on, write more letters before you can get someone to even see you.

We keep having battles, and I think there are some more coming because the chap who we battled to get, I'm not convinced he is the right person. He is all we have got and he is leaving at the end of July. They don't know what to do with Neil, really, they keep talking about, "We will have a meeting." Well, we have been having a meeting for two years and they are talking about moving him on to adult services. I don't know; we will just have to play it by ear. The unit we go to is for child and family psychiatry; he is a clinical psychologist.

Kay:
Anna went to St Giles' School for children with physical disabilities. She liked it there and did well until she was 16 and then went to Treloar, a college in Hampshire. We were advised to go and look at various places. The trick was to know what you wanted, then just go for it, keep on. So she went there till she was 19. And from there was an even worse battle, as to where she should go next. Everybody agreed that she shouldn't come home because she had done well and was independent, and it would be wasted if she came home. Treloar suggested a Queen Elizabeth Foundation place in Leatherhead, which we looked at and it seemed perfect. But the first meeting with the social workers – they hadn't even seen it, mind you – they said, "Don't go there!" And we said, "Why not?" and they said, "Well, we can't fund it." That was like a red rag to a bull, so we just made a case, we just kept on and on and finally in the end the social worker did go and have a look at the place, and did agree that it was lovely. Eventually we made a case, but it was a long battle. She is still there, hopefully for another year. You know, they fund these things yearly, but she can't stay there forever, she will have to move. Croydon Social Services and Housing will need to work together and provide something. They have nothing at the moment. Meanwhile she can stay where she is, which suits me and suits Anna. Whatever happens next will be for the rest of her life. That will be the next battle.

Daphne:
It was a full-time job with Philip, all the trips you had to make. We did speech therapy with him and after he had his first appointment when he was about five, there was no speech therapist assigned to him here. They said, "Oh you will have to be trained yourself to work with him." I said, "Hang on a minute, I'm a teacher, not a speech therapist." So we managed to find the lady who had referred him to the Ear, Nose and Throat Hospital. She was on maternity leave, and we had a private arrangement whereby I would look after her baby, in fact

I looked after all three of her babies. If we added up how much she cost us – well, we daren't. I actually went to work as a home tutor to pay for him to have speech and language therapy because we thought it was so important. We used to get him there before eight o'clock in the morning before he was exhausted with school. It didn't matter whether we were exhausted, we got him there. And then I took him along to school and he would always miss a little bit of something, but nothing really important, and our battle was really trying to get people to appreciate that in order for him to access the National Curriculum he needed speech and language therapy in the school.

Kay:

I really did battle with the statementing. The speech and language therapy came in part 5, which means you don't have to have it, but if it can be provided it would be nice. We really battled to get it into part 3, where it is then part of the education service, and they had to provide it. But this was Croydon, and we had to get a private assessment and we did all that. We shamed them into providing it, but they shamed us by saying, "You realise we are funding Anna's speech therapist but our funds are very limited, so someone else will suffer."

Daphne:

We took Kingsley's big briefcase to Philip's review. He always used to come to meetings with me and at that time he was working at Her Majesty's Treasury so he had a really nice big briefcase with official government letters on. So we'd go in with this because he'd never leave it in the car and I'm sure it had an impact, because people saw that and didn't dare start arguing. At one stage, there was this debate about Philip's speech and language therapy, and I knew how much it cost for a youngster to go away to a residential school – which was part of what they said they would do for him. We said, "How on earth is it as much as £25,000–£35,000 a year? Speech therapists don't cost that much do they?" And it was logic they couldn't argue with. But it was different pockets of money. So you get there in the end, but it is the sort of battle that you know very few people have actually won. It actually has a negative effect because they have had to work in school for so long without support, by the time they actually get it it's next to useless.

Maureen:

We had a specialist health visitor, she was the first person who actually gave me some hope. She came to the house and said, "Mrs Wright, this is the beginnings of what we are going to do for this child." And it was like, "Oh good, what are we going to do?" She gave me encouragement every time we saw her, she gave us exercises to do and encouragement – "You are doing really well."

She was fantastic, and when she left I wanted to cry because I thought I'd never get anyone else to do it. She said, "I am sure the next person will be as good as me." And she was, yes.

Colette:
I had the first specialist health visitor come to visit me at home and said, "I don't know what I am doing, I'm just learning. You will have to help me!" And I had to help her. I can't remember her name.

Marilyn:
You come to be seen as difficult parents. I think we are still seen as difficult. When Adam was being bullied, we even got on to the police in the end because the school wouldn't address it. The primary school were fine, they did everything they could to help Adam. But it took us three years for the secondary school to acknowledge that he needed some help.

Patrick:
They had a bullying policy but it wasn't clear how it worked. He had been bullied by several kids, but also by one particular child who was quite a big lad, so I got fed up in the end and telephoned the police in Croydon. I asked how they considered treating bullies, because I wanted to tell the school that I had reported it to the police. I said, "Will your school liaison people go down to the school and tell them that you have heard there is a problem before I make a formal report?" They could understand the seriousness and they did, and the bullying stopped.

Daphne:
Once they get to 25 of course the further education has gone and it is very difficult to know how to attack and go into battle with social services. It's difficult to know how much a parent should expect of them.

Coping with transitions – leaving school/growing up
Daphne:
At the moment Philip is at college in the New Forest which is supposed to be therapeutic. I am not sure whether he is there for the therapy or the horses. We had quite a lot of work to do in the transition from that, to what will actually be a 52-week-a-year placement in Somerset, because again there is nothing in Croydon. We said we were happy for him to go there, where he will do another college course around animal care, and a couple of days working with either dogs or horses, which will suit him down to the ground. Then we want him to decide whether he wants to come back here to find a more permanent residence in

a place that he thinks of as home. But he is quite comical in that having been through mainstream, the last two years are the only time he has actually been with people with special needs. Philip comes out with it, telling us quite clearly, no, he doesn't get a disability benefit because he is only half-handicapped. He is working it all through so that he can learn to drive the car and all the rest. So there are side bits to inclusion.

Marilyn:
Of course, Adam looks quite different. Life is tough. And everybody assumes that because he looks like he does he is not quite the ticket as well, which isn't true. He is quite bright, but obviously he finds it difficult to see things and he is quite slow and he gets very tired. And he is left-handed as well, he doesn't write very well.

Patrick:
He's blind on one side. He couldn't take notes at school, he had to turn like that and it slowed him down. But he does quite well. He finished school yesterday.

Marilyn:
Of course, one of the problems I have now is that after devoting years to Adam, it really put his nose out of joint because Neil got ill. And now he is saying to me that Neil is my favourite. He doesn't remember all those years; it was awful really. So I just say to him, "Well he doesn't give us grief like you do! If he was your son he'd be your favourite, too!"

Patrick:
Neil was always very good at school, academically he did quite well. Then when he lost his memory, of course, he can't retain things, you see but he works really hard. Of course it is not a problem you can see, whereas Adam, you can see he is disfigured. You can't see Neil's problems and people just assume they are not there, especially people who have not known him so long.

Marilyn:
We can't get any rehabilitation for him. And then we had the problem, "We don't treat children, we only treat adults", and this is all still ongoing really. He doesn't fit into any category at all. Memory loss, amnesia, they only happen to adults – not to children! Everything is about money. But Neil was very calm about his exams, I was very proud of him. We were very anxious about his perception of how well he has done and what his results show.

Patrick:

Now we are at a transition, trying to find a college, as there are virtually no sixth forms in Croydon. Adam is going to school with a sixth form because it will be better for him because of his disfigurement. He is also small and I don't think he can go straight into a college where everyone is a stranger. Neil is going to Carshalton to do IT.

Marilyn:

Adam has a very big face, and one eye is actually now closed, but he couldn't see out of it anyway. The operations don't seem to achieve very much, sometimes they give you other problems. Like last time, they operated on his forehead, they compromised his scalp, so he ended up with this great pussy wound and he lost his hair. He had a big bald patch in his hair, and where the hair has grown back it's all frizzy. He doesn't look any better. You wonder about the benefits: it's all cosmetic – none of it was life-threatening. He has said he doesn't want any more operations.

Colette:

I am really proud of my son! The fact that he is partially hearing and he has great difficulty with communication, and yet he travels independently. That makes such a difference to life to be able to go and travel, and get some self-esteem. I am really pleased, you have got to take calculated risks all the way along the line otherwise you protect them too much. He has his second day at McDonald's today. He was in the kitchen, filling the dishwasher, packing up the iced juice, washing the floor, he had different routines to do.

We have Status Employment here, a wonderful charitable organisation started by two young social workers a few years back. Now it is quite a thriving concern. What they do is they train them, they shadow them for however long it takes them to get used to the job. Then gradually they are trained and travelling, they know what time to leave for the bus. It's a charity.

Daphne:

Status Employment is a wonderful example of something that was joint-funded through the Disability Forum and then locally they decided they wouldn't fund it anymore because it wasn't new. So they spend the rest of the time finding the funding. I mean it is nationally accepted as one of the best, and they have spent a lot of time doing work nationally with the National Development Team. But there isn't enough. And what really makes you cross is that professionals say, "Oh, Status Employment" and the authorities say, "Oh yes, wonderful", but they don't write any cheques out. They don't understand there is a waiting list for Status Employment. They do a lot of proactive work in schools and colleges as well, and they even send teachers out to see what a day's work is like.

Kay:

Anna went to a development centre, in a residential college. She had a structured timetable, and had training like schools.

Colette:

Gershwin goes to a day centre. He has that as an anchor but he doesn't spend much time there. It's because I am teaching full time, it is where he goes for a base. He also goes to classes at the local college and he has got his work. I got a job in an ESN(M) school partly to get my son in. It was the place to go rather than the ESN(S) school. They had a new head in, because the old head said, "Oh the children will never read and write." She was a very nice lady but had that idea, and the new head came in and was really very good, had very good, new ideas.

My traumatic time was at the end of school and deciding what he was going to do. I happened to be having counselling at that time and we thought we quite liked the idea of a Steiner set up. We'd been to Botton Village, and thought that was nice. Having said that, we were talking to the school and the head actually suggested something up in Oswestry. She said, "Oh, that sounds rather good", and so of course we had a look and it was near the grandparents, and we thought that would be nice. We had the social worker round and said we liked the place, but the social worker said, "I don't think so." So I said, "Let's go to Steiner and have an interview with them and see what they have got to offer." And so he ended up going to a place near Gloucester, and they were very much in favour of that and he went down there.

It wasn't a happy experience from my point of view. I'm sure he was OK but I couldn't get the communication, it was a long way away, and I felt it was more really for children with autism. They weren't allowed to watch TV, or have sweatshirts with labels, normal teenage things. I felt he needed to be with his peer group at college. We had to struggle to get him out, and that really traumatised him for a bit. He went to college, loved it, and I thought, "I am never going to get funding again." I knew I would be fine with him when he was small but I didn't want to be the parent of an adult mentally handicapped, you know, you have seen them. So I don't know where we go from here, because I am on my own at home. There is another crossroads fast approaching, retirement, so what do I do?

Daphne:

It is awful when you have to say to someone like social services, at a review, I refuse to have Philip come and live with us at home. That breaks my heart, but you have to be absolutely clear that for him, progression will mean moving elsewhere. To him, yes, there is always going to be room for him at home. But for his sake, at my age, I feel very strongly that he has got to have something established for him. That is partly because I managed to get him into a college that had a residential home that was paid for by the FE funding, and they can see the progression. Parents who have put them in local colleges and things have now got this situation where they have got to try and move them on and it is very hard.

Kay:

The thing we have with Anna is about 'when is it me and when is it her?' The people in the Foundation, there are about 25 there, but only about ten who are really older – because the Foundation has a commitment to them. But from now on they say it's a transitional place and they can't keep them. The philosophy is to help them learn to manage their own life. They should do their own thing, such as ring up the DSS. It is very difficult for a parent to know when to sit at home and watch it all happen and when to step in. Anna rang up to say she had a letter about housing benefit and had to fill in a form. It is very hard to sit on the edge and watch it sitting in her room for three weeks, for six weeks ... I found it very difficult when she first went, I thought they were putting on them too much. You have to get to the point where you stand back and say, "Well she is there and that is going to help her to actually manage, even though she's bound to fall over a few times and things are going to go wrong. But that is how she is going to learn." But it's scary!

Daphne:

It's quite difficult for me at the moment, because Philip is going into a full-time residential place in Somerset. It's at least three hours' drive away. I have to actually hand Philip over to somebody who is going to be his 'mum', as it were. It's quite traumatic.

Kay:

I still feel awful. Every time you drive away you think, "I have put her in an institution." It's a nice institution, but you still feel it.

Colette:

If Gershwin had been happy there then I would be fine, but he lost half a stone while he was there. Funnily enough he doesn't eat bread, and that was their staple thing within their philosophy and so he lost this tremendous amount of weight, and it was far too quick. His ears had lots of infections and we caught them out because they hadn't actually got the doctors in, and things like that. So when things like that happen you get worried.

Daphne:

But it is the quality of life for them that you should worry about. Are they going to manage? Philip needs a tar bath. And you worry if this woman will be happy to have this smell in her house. We've got used to it here. It is all the daft things you worry about. It is the silly things that you worry about and say to them.

Chapter 27
We have come a long way down the road together

Shirley Colquhoun

Susannah Chappell interviewed Shirley Colquhoun for the first time in August 2001 and I carried out a second interview a few months later. The following account is taken from both these very rich interviews. Shirley Colquhoun and I have together transformed the interview transcripts into a narrative of her life with her grandson Alex.

Melanie Nind

Early years

Alex, my grandson, was born on 14 October 1973 at Queen Charlotte's Hospital in Hammersmith. He was very much a wanted baby and my daughter Gillian and his father Jonathan were delighted to have a boy. My husband wanted Gillian to come to England to have her first baby because he knew the problems being born in another country could cause in later life; they were living in Switzerland at the time, for Jonathan's work.

Gillian was looked after by Mr Lewis, who had looked after me at Guy's Hospital when she was born in 1948 and who was now a senior consultant at Guy's and Queen Charlotte's. As far as we knew it was a perfectly normal pregnancy and perfectly normal birth. At first Alex seemed all right, but then they found he was mildly jaundiced and he lost weight and was not feeding properly. They took a specimen of urine and, as Gillian and Alex were home at my flat by then, the head paediatrician came rushing round about 9pm and said that he was to go on to an antibiotic at once as he had a severe infection. This worked, and he stayed on it for three weeks until he was fit to fly out to Switzerland.

Queen Charlotte's Hospital then handed him over to be looked after by Professor Gautier at the Cantonal Hospital in Lausanne so that Alex could have regular check-ups. In May 1974 my daughter rang me from Lausanne to ask for help as her husband was in America. Alex had been for his check-up at the Cantonal and Professor Gautier had told her he thought that Alex should have an operation for a large reflux in the right side. I asked Gillian to send the X-rays by air at once and I would get them shown to Professor Williams at Great Ormond Street. Queen Charlotte's felt that we should let the Cantonal go ahead with the operation as they were in a better position to judge his condition. So on 12 June Dr Mayor operated on Alex, and we must be thankful that there were no complications after what was a long and difficult operation. After a few months of tests at weekly intervals they said we could stop testing and he has never had any more trouble from his kidneys.

In September 1974 I went out to Switzerland to stay in my daughter's flat in Lausanne to look after Alex for three weeks while my daughter was on holiday. As he was rather backward in crawling I was asked to take him to the gym twice a week. This I did for the first week, but then I was rung up and told not to come as the woman who took him for gym was ill. So I thought I would try at home and simply put some jointed, silver fish from a table that he wanted very badly some way ahead of him on the floor and waited to see if he would try to move. In no time he had got to them and then I put them further and further away and tried other things he liked and he never looked back. In fact it had been more peaceful when he was just still. If I had to leave him I always put him back in his playpen for safety.

My husband came out to join me for the last weekend and Gillian was back and we went out and bought him a nice new highchair and some toys to help get him moving. I did not find him difficult to look after and I had not looked after a baby for about 25 years, except for a few hours. The worst problem I found was that he dribbled a lot, but with plenty of bibs one coped and stopped him getting his nice clothes wet. An old family nanny said he sounded like other Colquhoun boys who, when they were young, tended to be rather lazy and sat down and were slow to crawl and to walk while the girls ran around. Gillian was told that he would be six months behind because of his operation and one accepted that.

In December 1974 Alex came over to London with his parents to spend Christmas with their families, and afterwards Alex was christened at St Michael's, Chester Square, where his parents had been married in March 1971. Gillian and Alex stayed on in London with us. In February they were moved from Switzerland to Johannesburg in South Africa by Jonathan's bank. It was sad to have to move and to be so far away, but for Jonathan it was a very good job and they were given a lovely big house and garden which was so much better for Alex as he could run around and enjoy himself. The flat in Switzerland had no garden and would not have been suitable as Alex got a little older. For the first year they took out a Swiss girl to help look after Alex and of whom Alex was very fond, as he had been with her in Lausanne. Then Alex had a very nice black nanny called Sarah. He was happy with her and soon also became friends with the cook who looked after him when Sarah had time off, as he could not be safely left on his own.

One day Alex was left while Sarah went to put something on in the kitchen. He was near the radiogram and he found something that looked like a toy, but was used to joining the wires from the radiogram to the lead from the wall, as none of the plugs from Switzerland fitted the wall plugs. Everything with Alex at that age ended up in his mouth, so he had a very bad burn on his lip and was taken to hospital by a kind friend who was called by Sarah. Only the fact that he was wearing rubber sandals prevented him from being killed.

Gillian's daughter Marisa was born in Johannesburg on 9 June 1976 when Alex was three. There were no problems and Gillian was so thankful to be told that she was a nice normal baby. In July 1976 my husband suddenly became very ill and he was told he must have an operation at Queen's Hospital. I had to tell Gillian, and she so wanted to see her father and to show him Marisa. Friends somehow got her on to the next plane with Marisa and they turned up at the hospital, having flown all night. Gillian was so glad to seen her father before he went in to have his operation that afternoon. He came through the operation and I was allowed to see him and I thought all was well. But I was rung the next morning at 6am and told that he had died. As after a week or two Gillian had to join her husband for a business trip that was arranged before David was ill, I kept both Alex and baby Marisa at my flat and had a nurse for Marisa.

When Gillian could return we had an appointment for Alex at Great Ormond Street with Dr Brett, a consultant neurologist. He was very kind and arranged for a psychologist to assess him too. They both felt that he should on no account be labelled at this young age and Dr Brett said he would be very unhappy for Alex to attend a school for severely handicapped children. The psychologist was particularly impressed by his good personality and his well-developed sense of his own identity.

Then they returned to South Africa and Alex went to an ordinary private nursery school, which he loved, and he rode the tricycles rather better and faster than the other children did. They said he was very good and came and sat down for their story with all the others, but he still had very little speech. In 1977 it was felt he needed more help than the playgroup could offer and he managed to get a place at a very good modern school, Forest Town School for Cerebral Palsied Children. Alex was happy there, as he always was at all the schools he went to; he liked being with other children and always made friends. He also needed the help of the very experienced teachers who understood his problems and tried to improve his speech. In 1978, after a year, Forest Town decided that, as he didn't have cerebral palsy and was taking the place of children who did, that we must find another school for Alex.

From some of my contacts I heard of Camphill schools and was told of Cresset House, Camphill Training Centre for Children in Need of Special Care.

This was outside Johannesburg and meant a long, hot drive twice a day, but it was a good school and the only suitable one. Alex went there from 1978 to 1979.

In June 1979, while they were out in South Africa, they noticed that Alex's toes had started to curl up and he kept falling over. He was seen by several doctors, as they first thought that he had muscular dystrophy. But to our great relief he was diagnosed as having bilateral cavas feet, in gait. On 26 July 1979 he had a Steindler Strip operation. I went out to Johannesburg on 4 August to look after Alex and Marisa and the house and dogs. This was because Jonathan had to go to Switzerland for his bank and it was important for Gillian to be with him as they were going to be moved to Germany early in 1980. So I took Alex backwards and forwards to the hospital to have his plasters changed. He was very, very brave and his father had given him a bicycle for being so good and he was longing to ride it. I asked the sister at the hospital who had put on his new plaster up to his knees on both legs if she thought he could try to ride his new bike. And she said, "Oh no, not possibly, he will be able to walk on carpet in the nursery." After lunch we went down to the front door for Alex to look at his bike, and then I had to go back for something and when I returned Sarah, his nanny, was standing there but there was no sign of Alex or the bike. So I said to Sarah, "Where has he gone?" and she replied, "Oh, madam, I couldn't stop him. He is riding his bicycle down to the gate." Well, he had ridden down to the gate and back safely, and from then on he never stopped riding his bike. He does not have a normal sense of fear.

Coming to England
In January 1980 Alex came to England and he became my charge. I have acted as his guardian since then. With all the best medical and educational psychologists' advice at Great Ormond Street and Riverside Health Authority, it was decided that Alex should remain in my care in London and go to a very good boarding school, St Joseph's Special School in Cranleigh, Surrey. It was a Roman Catholic school for boys up to 12 years. I was told of it by a friend at Mencap, who knew of a doctor in Kensington who had a boy of Alex's age who was very happy there. My daughter brought Alex to London and we all went down and looked at St Joseph's. I had been before and liked it very much; it was very much like so many other boys' prep schools I had visited. Alex was shown everything, his bedroom and a lovely nursery, and a sweet nun, Sister Gerard, who looked after the younger boys. They all had photos by their beds and teddies to make it seem as much like home as possible. We went to see the classrooms, which were modern buildings at the back of the house. They had a good playground with swings and slides and a pet donkey.

Alex settled down very happily at St Joseph's and soon made friends. It had been a school for boys for 31 years and very well known, and so it was a dreadful shock to have a letter from the bishop saying he would have to close the school in July 1981, as he could not get enough nuns and he could not afford lay staff. In the meantime the fees would increase from £3,000 to £6,000 and, if taken over by Surrey County Council, they would rise to £10,000. This increase was also because of the price of oil for heating a very old and large country house. I discovered then, which I had not known before, that we were one of very few parents paying fees. We then had another letter from the bishop saying that they would stay open until 1982. That gave us time to think. I now had time to talk to our doctor, and his advice was to get into the state system as the small homes and schools could close down and they could not offer the wide range of back-up that the National Health and ILEA could provide in their schools.

In November 1981 my doctor sent Alex to see Dr Jazeel, the principal physician for child health at St Stephen's Hospital. Dr Jazeel then arranged for Alex to be seen by Miss D'Aeth, their educational psychologist, in order to assess his educational placement and make recommendations to the ILEA. Before he returned to St Joseph's for his last term he was also seen, in my flat, by Mrs Mary Hardy, the senior nursing officer and coordinator of the District Handicap Team, which was based at the Cheyne Centre for Spastic Children. The team was to monitor Alex's progress and Mary Hardy was wonderful. She took great interest in Alex. He was put on the Kensington and Chelsea register, because they were trying to plan ahead. It was amazing how many professional people one had to deal with and organisations one had to join to do the job of being a grandmother and guardian properly. I used to spend my entire life at coffee mornings to raise money all over Kensington and Chelsea, and we all met at Mencap meetings.

On 7 April 1982 I took Alex down to Ongar to see Great Stony School, meet the head, Mr Barnes, and most important, to see the junior house, Bowes, and Mrs Hicks, who was in charge of the young boys. Bowes was made as homely as possible and teddies on the beds were encouraged. Mr Barnes said he would take Alex, and in due course I was sent a nice letter from the ILEA at County Hall telling me to take Alex to Great Stony on 4 May 1982. Alex was there from 1982 to 1990, from when he was eight to 16.

Alex got his 'statement' in 1984. For some reason they were very behind with statements. It named Great Stony. We could not ask to go to another school in the country because Great Stony had lots of places and needed the pupils to help pay for the cost to the ILEA of maintaining such a large school.

*The school covers curriculum areas of a wide-ranging nature
to help the special needs of young and immature pupils with
learning difficulties and which can best be met in a boarding
school environment. [It] aims at meeting Alex's need by the
development of a secure and structured environment, a social
and adjusted set of values and a realization of what is right
and wrong. The needs also for stability and the shaping of
peer group behaviour are further being met by added attention
being given to his rather severe learning difficulties which need
a more developmental curriculum.*
(statement of special educational needs)

In the ILEA the people were all first-rate teachers with the patience, and
the training and the knowledge. Alex wanted to learn, he wanted to learn to
read, but a lot of them did not, they were the failures of ordinary state schools,
they weren't severely handicapped, they weren't very mentally backward.

The headmaster said he would make Alex literate, which I rather laughed at,
at the time, but he did. He got reading books from America because the English
reading books that they had failed on they didn't want to know. They were
well taught in class and when they finished a book they then had to take it to
the headmaster. He didn't trust the staff to say, "Well, he can read that book."
If they read it properly they got a sweet and a pat on the back, and a hug,
I think, if they were a girl (you couldn't do it now), and then they were proudly given
the next book. Whether they picked up Americanisms I didn't quite understand.
It worked, anyhow. Alex can now read *The Times* if it is about Liverpool
football club. I couldn't think why he would say, "Did you buy *The Times*?",
and I would say, "Yes, Alex, did you want it?" "Yes." I said, "What did you
want it for?" "I want the football." So the football is always removed from
The Times when he is staying with me. The football correspondents write with
the most long, flowery words they can think of, but Alex will get the gist of it
and he is happy.

At Great Stony there was this enormous black boy, who is now a plumber;
he was quite clever. He took Alex under his wing, probably because Alex liked
him and didn't call him names; some of the other ones called him a Paki.
Nobody would ever dare do anything to Alex because this boy would have
come down on them; it was like any ordinary school.

Great Stony was so good for the children, they were frightfully well fed
and it was spotlessly clean. When they returned to school at the start of a new
term they wore their own clothes, and after lunch they were given a bath or
shower and dressed in their very nice school uniform; they had nice green
blazers and had to learn to tie a school tie every morning. Alex was taught to

write by Mr Monroe, who wrote a letter for Alex and Alex had greaseproof paper over the top and traced the writing through the paper. As Alex was left-handed it was very difficult for him, but he learnt and could soon write on his own. Mr Monroe wrote 'lovely writing' on one of his letters. Mr Barnes made everyone write a letter home every Monday; if it took all morning it didn't matter.

They had a very full and good life at Great Stony. Alex joined the Ongar Scouts, which Mr Barnes ran. He went camping with them and went on wonderful holidays. Alex so enjoyed going on an Adventure course at the Dartmoor Centre that included climbing, caving, canoeing, pony trekking and sailing.

Moving on
When we had to find a good college for Alex to go to from Great Stony from 16 to 18, I was very lucky that everyone agreed that if he were accepted, Lufton Manor Rural Training Unit near Yeovil in Somerset would be the best place for him. Because it was run by Mencap, and the Queen Mother was its patron and the Archbishop of Canterbury a vice-president, I did not think anyone would dare close it down. We filled in all the forms and Mr Paddon at Great Stony and Mary Hardy and others all wrote nice letters recommending Alex for a place.

Then I was given an appointment to take Alex for an interview and for him to stay overnight at Lufton and the next day, to see if he would fit in. I drove down the day before and spent the night in a hotel not far away so that Alex would be fresh the next day. Alex did not feel like his breakfast so I knew he was feeling a little nervous. Alex had made up his own mind that he wanted to go to Lufton when I had been able to take him to an Open Day in the summer and he had been able to see it without being under the pressure of an interview. I left him at Lufton with his night bag and was told what time to collect him the next day, when I would have an interview with the headmaster, Mr Brooks. When I collected him he looked very happy and Mr Brooks said he would take him and he could start in May.

It was a great relief and wonderful news for us all. If he had got a place at Oxford it could not have meant more. At Lufton you spent a few weeks in the big house and as soon as the staff thought you were ready you moved out to a chalet in the garden. You had your own room, but they had two boys to a chalet. Alex liked life at Lufton and enjoyed work in the garden. He loved best being asked to dig the foundations for a new chalet. He dug huge trenches and got deeper and deeper down until you could only see his head above the trench. Later on, Alex was moved to a flat at Manor Farm and was in charge of it with two other boys, and kept it very well.

The present and the future

After Lufton Alex was able to move on to The Stables Family Home Trust at The Stables at Bisterne, near Ringwood, where he's been for nine years. Because it is a trust with very good trustees it is secure, and I hope it will be able to give Alex a safe and happy home for the rest of his life. Alex has family who live not too far away who will be kind and have him out when I am no longer here.

They live at night and on weekends in groups of eight in three houses. Every weekday they go in minibuses to The Stables, where they have various workshops and the gardens to work in. Alex changed from gardening to wood-work in his first year. He likes being part of a group all working at different things but able to talk; football is Alex's favourite subject and he is a great supporter of Liverpool. They have a very good hot lunch cooked for them at The Stables, and some of them work in the kitchens.

Alex now has what he wanted more than anything – a nice, large room of his own with a shower and loo. They had to move to a larger house so that everyone has a room of their own. I was allowed to have it decorated and furnish it. Alex made lots of shelves for his Liverpool mugs and videos and CDs. He loves his new room and takes great pride in it. He keeps it very clean and tidy; he has a small electric cleaner he keeps in his room and uses all the time. All his Liverpool things are around him, from a rug on the floor, paper basket, and a lamp with Liverpool shade to his duvet covers.

Alex, Liverpool supporter

Once a year he goes to watch a match at Liverpool with his father, and comes back laden with presents from the team of signed shirts and balls and things he has found in the gift shop. Everyone up there is so good to him.

In May 2001 Alex went on holiday to Malta and for the first time since his operation in 1979 his feet really hurt him. And he could not carry anything or walk for more than a few yards. When he got back to England we had to wait a long time to see Mr Farrar, a consultant on feet, and he finally operated on 12 January 2002. Now, in June, he has been for his final check-up on his left foot, and he is free of pain and has a normal-looking foot which he is thrilled with. Mr Farrar will operate on his right foot, which does not hurt him, to straighten his toes only, in December.

His latest report states he has a stable relationship with his girlfriend, as they live in the same house they see more of each other than he did previous girlfriends.

They have wanted to have a shop in or near Ringwood for some time so they could sell the things they make and run a café. Clare Davidge, the training officer, took Alex and Charlaine and others in the shop project to London for an interview with the Millennium Commission to ask for help with starting a shop. Clare felt they had done well in putting their case and they have just been told that they have been awarded £10,000 towards their café project. While waiting to hear from the Millennium scheme they had marvellous news that the Owl Sanctuary, in connection with Barclays Bank, had offered them a room to turn into a shop, and when the café has been done up by Barclays it will be staffed by residents from The Stables. They will have a share of the profits. Alex and his friends are so thrilled, and Alex is going to work on Saturdays and is already cleaning the shop out and washing it down before they paint it. There is to be an opening on 1 July 2002 and we are all invited.

Alex worked at B&Q before his operation in January and they have very kindly kept a place for him and he has now returned to work on Mondays, which he loves doing, and he takes himself there and back on public transport.

In the past nine years Alex has been on every possible college course and he has all sorts of certificates from Brockenhurst College, and even two silver cups which he won for courses on football.

I am now 85 and Alex will be 29 in October, so we have come a long way down the road together. I think, looking back, that it was probably a good thing that I knew nothing about children with learning disabilities as, apart from his schoolwork which I knew would be very difficult for him, I saw no reason why he could not learn to behave as well as other children. As he was always very independent and liked to do things for himself it worked well for Alex. He was asked to normal children's parties. He flew home to South Africa for school holidays with only an air hostess to look after him. Because he could be trusted to behave he had a far better life than otherwise would have been possible.

I know I was lucky in having a niece in the country with five children and two boys, one a little older and one a year younger than Alex. For them it was a treat to come to London and stay with me and Alex and be taken round every possible suitable sight and museum. When he went to Lufton he had a friend up to stay and we took him round and Alex liked showing off his knowledge of London. Alex also has a great friend, Jimmy, who lives very near us and is able to come round and have a meal when Alex is in London. They go shopping and even went to Liverpool to a match when, at the last minute, Alex's father was unable to go. Jimmy is a normal young man, but they rode their bikes together as small boys and I took them in the car to Battersea Park and they have remained good friends.

Chapter 28
Wherever we went we would bump into somebody who knew Mark

Mark's mum

Mark Bellas was a Director of Carlisle People First. He died on 9 April 1999. His mother kindly agreed to take part in the interviews in memory of Mark's life and this chapter is drawn from the interview transcripts.

Rohhss Chapman

We wanted another baby, and he arrived

Mark was the first boy in the family, so that was our family complete and he could carry the name on. However, when he was born and in hospital he was awfully sick. I already had one baby and I knew this was wrong. Anyway, we came home and I went to the doctor's, and he still wasn't putting weight on. I took him back and we got an appointment at the hospital, and it was something to do with a loose valve in his stomach. We got the result when he was about 16 months old. We also noticed his hands would go round and round when he cried a lot. He wasn't a happy baby, you could tell there was something.

He was about 16 months when he walked and he was late sitting up. His speech was late. I asked a health visitor about the speech a few times and she sent us to a clinic. They did a test to see if he was deaf, and that was all right. So, we went a few times and she said, "Oh, I think he is OK", so that was it, we didn't bother any more and she signed us off.

Starting school

I was at the doctor's and we mentioned that we thought he was a bit behind, but he said, "Well, just leave him until he starts school, and then we will see how he progresses." So, he started full-time school the day after his fourth birthday. After a few weeks the headmistress asked to see me. She said she thought there was something up with Mark; she said, "I think he is part spastic." I got this feeling, as if someone had just kicked me.

He knew where to put a piece of jigsaw but he couldn't coordinate putting the puzzle together, it was fine movements that he couldn't do. The doctor said he wasn't spastic, but he made us an appointment at the hospital to see a paediatrician. He was diagnosed with apraxia, a condition that affects fine motor control, and denotes coordination and learning difficulties. There were other things like his letters, he used to get 'b' and 'd' mixed up, 'u' and 'n', 'q' and 'p'. We tried and tried with them until he got it. There were buttons, he would start on big buttons and work down to small ones. The doctor suggested we used Velcro as a fastening, but we wanted to persevere so Mark wouldn't appear different to anyone else. All along he would have bed-wetting sessions, sometimes twice a night up until he was about nine years old. After that he had to go and see a psychologist, who said he could have extra help at school. The teacher was lovely, but sometimes Mark would be in a world of his own, looking out of the window.

It's just a squint

Just after he was nine years old we noticed that when he was sitting watching the television he would lift his whole head back rather than just his eyes. I kept saying, "Mark, you are sitting too near the television." I thought I would take him for an eye test and the optician tested him, she said, "It's just a squint." I came out and made an appointment at the doctors. He thought it might be a migraine but to be on the safe side he got us an appointment with the specialist. The school phoned us and said that they were concerned about Mark, and they had noticed the same thing as us. He got really bad headaches, and I took him to the doctor and he said, "It is a migraine; I will give you something." That was on the Friday, but over the weekend he got worse and he was getting pains in his lower back. We were awake all Sunday night, because he couldn't settle and we phoned the doctor first thing in the morning and luckily our own doctor came and he sent us right up to the hospital. And then from there the specialist said it could be serious, and we would have to go to Newcastle.

He was lifting his head because of fluid build-up in his brain, which was pressing on his optic nerve. This is why his eye movement was impaired. The tumour was a very rare one, deep in his brain, so it was inoperable. A shunt had to be put in to take away the fluids. Then he started the radiotherapy, and he was really ill with that. He couldn't keep any of his food down. Eventually he was allowed home for Christmas, and every weekend. But sometimes he really was ill, coming back and forwards in the car; he was sick such a lot. We had to give him his medication by suppositories, and all his hair fell out. It didn't bother him, he just made a joke of things, and luckily it was in the winter and he would wear hats.

Nobody told us about benefits

While we were in the hospital, this lady, a social worker perhaps, came round and had a form. I saw 'cancer' written on it, and it was the first time it really hit home, you know, I don't know why, but once I had seen 'cancer' it floored me.

She asked us if we were managing financially, and if we had any HP, debts and mortgage. She said we could apply for benefits. I said, "We won't be entitled to any benefits as my husband David is working and I have worked part time."

Nothing was mentioned about Mark's illness and whether he might be entitled to benefits. The way she was speaking it was all about Mark, not us. I didn't know you could claim for a child with a serious illness, nobody mentioned anything like carer's allowance or disability payment for Mark, despite the fact the doctors told us he only had a 40 per cent chance of survival. We thought he wasn't entitled to anything but now we realise he probably was. I feel that we weren't given all the information at the time, which had a big impact later on and right through Mark's life. The fact that we hadn't claimed then seemed to make a big difference later on.

After his initial treatment the doctors told us that if he survived for the next five years that would be progress and ten years would be excellent. It was only then that we fully understood Mark would not live to a ripe old age.

Schooldays

After Mark came home he went to a special school. He was put back a year at school because of what he had missed through illness. A year later, when it came to going to secondary school, we were advised to choose a small school. We had to go before a board because it wasn't our catchment area. He got into the smaller school and it was a really nice place, the teachers knew all the children and it was more like a family school, Eden School.

When he was leaving the junior school I asked the headmaster to send on a report on Mark's health and progress, which he told me he would. But a few weeks after Mark started I got a phone call, I think it was the deputy head saying he was concerned about Mark, in the way he was looking at them. Anyway, I explained and it was clear they didn't know anything at all about Mark's medical history; I felt I had tried my best to make sure the information was passed on. Overall the teachers said he was a helpful boy with lovely manners, he wasn't any trouble.

He loved the plays and every year he would want to be in the school pantomime. We used to get a laugh because he was always late getting on to the stage, and it took him that long, you would see somebody push him and he would still be getting into his position when the curtains opened up. But he loved it; he used to say, "I am going to be on the telly. Mum, I'll be a comedian." He just did three GCSEs because they said it would be too much to try and do more so he did maths, English and art. He got low grades but we were proud as punch of his achievements.

Leaving school

Mark used to go to the technical college in the evening, to a class for physically handicapped people and people with learning difficulties. Then he got on to a course in the day, he did joinery and cookery and things like that, he would do a bit on computers and had two or three days' work experience. I never thought the kitchen was really a safe place for Mark so when he got his job experience, guess where they put him? In the restaurants, and kitchen work! The restaurant rang up one day to say that Mark wouldn't cut onions, and I said, "Well, the only thing is that he is clumsy with knives, and onions are slippery anyway. He's not being awkward; he just doesn't have the coordination." One day they were baking scones and he had forgotten to put in the sugar; he still had some days where his concentration was poor. He would have to organise stock cupboards and then he would come home and my larder got sorted out! He would go through and check all the 'best before' dates. When that course ended there didn't seem to be any job opportunities available to him so he made an appointment to see the Employment Liaison Officer by himself.

He was told by the officer to go round to the employment office, "But don't say you have been here first." I felt like he was fobbing him off, but they seemed to disregard the fact he had special needs. So in the end I went with him and they told us at the employment offices that he did need a sheltered work placement. So we thought, "Where do you go from here?" You are told to go to one place and then to the other, and then you are told he needs something else, but you are left in the middle and you haven't a clue where to go.

Aged 22, Mark has a stroke

I made tea and I said to Mark, "Come on, get up, have your tea", and he said, "I can't get up, Mum", and I said, "Don't be so flipping daft", and he was laughing. I got him to his feet and his arm was floppy, and then his speech was a bit slurred and I said, "Are you pulling my leg?" I said, "Stop it", because he was still smiling. The doctor came and said we should take him up the hospital. We said we would just put him in the car and go up. Well he couldn't move, and we had a heck of a job trying to get him in the back of the car but he was just laughing as usual. When we got him there they said he had had a stroke.

So, he had to go over to the hospital in Newcastle again. He was put on steroids and given a lumbar puncture. His speech came back a bit, but it was fast and you had to try and listen carefully to what he was saying. They couldn't find out what had caused it, and said it could have been a virus and that Mark would need a lot of rehabilitation, he couldn't walk and had lost the use of his right-hand side. There wasn't any proper rehabilitation place in Carlisle, but the doctors made us an appointment in Newcastle to look around Hunters Moor rehabilitation.

We went to have a look at it, and it was marvellous. They had tools for gardening and a greenhouse. There was a room with art in and cookery and table tennis. Mark was offered a place there, which meant living away from home for ten weeks, but he would learn self-help skills and become more independent. Staff would take the patients out to the pub and watch them to see how they were getting on, you know, it wasn't just a day out, they were seeing how they managed, and all that kind of thing. They had speech therapy and physiotherapy and all kinds of help. They said Mark could have the next available place but then, all of a sudden, he got sent back from Newcastle to the Cumberland Infirmary in Carlisle. We rang to ask why and they said they couldn't accept him at Hunters Moor until they had agreement from Robert Marks in Carlisle. We didn't know who Robert Marks was! We asked time and again to see this elusive Robert Marks and kept missing him or not being told when he was there, it went on for ages, we got nowhere. All this time was being wasted when Mark should have been getting rehabilitation. He missed two beds over in Newcastle and we knew that the more help you got straight after a stroke the better. It turns out there might have been a funding issue between the two hospitals and we were caught up in it, but we certainly didn't know what was going on.

When you are worried about somebody you don't need extra stress and pressure. All we wanted was the truth about the situation and the best care for our son. If you are not a pushy person it is really hard. We felt if we didn't push for Mark, nobody else was going to bother. You feel as if you are a troublemaker, it really did make us feel uncomfortable to be continually asking questions and not being allowed to speak to the decision-makers. Finally, after weeks of struggling, Mark got his place at Hunters Moor.

Mark gets a job at People First
I think it was our occupational therapist, Maggie, who got Mark involved in People First, an advocacy group for people with learning difficulties. He started going there to the meetings. He loved it and then there was the chance of a job coming up. I thought he would never get it; I didn't know what it entailed, but we got him all dressed up in his jacket and tie for the interview and he got his CV together in his case. When he was offered the job he was over the moon, and we had a celebration. This was really therapeutic employment and seemed suited to someone with Mark's difficulties and talents, as it was PR-based!

I thought I had better go and tell the DSS that he had a job. He had been employed for two weeks, so I gave them the date he had started. The person I spoke to asked where the doctor's note was, and that we should have had it before Mark started the job. It was back to all the rules and regulations that you don't even know exist. Then we got a letter back from the DSS saying there was a controversy about the job Mark was doing. In the end we had to go to tribunal.

Mark, Director of Carlisle People First

Problems over benefits

Instead of taking any rent off Mark we let his benefit money build up. He was earning £15 a week doing his job at People First. However he wasn't supposed to have more than £3,000. We wanted Mark to have money for himself in case anything ever happened to us and we didn't realise this was a problem. After filling in a DSS form they told us that Mark had well over what he should have. I tried to ask them what was going to happen if we couldn't look after Mark – if he was only allowed £3,000 he was never going to be able to afford even an electric wheelchair.

He didn't have life insurance, because with all his medical complaints the premium would be too high, so that is why we wanted him to have money set aside. We were told we would have to pay back a substantial amount. Mark had been on benefits for three years. It was quite a carry-on from the January to October and we were worried sick all this time. I asked if there were any other benefits he could go on so that we could look after him financially, but we were told no. The DSS said we couldn't ensure that Mark would have a secure financial future. You feel belittled. They seem to know everything you can't do, but they don't know what you can. They don't tell you anything clear or where to go, and you never get to deal with the same person for any consistency.

We did think about moving to a bungalow and we thought some of that money would go towards making him a proper shower room where he could be more independent. Something that he could live in after we got older, because we used to have to bring the bed down when he wasn't well and we were worried about him going up and down stairs because we were frightened that he was going to fall.

Eventually we got a bill for £2,900.60 and so we paid that back, and that was in the October, and then in the January there was a phone call, a woman was coming the next day from the DSS. She had a great big A4 sheet on a clipboard and there were three things written on it; there was his bank account, his little post office savings and his benefit. She was filling this form in.

They told us because Mark was on the middle band of disability payment that he couldn't move from that to the severe sickness benefit, which would not have been means tested. I later discovered from the Benefits Advice Centre that this was completely incorrect.

Finding things out

I feel stupid myself because I had let Mark down, and then the people who actually work there don't tell you things you really need to know. You just get the feeling that they think you are scroungers. I feel we let Mark down because we couldn't make sure of his future financially, because if we left him money in a will he would lose his entitlement to benefits. That seems so ludicrous to me, because inheriting money doesn't stop him having a disability. It's like Catch 22 the whole time. I went all over the place to find information, I went to the Citizens Advice and got books out. Nobody wanted to know before the stroke, it was as though he was perfectly healthy up until the stroke when he was 22, because we had never claimed anything prior to this. In the end I went to a solicitor. We were in there for 20 minutes and it cost £228 and she just went through and said, "Yes, you are over the limit." But she just went through everything and said, "If Mark wants anything you are entitled to get it." We were trying to save up and so we got him a computer, and we were going to get a new wheelchair, a motorised one so he could go out on his own.

You feel as if the money isn't yours

When the man from the DSS came I remember he said, "Oh, that is a lot of money you've spent", as he went through the bank book. I said, "That was to pay for Mark's computer", and he said, "Oh, that must be some machine." We wanted the computer to help Mark write more legibly. Mark never went out drinking, he would never be able to have a car, he didn't even have a swish wheelchair, he couldn't go on holidays like us and yet he came out with that remark that really made me annoyed. You feel as if the money isn't yours and you have to justify everything. You feel degraded, you really do. And you just think, "Well, where do you go for help?"

Once, after a lady from the DSS visited, I asked who was in charge of the office, and I needed to speak to somebody senior. She looked at me and she said, "What do you want to know that for?" I said, "Well, I have asked you questions, I have asked the other man who called questions", and I said, "You can't tell me the answers", so I said, "If I could speak to somebody senior I might get some answers." She said, "Oh, just ring the office and somebody will see you." You go in, and one time it is one person and another time it is another and you end up explaining everything over and again.

Even when the social worker came, she was asking Mark the questions for disability living allowance, and I thought she would have read through all his notes and know all about his illness. But she said she didn't think Mark would get it because he wasn't bad enough. I wondered if he would need to be bedridden! She really didn't know that he had to be helped with everything, she hadn't read any of the notes, I had been doing all that since he was a baby! When he took ill for the last time we were still trying to sort it all out.

It was never resolved

It was never resolved. It is really upsetting. David says to forget about it but I can't, I just feel I need answers. If I could just sit down with somebody, it could be resolved in no time. I would have been more than willing to go for a medical with him, and get a consultant report and things, but they just fob you off. Your responsibility is there all the time when you are looking after somebody. You know you can't switch off, can you? It is heartbreaking.

Mark's last illness

So, when he was taken ill for the last time he was only supposed to go into hospital in Newcastle for four days, when he had had another stroke. He was going to have a lumbar puncture and more steroids and then he was to come home.

David and I noticed for a while that he didn't seem right ... there were little things that you can't quite put your finger on and he would be a bit breathless when he was getting up and down. He was a bit shakier. When we had been on holiday he was getting these spasms more. He would still get loads of headaches, he would get dizzy spells and I always said to him, "Mark, if you get dizzy shout at us, or get down and come down on your bottom on the stairs", you know. Now and again he would shout, if he was going upstairs he would get them, and I said, "Just lean forward", and they wouldn't last long.

One day he had a really bad one in the kitchen, and he shouted, "Mum, I feel funny." I got hold of him and I got him sat down on the chair and eventually he came around all right, and he turned round and he said, "Mum, I think I am going to die." I said, "Don't be soft, we will take you to the doctor's." He did all the tests; I couldn't have faulted him. We were concerned about the dizzy spells. He had double vision all the time. They said they wouldn't operate on him, it was too dangerous and the risk wasn't worth taking. So, anyway the doctor said, "Bring him back in a fortnight if you are not happy about him." Neither of us was very happy when we came out, and then the next day he was going somewhere with Karen, his support worker at People First. Karen was going to pick him up. He said, "Mum, I have got another clonking headache", and I said, "Well, if you don't feel well I will ring Karen up", but he said he was going to go with Karen. When he got home he wasn't well at all; I could tell. I had noticed a few weeks before it seemed as if his tongue had curled a bit sidewards, just little things like that, and you think, "Well, if he does it again, I may be imagining it", so I kept watching him. It's like living with a time bomb, all the time looking for signs that something might be going wrong again.

Anyway we went to see the doctor and as soon as he went in, he said, "Mark, you are not well, are you?" He said, "I think we will have you at the hospital", and so I told him what had been going on and he wrote us a letter. He was in there a few days, then Dr Jackson called through and she said she would have him over at Newcastle. He was only supposed to go from the Wednesday to the Friday or Saturday, depending when he got the lumbar puncture. So, they did tests and then the doctor had gone home and a young doctor was on and he said, "I don't know what to do with you; the blood tests don't show what we would have thought."

Mark still had these funny turns. We had a phone call from Dr Jackson who said that Mark had had a rough morning, and she thought that if she rang instead of just waiting until we went up, she said, "He had a few bad spells and we think you should come over." So we went over and they found out it was one of the main blood vessels into the brain that had been damaged by the radiotherapy treatment that had cured his cancer 16 years before. The blood wasn't getting through; she said there was only 20 per cent of the oxygen his brain needed getting into the brain, so no wonder he was having really bad spells. They decided to give him something to thin the blood to make it easier to go through the vein. But not only that one was damaged, there was some damage to the next of the four major ones as well. But the thinning blood caused a major bleed internally. Then he was paralysed and his voice started to go. We were told when he first had the tumour when he was ten if he got five years that was good, you know. And ... when it got to ten years it was excellent, they were really pleased. And in between times sometimes you have to rush off to Newcastle and when he was getting bad heads and things like that, you always have to be kind of prepared. We knew it was going to happen someday, but we didn't live like that. It is a horrible thing, but when we were going through the thing with the DSS I used to say to Dave, "I hope he does go before us." I didn't mean as soon as that, but you just think, "Who would care about him?", because nobody seemed interested at all.

The impact of Mark

He brought a lot of love and happiness for us. He was a proper character. I mean, with him being hyperactive when he was little he was never still, but the things he used to do, you couldn't help but laugh at him. He liked travelling. It was when he didn't have any friends of his own, not knowing where to go for help, we took him everywhere, it was like three in a marriage, he was always with us, you know. But you used to feel it would be nice if he had his own friends away from us, and got out.

My mum ended up with a brain tumour as well and bone cancer, and if she was going through an operation she would say, "If our Mark can do it, I am going to be all right", and Mark would say, "Think positive." That was his saying: "Think positive." He had such a lovely nature; if you were a bit down he would give you a cuddle or he would come in and say, "Mum, I have got us a treat" – may be a cake, because he wasn't supposed to eat cake. He was a thoughtful little lad, even when he was small, he used to go Auntie Renee; she used to live two doors up. When her husband died Mark used to go every day, and she said, "Do you know, if he didn't come in, sometimes I would never see anybody." He could talk to old people and young people.

He seemed to get on with people really well, even on holiday, if you went anywhere you would get in a lift, and people just stand and they don't say anything. Well, the next minute Mark would say, "Are you having a nice holiday?" and they would answer, and then, "Yes, the weather is nice and we are going to so-and-so." And then for the rest of the week they are like his friends, you know, if he would bump into them, "yak, yak, yak", that was Mark. Wherever we went we would bump into somebody who knew Mark.

Future

Now that there is greater inclusion of children with disabilities in mainstream schools I think it is really important that, as they leave school at 16, they are given medicals. If their illnesses are documented before the age of 20 they can be put on a non-means-tested benefit, which means the families will not have to go through all of the stress with the DSS that we did. They should be given a caseworker at the DSS, someone who knows them, knows what they are entitled to and can point them in the right direction.

You shouldn't have to fight all the time. Mark's life was hard enough and too short to endure all the extra upset that this created. Because his disability didn't categorise him he didn't fit into a tick box. We felt that he didn't get the support he needed from the agencies involved.

Conclusion: emerging themes

In these more recent life stories a sense of pride, celebration and progress is frequently interwoven with continued experiences of personal struggle, frustration and confusion. From the beginning of the period, with the White Paper *Better Services for Mentally Handicapped People* through to the very recent White Paper *Valuing People*, this has ostensibly been a period of positive policy and written commitment to advancing community participation for children and adults with learning difficulties. The official history tells of a time when institutions were closed and increased emphasis was placed on supporting people with learning difficulties at home within the family. It tells of the development of community-based resources; the stress on ordinary living, with equal access to primary and acute health services, and latterly of growth of advocacy and self-advocacy; an awareness of other dimensions of difference such as ethnicity, gender and sexuality; and an era of rights. Education policy brought new access to education for all, and gradually greater access to mainstream schools.

We see evidence of these trends in the personal accounts. There are recurrent themes that emerge from the narratives, however, that emphasise the issues that the families have seen as important rather than the issues that have assumed dominance in the policy framework and professional literature. There is, of course, some overlap here, but by starting with the emerging themes from our witnesses' stories rather than from the official history, we get a different picture of key issues of change and continuity across the period.

The themes that emerge in Part 3 are:

● beginnings

● family networks

● struggles and battles

● changing labels, changing attitudes

These connect with the official themes of:

● community – segregation or inclusion

● an ordinary life

Beginnings

When asked about family and community life with a relative with learning disabilities, it is a natural tendency to start the story from the beginning. The stories of birth and diagnosis told for this period do little to indicate an era in which attitudes and practices are much changed. The birth of the children was not seen by professionals as something to celebrate; for them the notion of disabled children being a burden is retained. Most of the children were born towards the earlier part of the period 1971–2001, but signs even of the beginnings of new approaches by medics working with new parents of disabled infants are elusive. These families, like families before them, lived with unclear information, lack of support and poor, unhelpful and uninformed prognoses in the early weeks, months and years. In 1971 it was suggested to Colette that she should leave her newborn son Michael, diagnosed with Down's syndrome, at the hospital. When Kay's two-year-old daughter was at last diagnosed with a rare genetic syndrome she was told, "she won't marry", and Maureen (Parents in Partnership) was told that all her son would ever do for her was "a bit of dusting". Even medics acknowledging the achievements of people with learning difficulties undermined such achievements. Daphne's paediatrician, for example, explained that although some people with Down's syndrome "can read a bit", "they don't know what they are doing, it's just a thing they go through". Unhelpful comments were followed by lack of helpful action: being patted on the hand and told, "You go away and don't worry about it" and feeling too frightened to ask (Maureen) and being "left to get on with it" (Elaine Monk).

In contrast to the earliest experiences, some of the stories in Part 3 do tell of more positive intervention in the pre-school years. Support did arrive for many of the families in the form of home tutors, Mencap nurseries, opportunity groups, physiotherapists and Portage workers. Support also came from other parents who both shared experiences and gave practical advice and help and who were "a tremendous inspiration" (Daphne, Parents in Partnership). The raised expectations in this era for children with learning difficulties are evident, if not in the outlook of some of the medical professionals, in the willingness to invest in provision for children in the early stages. The gratitude of parents for this support is touching. Maureen says of her specialist health visitor, "She gave me encouragement every time I saw her … she was fantastic, and when she left I wanted to cry because I thought I would never get anyone else to do it." The statutory and voluntary services had something to offer, and if this did not match with the families' aspirations they were often proactive in finding solutions for themselves, such as Elaine Monk's family privately funding support for Rachel.

Family networks

Clearly evident in the narratives is the role of family networks in providing (or sometimes not providing) webs of support. We see grandparents taking on important roles, from being the main carer in Shirley Colquhoun's case, to offering forms of shared care and sometimes alternative perspectives on how things should be. It was Elaine Monk's maternal grandparent who offered her support with "Rachel's constant crying", filling the place of absent services in her early years.

We also see much concern given to siblings, with families rather than professionals attending to the rights of siblings of the children with learning difficulties. They relate their awareness of how a sibling can feel left out and tell of attempts to keep them involved. Joyce Mays recalls, "I felt guilty about Mark for a long time until it dawned on me that he was more than up for the challenge. Having had Emma for a sister has contributed greatly to the generous giving adult he has become." Parents also recognise the role of other children sometimes in keeping the family going and in offering practical support as they get older. We gain direct insights from some of the siblings and see how their lives are touched – sometimes, like Jennie Harris, building on their experience to seek careers in the disability field.

There is also evidence of differing attitudes and a continuing gender division in caring roles and responsibilities. In some of the families, the women are sole carers for much of the child-rearing and simply get on with the job of caring, even into the person's adulthood. This is the era of care in the community and we see this as largely translated as care by the women of the community, with some support by personal networks and the voluntary sector and patchy support by statutory services.

Struggles and battles

The accounts from Parts 1 and 2 of struggles and battles to get basic needs met are somewhat echoed in these narratives. Interactions with professionals, whether medical, educational or from social services, vary greatly in quality. Greater openness is far from uniform, but lack of communication is widespread. Mark's mother describes being made to feel uncomfortable for asking questions and her frustration at not being allowed to speak to decision-makers. Sue Wilson tells of a fight for respite care for her son James, and Kay (Parents in Partnership) describes her interactions with professionals as a series of "battles". Marilyn reflects on how battling means "you come to be seen as difficult parents" and similarly, Mark's mother reflects, "If you are not a pushy person it's really hard. We felt if we didn't push for Mark, nobody else was going to, you feel as if you are a troublemaker."

The families here have struggled with discrimination, prejudice and ignorance. Jan Thurlow was given the wrong information based on her daughter Clare's physical appearance – "she won't talk because she has a big tongue … they don't usually live beyond the age of five". From their children's birth we see parents coping with negativity and a cycle of low expectations. Jet Isarin describes her son, aged seven, "beginning to realise that to be stared and laughed at is not the way things ought to be" and his "wonder at not being asked for football games and birthday parties". Rachel had her 'talker' switched off when she was at college. Simon's lacerated lip would not be sutured because the medic presumed his learning disability meant he would not care how he looked in the future.

The family stories also tell of the struggle with the practicalities of giving care and the resulting tiredness and physical strain. From the stories we see the tremendous expertise and detailed knowledge family members build up to support their relative almost without noticing and yet, in spite of this, the continued lack of responsiveness on the part of services when they were needed. There seems to be little evidence in the stories of services harnessing such detailed individual knowledge and working with the person with learning disabilities and their family and community networks to develop plans that involve and respond to people's individual circumstances. We see parents expected to fit into models of service on offer, such as long-term fostering, rather than the real respite Jan Thurlow and Sue Wilson actually wanted.

We get the impression, not so much of the children being a burden, although families are 'mentally worn out', but of a fatigue born of having to fight so many fights over the years to get what they need, such as the vital medical services sought by Jayne for Trudy and Simon. Mark's mother sums it up: "When you are worried about somebody you don't need extra stress and pressure." The joined-up services so talked about in the latest policy discourses were sorely lacking for Marilyn, who laments, "You go from one person to another to another – they say, 'we don't do that here', so you have to go a different day to see to his skin, a different day to see his neurologist and a different day to see the facial surgeon." Elaine Monk sought out private facilities in response to feeling "helpless"; other families similarly responded to or pre-empted this feeling by continuously looking for their own solutions. Parents living in the latter part of this era are expected to be 'active consumers' of services (Norris and Lloyd, 2001), but for some, battles were not won and families felt their children suffered from not having all of their complex difficulties detected or futures secured. Mark's family spent years trying to resolve difficulties over benefits to secure a financial future for him, but "it was never resolved".

Changing labels, changing attitudes

Many of the authors of the personal accounts are acutely aware of the changes to labels and language they have witnessed in their lifetimes. We see the ways in which the terms used to describe the people they live with and care for are not of their choosing, but part of a separate discourse. Ann Tombs, talking of her son, remembers, after seeking a second opinion for her son's slowness, "That was the first time that someone had specifically said mental handicap." She talks of using the term and finding it more helpful than the term 'learning disabilities', which she regards as a kind of euphemism. In several of the stories we see the ways in which the narrators interact with these changing labels and changing attitudes, influencing and influenced by them. Jet Isarin reflects on the various professional labels describing children's defects and deviations and how these labels can be both useful for parents who want to understand their children and obtain the support they need to raise them, and at the same time obscure the person beneath the label. Sometimes the labels are shocking, as Mark's mother explains: "When the headmistress said, 'I think he's part spastic', I got this feeling as if someone had just kicked me." In this period we can also compare the differences emerging between the attitudes of some carers to labels and the voices from people with learning difficulties themselves, with the People First self-advocacy group's campaign, 'Label jars, not people'.

Similarly, there is a concern for some carers, who have themselves been very active campaigners for integration and equal rights, that the right balance is struck between what Anne Tombs refers to as "progressing towards normality" and the protection of a potentially vulnerable person. For some carers, after years of pushing for improvements in opportunities, for their children to be confronted with the reality and risks an ordinary life affords brings a new set of worries and dilemmas to work with. Yet there is also an acknowledgement from many carers who have worked as campaigners for change that their contribution is part of a bigger transformation continued through generations of carers and now also people with learning difficulties themselves.

The narrators are also aware of the changing attitudes within and around them. James' grandfather, Jim Broadway, questions the idea that it is rewarding to look after a child with learning disabilities; Elaine Monk comments, "I see a lot more parents walking their children to ordinary schools and buildings getting changed." Shirley Colquhoun describes happenings in Alex's life now – like working in a store and being involved in a business enterprise – that she would not have foreseen when she set out on her journey of caring for him. We are led to wonder if medics at the side of new parents in the twenty-first century portray these opportunities as part of the future picture for children with learning disabilities. With the *Valuing People* White Paper comes the call for 'nothing about us without us'. Individuals involved in People First and campaigning are finding that change is possible. Elaine explains, "I wouldn't put anything past Rachel", and Rachel herself is suing over mistakes made at her birth.

Celebration – a sense of pride and achievement

Alongside the accounts of struggle our witnesses to change also tell celebratory stories. In talking of Mark's impact on their lives, his mother says, "He brought a lot of love and happiness for us; he was a proper character." Elaine Monk reflects that "Rachel has changed our lives but she has really enriched them"; her family like "the person she's turning into" and "wouldn't swap her for anybody else". Colette remarks, "I am really proud of my son!" and Joyce Mays concludes her story by saying, "I can honestly now say I am grateful for Emma exactly as she is" – "We are very very proud of her." Not all of the families are so clear that they wouldn't have had their family member with a learning disability any other way, but they still communicate a pride in what has been achieved.

These families fought back against low expectations. Daphne recalls walking back into the office of the paediatrician: "Some years later we took her a little book in which Philip was featured and showed her, 'This is our "common or garden" Mongol!' I was so angry that he wasn't a person to her." Maureen combines her sense of defiance in wanting to prove the doctor wrong with her feeling of pride: "I came out and thought of it as a challenge. Let's get on with it. And you know he's lovely. He has done well. I did prove him wrong!"

These family members, like those of previous eras, have been fierce advocates for their children/grandchildren/siblings. But they have also faced the growth of self-advocacy and the challenge of listening to what the individuals with learning disabilities want for themselves. This is not always easy. Some of the sons and daughters, such as Mark and Rachel, have worked for or been involved with People First. A recurring theme, however, is that these narrators have not just nurtured and given support, but have learned and gained themselves from their relationships with a family member(s) with learning difficulties.

Community – segregation or inclusion?

The official history of this period is characterised by emphasis on the community. The rhetoric has been (somewhat confusedly) about care in, by and from the community. The stress has been on involvement in the cultural community, the neighbourhood locality and local schools, as opposed to the segregation of the past. However, our families have very differing experiences of community life. Elaine Monk with her daughter and Ann Tombs with her son have felt part of community, whereas Sue Wilson relates feelings of rejection. Jan Thurlow, Joyce Mays and Jayne Clapton's stories show how community life is something that families move in and out of at different times; they are neither fully included nor excluded.

Aside from the early lives of the children in Jayne Clapton's story, the people in these families do not have the history of incarceration in institutions of many in previous generations. In spite of the legislative and policy moves to end the practice of admitting young children with learning disabilities to institutions, however, institutional care was suggested to Gershwin's parents (Parents in Partnership) and, as late as 1977, Jan Thurlow was advised that her daughter would need institutional care by the time she was five. We still see the spectre of the institutions touching the families' lives with the special school nursery located in the grounds of a long-stay institution behind iron gates. Giving a more international picture, Jayne Clapton highlights the institutional deprivation suffered by many children with difficulties growing up in Australia in the late 1970s and 1980s and latterly how her children were not included with their peers in Sunday school. For many of the carers telling their stories here, segregation was something they fought against in their campaign for various kinds of social inclusion. This was also reflected in choices of schools.

An ordinary life?

Normalisation ideologies were espoused for much of this period of recent history and they clearly had their impact on families' aspirations as much as on services. Elaine Monk observes that without her determination her daughter "would have probably gone into the system … and into a special needs school and stuff like that". Mrs Colquhoun records her strategy to surround Alex with able peers who could provide him with good role models, and we see her various means of making his life as ordinary as possible. Jan Thurlow reflects on her reaction against the special school when she first saw it: her parental instinct that her child should not be segregated and the conflicting pressures for the ordinary and the special. The desire for the children to access ordinary services and experiences was, for many of the families, part of the raised expectations for a sense of normality. As Elaine Monk comments, "right from the start I was not going to have her made different from anybody else. I didn't want her treated differently from anybody else." Mark's mother, also feeling a need for normality right from the beginning said, "we wanted to persevere so Mark didn't appear different to anyone else".

Michael Tombs describes the drive towards the right of people with learning disabilities to access affordable and ordinary housing in their own right through tenancies with housing associations. Jayne Clapton tries to capture this concept of 'ordinariness' in the lives of people with learning disabilities, arguing that what makes it so important is the underpinning message of acceptance.

An era of rights?

Michael Tombs emphasises the landmark nature of the 1970 Education Act which opened this era: "to my mind the key event of the last 50 years has been the opening of the schools for the children". We would expect, then, to find discontinuity with previous eras in the educational experiences of the children during this period. After 1983 there was much rhetoric about the (conditional) right to attend a mainstream school, and some of the children did. We see clearly how expectations about schooling were raised, but that enacting parental choice could still mean battles with the authorities and internal turmoil. The stories show, in a way the official history does not, how transitions between schools and from schools into adult services are difficult times when the quality of support and range of options varies enormously.

A strong theme in the narratives is the importance for these service users of the words and acts of individuals they come across who could make a difference. This contrasts with the new rhetoric of the rights framework, which stresses that services should not be dependent on individual acts of kindness, goodwill or even professionalism. However, the discourse of rights comes late in this era, and instead we see illustrated over and over again the power of the individual within systems that work for or against people. These carers tried to build a network of key contacts and people of influence who could help them to negotiate the complex services that made them feel like outsiders to the system. Shirley Colquhoun remarked that it was "amazing how many people one has to deal with to do this properly". For her, careful "work behind the scenes" meant that she did not have to fight for Alex; her efforts to recruit and work with allies in the system were ongoing and effective. Michael Tombs emphasised how important the interest of the Director of Social Services was in their Mencap work: "I think we were fortunate in having someone who was prepared to take a real interest in the field … [who] made a very big difference to the development of services." Similarly, Elaine Monk notes the importance of the educational psychologist who "told us he would get Rachel to college before he left, and he did". She sums up, "it all depends on the person really. I found that a lot over the years."

Witnesses describe the campaigning and advocacy role of such key individuals, who often originated from outside the families' networks (several from professional contacts), in the local evolution of support and services. They highlight again how the lived experiences of contributors and their perceptions of "what really helped and moved things on" often contrasts with the official history of policy development. Evidently also, a lot of parents and carers are still having to sort things out for themselves. Colette remarks, "The thing I found was you had to find out your own information. You had to go to libraries, you had to read things in magazines and find everything out yourself."

Mark's mother spent time trying to work through a maze of confusion regarding benefits: "They don't tell you anything clear or where to go, and you never get to deal with the same person for any consistency." She reflects, "You shouldn't have to fight all the time. Mark's life was hard enough and too short ... we felt he didn't get the support he needed from the agencies involved."

Our witnesses to change may have seen changed attitudes and new opportunities, but they have not lived their daily lives within a safe rights base. They have a sense of the entitlements of their family members, to education, for example, that may not have been enjoyed by previous generations, but they know that they still have to work hard and use allies where they can to access any such entitlements.

Summary

It is easy to become lulled into seeing history as a fairly smooth journey of progress. These narratives alert us to the inaccuracies of this image. Despite the ending of the institutional era and the growing sense of the right to community participation, not everything was better for these families. They went through much that families in the 1930s and 1940s went through. What was largely new, however, was that now it was not just families fighting segregation, but people with learning difficulties were themselves becoming active campaigners.

Poems by Tom Hulley

plans

plans are put into place
carefully layered
dovetailed through the day
slipped between appointments
and arrangements neatly
when a friend calls
you never miss the chance
to fix the next visit
never let a calendar hang
without its pages filled

celeb.com

everywhere we go people greet you
once in edinburgh a woman said –
excuse me are you sam? forever
famed beyond your borders
in the town centre someone stops
ignores me but hails you like
a forgotten friend reaching the realm
of twins separated at birth
brought up by howling dogs
perhaps one night we will travel
along the secret trails to samarkand
no doubt hearing a soft voice
calling in the urgent darkness
samantha samantha what a joy
to find you here after travelling
so far waiting for so long